CHANGE AND HABIT

THE CHALLENGE OF OUR TIME

Change and Habit

THE CHALLENGE OF OUR TIME

by

Arnold J. Toynbee

1966

OXFORD UNIVERSITY PRESS

NEW YORK AND LONDON

#619402

Second printing, 1967

Copyright © Oxford University Press 1966
Library of Congress Catalogue Card Number: 66-25824

PRINTED IN THE UNITED STATES OF AMERICA

4|67

CONTENTS

PART ONE

THE CHALLENGE OF OUR TIME

PART TWO

THE OVERRIDING NEED IN POLITICS FOR ORDER

PART THREE

THE CONTINUING SCOPE IN RELIGION FOR FREEDOM

PART FOUR

THE IMPACT OF TECHNOLOGY ON LIFE

PREFACE

Most of the topics of this book were the subjects of lectures that
I gave at the University of Denver, Colorado, in the last
quarter of 1964 and at New College, Sarasota, Florida, and at
the University of the South, Sewanee, Tennessee, in the first
quarter of 1965. The notes for these lectures have given me my
starting-point for writing the book, but the lectures themselves
are not reproduced in the chapters into which the book is
divided. In the course of writing the contents have been re-
arranged.

Arnold Toynbee

New College, Sarasota, Florida,
   1 March 1965

PART ONE

THE CHALLENGE OF OUR TIME

I

Light from the Past: Its Value and Limits

The question of our human race's destiny does not always loom large in people's minds. When life seems satisfactory and secure, most people, apparently, are not moved to peer into the future farther ahead than is required for present practical purposes. As a rule, people feel acute concern about the future, beyond the horizon of the present, only when the times are out of joint and when the prospect looks menacing. In our generation we are living in one of these times of unusually intense stress and anxiety. What awaits us? What are we going to make of it when it comes upon us? In our present situation, such questions force themselves on our attention.

Since the future is hidden from us till it arrives, we have to look to the past for light on it. Our experience in the past gives us the only light on the future that is accessible to us. Experience is another name for history. When we speak of 'history', we are usually thinking of the collective experience of the human race; but the individual experience that each one of us gathers in a single lifetime is history, just as truly. In private life, as in public life, experience is highly esteemed—and rightly, because it is generally recognized that experience aids our judgement and so enables us to make wiser choices and to take better decisions. At all times—in good times as well as in bad—we do, of course, have to plan for the future in our conduct of our human affairs. We plan for the future with an eye to controlling it, and shaping it to fulfil our purposes, as far as we can. This conscious attempt to control and shape the future seems to be a distinctively human activity. It is one of the features that distinguish us from the other living creatures with whom we share our home on this planet. We cannot plan without looking ahead, and we cannot look ahead except in so far as the light of experience illuminates the future for us.

Unquestionably, therefore, the light derived from experience is valuable. It is the only guide for dealing with the future that we have. But, when the field in which we are peering into the future is the field of human affairs, we have to ask ourselves: How trustworthy, in this field, is the information about the future that the light of experience brings within our ken? In this field, does the past give us such accurate and such precise information about the future that, on the strength of it, we can make predictions about the future with confidence that these predictions will vindicate themselves by coming true in the event?

In our dealings with non-human nature, as distinguished from our dealings with each other and with ourselves, this question is not an open one. Here successful control—or successful prediction in provinces still beyond our physical reach— is a matter of everyday practice. We can set in train a chemical process and be sure of the result if we carry out the operation correctly. On the same condition, we can construct a machine and be sure that it is going to work. In the province of astronomy we have only just succeeded in making a physical impact on our planet's near neighbour and satellite the Moon; but, during the last 2,500 years at least, there have been astronomers who have been able to predict eclipses of the Moon with an accuracy that is astonishing to lay minds. This became possible when Babylonian astronomers had accumulated a series of accurate observations, extending over a long period of time, of the relative positions of some of the heavenly bodies. In the light of this past experience in this province of inanimate nature, astronomers have been able to forecast successfully what the relative positions of these same heavenly bodies were going to be at particular moments in the future. Creatures that are alive, though not human, are more tricky to deal with than stars are. Yet farmers who sow seed in the expectation of reaping a harvest are rewarded for their labours more often than not, in spite of the vagaries of the weather, unless they are trying to cultivate a soil that is prohibitively dry or chemically unpropitious; and breeders of livestock often succeed in breeding successfully for the points that they wish to develop, in spite of the rudimentariness of our understanding of the behaviour of genes. The breeder and the farmer are successful on the whole because they too, like the astronomer, the engineer, and the chemist, are acting in the light of experience. Evidently these successes, whether complete or only partial, are possible because, in all these fields, Nature is more or less uniform in her structure and regular in her working. Here, on the whole, 'as things have been, they remain'.[1] Consequently, in these fields, the value of experience is virtually absolute. Experience here enables us to predict with assurance.

By contrast, in the field of human affairs, experience enables us merely to guess. In this field, what has occurred in the past may, of course, recur, but it is not bound to recur and, indeed, it was not bound to occur in the first instance. Experience informs us of one or more alternative future possibilities; but, however many of these it discloses, we can never be sure that the inventory which it has given us is exhaustive. Again and again, what actually comes to pass proves to be something that has no recorded precedent. Thus, in human affairs, the light thrown on the future by the past is a less trustworthy guide than it is in any of our other fields of action. In private life, no sensible person expects that his past experience will enable him to predict the future with mathematical precision. Personal experience can improve one's flair for guessing—that is all; and the collective experience that we usually call history can do no more for us than that.

What element is it in human affairs that makes impossible, here, the exact mathematical prediction that is so brilliantly successful in our calculations about non-human nature? Evidently our unknown quantity in the realm of human affairs is a human being's apparent power of making choices.

No other human being can foretell, for certain, what his neighbour's choice is going to be in some situation in which it is apparently open to this human being to choose. I may have studied my neighbour's behaviour carefully and closely over a long period of years. I may have observed that he has reacted to a certain frequently recurring situation in a certain way with a regularity almost comparable to the Earth's in its annual circuit round the Sun. In the light of this experience, I may have formed a mental picture of my neighbour's 'character', and, on the basis of this apparently fixed and permanent

[1] Arthur Hugh Clough, *Lines Written on the Bridge of Peschiera.*

structure of his personality, I may venture to prophesy that, when the familiar situation recurs once again, he will once again react to it as he has invariably reacted before. If my neighbour were a star or a chemical element, I could be certain in advance that my procedure would be vindicated by the event. I could still be fairly confident of this, even if he were a domesticated plant or animal. But, since he is a human being, I shall rely on my experience of his behaviour at my peril. If I do rely on it (and it is all the light that I have), I am going to be caught out sooner or later. His reaction may have been identical one hundred times running, but, on the one hundred and first occasion, he may make nonsense of my method by playing a practical joke at my expense. He may choose, this time, to act differently from the way in which he has consistently acted hitherto. Indeed, how can one expect to be able to predict what another person's choice is going to be when one has observed that the chooser himself often does not know which of the alternative possibilities open to him he is going to choose until his decision has actually been taken? We have all had the experience of the anxiety, or even agony, that a human being suffers when he has to make a difficult choice on an important issue.

This apparent freedom of a human being to make unpredictable choices raises the theological and philosophical problem of free will. Is this apparent freedom of human wills a reality or is it an illusion? Of all the intellectual controversies in which theologians and philosophers have ever engaged, this one has been perhaps the most inconclusive. Possibly the question cannot be answered in terms of theology or of logic. Psychology, translating the question into its own different terms, may or may not be more successful. As it extends its exploration of the subconscious depths of the psyche, psychology may discover that, at this level, a human being's psychic activity is governed by 'laws of nature' that work with a regularity comparable to that of the physical movements of the stars. Yet, at the level of consciousness and will, the psyche will still appear to act spontaneously and autonomously; and, at this still early stage of our exploration of the human psyche, we cannot guess the eventual answer to the question whether this apparent freedom of human wills is a reality or an illusion.

Fortunately, for the purposes of the present inquiry, this

question can be left in suspense. We need not look beyond the fact—and this is an unquestionable fact—that human beings do not have a foreknowledge of future human choices. In this field, therefore, we cannot make infallible predictions; we can only hazard guesses. This human inability to forecast what courses of action are going to be chosen by human beings makes it impossible for human minds to foresee the future course of human affairs on the basis of our knowledge of past human history. This conclusion will hold good, whatever the relation between the consciousness and will and the other constituents of the psyche may prove to be if and when the vast unknown world of psychic nature has been effectively explored by the psychological approach to the study of human affairs—an approach which, in our time, is less than one generation old. The unconscious constituent of the human psyche may prove to operate with as rigid a regularity as the physical matter of which the human body is composed. The operations of the human subconscious and the human body may also prove to be tightly geared together. Yet, however methodically Nature may have stacked the cards in this psycho-somatic pack, and however successful a student of human nature may be in discovering what Nature's method here is, any attempt to make infallible predictions of a person's future actions on this basis will be invalidated by the presence in the pack of a 'joker' that cannot be eliminated and cannot be counted on to behave in the future invariably as it has usually behaved in the past. This intractable 'joker' is the apparent freedom of a human will to vary its response to an identical challenge when this identical challenge is presented to it on different occasions. On the plane of consciousness and will, challenge and response seem not to be geared together in the unvarying and therefore predictable relation of cause and effect.

If it is true that the future course of human affairs is unpredictable—and this perhaps intrinsically, as a consequence of the constitution of the human psyche—are we to conclude that, for an understanding of human affairs, the experience of the past is unilluminating and that the study of human history is therefore unprofitable? In our approach to the past, shall we dismiss human history as 'bunk' and concentrate our efforts on recording pedigrees of prize bulls and breeds of wheat, or on compiling tables of astronomical observations? Students of non-human nature, who are accustomed to the strict regularity that they can count on in this realm, may be inclined to suppose that this is an indispensable condition for effective study in any field, and they may therefore go on to conclude that the study of human affairs is impracticable. It may be agreed that there cannot be a science of human affairs, if by science we mean (as we usually do mean by the word nowadays) a method of study that yields a possibility of infallible prediction. But to abandon the study of history on this account would be to pay excessive deference to scientific scepticism. Study does not have to be scientific in order to be illuminating. Where prediction is impossible, guesswork may be valuable so far as it goes—on condition, of course, that we recognize the limits, as well as the value, of the light thrown by the past on the future when our field of study is the field of human affairs. In this field too, as well as in genetics and in astronomy, an answer to the question 'whence' does give us some light on the answer to the question 'whither'.

The bearing of 'whence' on 'whither' in the realm of human affairs is, in fact, the theme of this book. We shall attempt to make a survey of the problems that are giving us the greatest anxiety in our time, and in each case we shall glance back over our records of the past to see whether these present us with any historical situations that may be relevant to ours. Our motive will be a presumption that, if we do find what look like genuine historical precedents, and if we do not mistake them for scientific blueprints, these precedents will enable us to understand our own present situation rather better, and may perhaps also help us to cope with it rather more successfully. Though this aim is a modest one, it may be worth pursuing nevertheless.

II

Stable Ingredients in Human Nature

One reason for thinking that the past may throw some light on the future, even in the realm of human affairs, is the existence of what look like stable ingredients in human nature. Like other kinds of living creature, mankind exhibits specific traits, the presence of which enables us to recognize the species to which a creature belongs. However, the discovery that all forms of life have evolved from, and through, a long series of successive forms suggests that the evolution of life is continuing and will continue, and this implies that, in any species of living creature, the appearance of immutability is an illusion produced by differences in time-scale. The length of the time taken by evolution is vast by comparison with the length of a human life and even with the aggregate lengths of the generations during which the phenomena of evolution have been under scientific study so far. For this reason human observers have not been able to catch evolution in the act. We know, however, that, on the time-scale of the evolution of life as a whole, mankind's arrival is a recent event. It is more recent still on the time-scale of events in the stellar universe, which are the subject of astronomy. If mankind did evolve from some pre-human species at a date that is recent in terms of longer time-scales than mankind's own, it is conceivable that eventually some post-human species might evolve out of mankind. Indeed, present-day biologists are hinting that specific variations on human nature may occur in a future that is not distant even in terms of our human time-scale. The man-made fission of atoms might produce unintended mutations in human genes, or intended mutations in human genes might be brought about by direct human manipulation of them. If biologists were to achieve this power, that would mark a new departure in the operation of the process of evolution. For the first time, an existing species of living creature would have created a new species out of itself on its own initiative, by a conscious and purposeful act of planning. This power to direct our own evolution would have greater effects on mankind's future than any power that we have acquired so far. Like previously acquired powers, this biological power would be likely to be used. For instance, we might come to the conclusion that, in the Atomic Age, the only way to prevent the human race from liquidating itself would be to condition human nature to be incapable of resorting to violence. This would be to deprive human beings, at least partially, of their apparent freedom of choice. We should be transmuting them into something more like angels or ants. We might do this on the ground that to condition ourselves would be a lesser evil than to extirpate ourselves. This might seem to be the best choice of life and good that was open to us. Evidently, however, this power, like others, could be used for evil as well as for good, and the prospect of our acquiring it is therefore a formidable one.

Thus the apparent presence of stable ingredients in human nature cannot be accepted at its face-value. Yet, short of being immutable, these ingredients have been stable enough, so far, to warrant the assumption that they will also be there in the future; and here we do have a basis for making guesses about our future in the light of what we know about our past.

Our oldest evidence for the presence, on the face of the Earth, of living creatures that are recognizably human is the material débris that these predecessors of ours have left behind and that our modern archaeologists have retrieved. This earliest evidence for the existence of human beings consists of bones and stones. The bones tell us that 'homo sapiens', the kind of human being that is represented by all human beings now alive, is the sole survivor out of a number of different species of hominid that have existed in the past. The stones that are here in question are stones that have been artificially shaped, however crudely, to make them more efficient for serving as tools than they would have been if they had been left in their state of nature. Where we find shaped tools in juxtaposition with bones, and where we can be sure that these tools were made, as well as used, by the creature whose bones have survived to testify that this creature was once alive, we can classify this creature as being human, even if its bones indicate that it was a representative of a different species of hominid from ours.

Early tools are far more plentiful than early bones, and they are also more informative. Artificially shaped tools, unlike natural objects that have been used as tools without having been modified, tell us that their makers and users were capable of planning, and this tells us in turn that they possessed consciousness and had wills. Tool-making has, in fact, been one of the distinctive characteristics of human nature from the earliest stage of human history that is known to us down to the present, and it is reasonable to guess that mankind will continue to make tools for as long as it continues to exist. Technology has been the field of mankind's most brilliant successes so far. Man is certainly 'homo faber'. He has lived up to this matter-of-fact label, while he has failed, so far, to live up to the presumptuous label 'homo sapiens'. Yet this other label, unwarrantable though it may be, does make a point that is true and important. It reminds us that Man, besides being 'homo faber', has also another side to his nature, and that this other side of it is a more significant aspect of it. Though Man's technology has been by far the most successful of his achievements hitherto, it is not the essence of humanity, and is not even the feature of human nature that is the most crucial for mankind's existence, survival, and well-being. These more important features of human nature cannot appear directly in the archaeological record, since they are not material but are spiritual. At the most, archaeology can bear witness to the existence of these spiritual characteristics of human nature indirectly, inasmuch as we can assume that, if these had not been present, Man could never have created the culture of which his tools are material evidence. This material evidence is trustworthy as far as it goes, but it informs us directly only about one part of human life, and this a part that is not the most vital.

The distinctive spiritual features of human nature, which are the most significant marks of being human, are known to us, not through any material products of human work, but through a human being's spiritual encounters with his fellow human beings, with himself, and with the ultimate spiritual reality in the Universe. One's encounters with one's fellow human beings are of two kinds. One has encounters with those of one's living contemporaries with whom one has come into personal relations, and one has encounters with other human beings, living or dead, about whom one knows something indirectly through visual or oral or written information. The reason why we are informed about some of those people that we have not met personally is because they have made, or at least are believed by us to have made, some impact on our lives nevertheless. Indirect relations may affect us more deeply and more dynamically than any personal relations. The late President Kennedy made such a vivid impression on millions of his contemporaries who had never met him that his death was felt, all over the World, as keenly as if it had been a personal bereavement for mankind at large. Yet President Kennedy's influence on his contemporaries cannot compare, in intensity and in effectiveness, with the influence exerted on posterity by the Buddha, Laotse, Confucius, Jesus, Muhammad, Marx, and Gandhi. These founders of higher religions and of schools of philosophy have influenced hundreds of millions of human beings who were still unborn during their lifetime. In innumerable cases, they have had a more profound influence on human beings who have never met them than has been exerted on these same human beings by anyone whom they have met in the flesh.

The outstanding distinctive spiritual features of human nature are at the heart of the subject of this book, and an attempt to survey and examine them must therefore be made at this point. Inevitably the survey will be incomplete and the examination inconclusive; for nothing within the cognizance of human minds is so enigmatic as human nature itself is, and the systematic study of it is still in its infancy, though it was started, more than 2,500 years ago, in India and in the Greek World simultaneously.

One of the spiritual features of human nature that is outstanding but is not distinctive is society. It seems probable that our pre-human ancestors could not have become human beings if they had not been social creatures already, but Man is not the only social creature on Earth. He shares this characteristic with some of his fellow-mammals—e.g. wolves—and, above all, with the social insects, whose social organization is as elaborate as Man's and is, for some purposes, more efficient than his. The superstructure of culture that Man has erected on the basis of his sociality is, indeed, something peculiar to Man. There is no counterpart of this in the social insects' life. For this reason, human culture is considered in this chapter, but human sociality is taken for granted.

The primary distinctive feature of human nature is consciousness, including a human being's consciousness of himself, as well as his consciousness of the Universe outside himself, in which his fellow human beings figure side by side with non-human nature, animate and inanimate.

Consciousness reveals the possibility of making choices, and thus evokes the will to choose. Man's apparent power to will —whether this is a reality or an illusion—is the second of the distinctive spiritual features of his nature.

The third of these features is his recognition of the distinction between good and evil. This distinction is implicit in the power to choose, since every choice that a human being makes is in some degree, however slight, a choice between life and good on the one hand and death and evil on the other. The distinction between good and evil seems to have been drawn by all human beings at all times and places. The drawing of it seems, in fact, to be one of the intrinsic and universal characteristics of our common nature. However, in the application of this distinction to the practical conduct of life, there has been, and still is, a very great diversity as between the moral codes of different cultures. Long before the beginnings of the systematic study of anthropology, this diversity in the field of ethical usage was illustrated by Herodotus in his story of the Persian Emperor Darius I's confrontation of some of his Indian subjects, who ate their fathers' corpses, with some of his Greek subjects, who burned them. When, at Darius's instance, each of the two parties, in turn, informed the other party of their method of disposing of their fathers' corpses, the other party was shocked, as Darius had foreseen that they would be. To pollute the pure and holy element fire was as shocking to the Indians as cannibalism was to the Greeks. Herodotus expresses his conclusion by quoting Pindar's dictum that 'custom is king of all'.[1] It would be nearer the truth to say that the relativity

[1] Herodotus, Book III, Chapter 38.

of different ethical codes is subject to an absolute belief, underlying all codes, that good and evil can be, and should be,
distinguished.

A fourth distinctive spiritual ingredient of human nature is
religion, and this, like the will to choose, is a spiritual reaction
to one of the findings of consciousness. One cannot be conscious
without becoming aware that one knows only a fragment of
the Universe, and that this fragment is not self-explanatory.
It confronts us with incongruities in human life that are painful
and that also seem unreasonable. Death, for instance, is incongruous with both our human ability to understand and our
human power to love. A human mind's range of comprehension
seems to be potentially infinite; yet *ars longa, vita brevis*; the
most potent and penetrating mind is soon put out of action by
death. A human soul's capacity for loving other human beings
seems likewise to have no limits; but, the greater the love, the
keener the pain of bereavement. *Video meliora proboque; deteriora
sequor.*[1] I often use my freedom of choice to act against my
conscience; and sin is more unreasonable and more painful
than bereavement and death; for sin is an incongruity that is
not imposed on me by God or by Nature; it is one that I create
for myself. These are perhaps the three most poignant of human
life's inherent misfits. One can think of many others.

All these misfits are left unexplained within the limits of the
fragment of the Universe that is observable by us; but the
human spirit will not readily resign itself to supposing that these
painful incongruities in human life are truly inexplicable in the
sense of being utterly meaningless and purposeless. It will
acquiesce more readily in a recognition of the feebleness of its
own powers of insight into the enigma. It will guess that the
explanation of the observable fragment of the Universe must lie
in the nature of the Universe as a whole, or in the nature of
some spiritual presence, greater than Man, that exists behind
and beyond the Universe and that is perhaps the source of the
Universe's being. The conclusion is that human life and its
setting are mysteries; and the emotional reaction to this conclusion is a feeling of humility and awe. We recognize that a
human being is not master of the situation in which each of us
finds himself as a consequence of having been called to life by

[1] Ovid, *Metamorphoses*, Book VII, line 20.

forces whose nature and working he cannot fathom. The recognition of this impels a human being to seek to make contact with these mysterious forces that hold him in their power. His motive is not just the curiosity that is another of the distinctive ingredients of human nature. His motive in seeking to make contact with these trans-human and super-human forces is a wish to live, as far as possible, in harmony with them, and he desires this because he recognizes that the last word about Man and his destiny lies, not with Man himself, but with these ultimate spiritual forces, whatever they may be.

This impulse seems to be common to all human beings, and all the historic religions are attempts to express it and to satisfy it. However, religion resembles ethics in the point that, in this field too, there is a very great diversity as between the doctrines in which an underlying common belief is expressed and as between the precepts for carrying out an underlying common endeavour. Ultimate spiritual reality may be conceived of as being transcendent or as being immanent in human souls, animals, trees, stones, mountains, rivers, or stars; it may be conceived of as being impersonal or personal or suprapersonal; it may even be conceived of as being a deplorable illusion (the Roman poet Lucretius, who took this view, was an intensely religious soul). As for the methods, prescribed by different faiths, for bringing oneself into harmony with ultimate spiritual reality, whatever its nature may be held to be, these methods range from the Buddhist's endeavour to liberate himself from Karma by extinguishing his appetites, his self-centredness, and perhaps his personality itself, in Nirvana, to the Christian's endeavour to attain personal immortality in the *visio beatifica* of a God, who, in Christian belief, is also a person.

The four stable ingredients in human nature that we have considered up to this point are, all of them, not only stable in themselves in the sense that they are to be found in all human beings always and everywhere; they also all make for stability in the sense of providing an element of changelessness and permanence in mankind's way of life at all times and places. There are other ingredients that are also stable in themselves but that, in their effect on mankind's way of life, make, not for permanence, but for change.

One ingredient in this second set is curiosity. This, too, is a distinctive characteristic of human beings. Curiosity is a wish for knowledge for its own sake, not just for the sake of accomplishing some ulterior 'practical' purpose. Man is curious about the heavenly bodies, about the human psyche, about the ultimate spiritual presence behind the Universe, about whether or not his own personality is going to survive death, and, in fact, about everything that comes within his field of consciousness. Curiosity has two important effects on Man's way of life, and both these effects make for social and cultural change. Curiosity is always enlarging Man's cultural heritage; and though—or, perhaps, rather, just because—it is not utilitarian in its aim, it sometimes produces 'practical' fruits that were unintended and unexpected.

A human being's curiosity, and the discoveries to which it leads him, would perish with the individual himself if he had no means of communicating with his fellows. Man shares with some other species of living creature the power of communicating with his fellows telepathically. In human society, however, this faculty has been pushed into the margin of intercourse by language. This more effective medium of communication is possessed by all human beings in all societies and is one of the distinctive marks of being human. In spite of our command of language, telepathy is still an indispensable means of communication for human beings too; and, if the use of language were ever to cause this 'sixth sense' to atrophy, we might find that language, unaided by telepathy, is an inadequate instrument. However, language is a more copious means of communication than telepathy is. Like telepathy, language can communicate feelings and impulses; but it can also communicate thoughts, which telepathy can convey, if at all, only when they have a strong emotional charge—and emotion is the enemy of intellectual clarity and objectivity. Some non-human species of social animal possess rudiments of language in the form of cries and gestures conveying meanings that are recognized by all concerned. But no non-human species—not even any species of social insects—has developed language, in the form of sounds and gestures signifying feelings, information, and demands, to a degree that makes these non-human 'languages' at all comparable to even the most rudimentary human languages that are known to us.

The faculty of speech has endowed human beings with a new, distinctively human, means of transmission from one generation to the next. In all species of living creature, including the human species, specific traits, psychic as well as physical, are transmitted through the act of physical procreation. Man, however, has an additional means of transmission in the form of education in the broadest meaning of the word. Education is the procedure by which a body of social and cultural tradition —accumulated by curiosity and communicated in language— is handed on to the rising generation by its parents and their contemporaries. The rudiments of education, as well as the rudiments of language, are to be found in the life of some non-human species of living creature too, but in human life the effectiveness, range, and role of education are so very much greater that the difference in degree is virtually a difference in kind. In human life, transmission through education has pushed transmission through physical procreation into the margin, as language has pushed telepathy. It is true that education alone would not suffice to keep us human if our humanity were not underpinned by the procreational transmission of those stable ingredients in human nature that are the subject of this chapter. This basic nature of ours is, however, overlaid by a thick deposit of tradition, and this even in culturally primitive human societies.

This relative importance of 'nurture', over against 'nature', in mankind's social life is an outstandingly significant feature of it, because this is the field in which human beings are free to make their choices, and it is also a field in which they are practically powerless to prevent change, even if they try their hardest. Nearly the whole of the behaviour of non-human animals—for instance, the social insects—is built into the psycho-physical constitution that is transmitted through procreation, and therefore it can be changed only by one of those genetic mutations that may or may not lead to the evolution of a new species. In human society, the adult generation can choose what it will transmit to the rising generation and what it will discard, and the rising generation can choose, though this to a lesser degree, to be more or less receptive to its education or to be more or less recalcitrant to it. Actually, a social and cultural tradition is never transmitted from one generation to another without some involuntary change in it, even when both generations concur in wanting the tradition to be transmitted intact. It is impossible, for instance, to freeze a language at some arbitrarily chosen stage of its development. The frozen form will eventually become 'dead' and will be embalmed as the 'classical' language, while the living language will depart from it progressively, with each successive change of generation, until eventually the classical language and the vernacular will have become mutually unintelligible. Nor can a society's way of life be frozen by the fiat of a government, however autocratic and however efficient that government may be. In Japan in the seventeenth century of the Christian Era the Tokugawa régime tried to immobilize Japanese life in all its aspects by freezing the established political and economic order at home and by cutting off almost all intercourse between Japan and the rest of the World. Yet, within little more than two centuries, Japan had undergone a peaceful but irresistible economic and intellectual revolution, and Western 'dangerous thought' had reactivated Japanese minds before Commodore Perry's guns browbeat the Tokugawa régime into reopening Japan's doors to Western bodies. These examples illustrate the truth that a social and cultural heritage is virtually bound to change continually in the process of being continually transmitted.

Subject to this limitation, however, human beings are free to innovate deliberately, as well as to do their utmost to conserve. Consequently, a social and cultural heritage is always precarious. As compared with a built-in psycho-physical constitution, it has the enormous advantage of being alterable at will. Habits and institutions that have become, or have been discovered to be, detrimental can be eliminated by making the necessary intellectual and moral effort. But the price of this advantage is that, unlike built-in nature, a social and cultural heritage may be lost either unintentionally or through a deliberate abandonment of the essence of it. In our time, we have seen the moral and religious essence of the Western Christian culture repudiated—and this in act as well as in theory—by the government of Germany, one of the foremost countries of the Western World. By the date at which Hitler came into power, Germany had been a Christian country for 1,100 years, and for longer than that in those German territories that had once been included in the Roman Empire. Since their conversion the Germans had played a leading part in the development of the Western Civilization. Martin Luther was a German; modern Western music is a German art. Yet the Nazi rejected Germany's Western heritage and jettisoned it; and, though there were individual Germans who suffered martyrdom in resisting this would-be reversion to pre-Christian German heathenism, the German people as a whole submitted passively to the Nazi régime, while a substantial minority actively supported it. The lesson of this Nazi episode in our modern Western history is that any element in our social and cultural heritage that we value has to be defended with eternal vigilance. If we ever take the preservation of cultural treasure for granted, we are likely to lose it.

It will be seen that Man's social and cultural heritage is the field of history. History, in the objective meaning of the word, is the process of change; in the subjective meaning, it is the study of how and why one situation changes into another. History is the 'living garment' that the Time-Spirit is always weaving for mankind on the 'humming loom of Time'.[1] At the social and cultural level of human life, time spells change, whether deliberate or involuntary. The past and future course of this flow of change in human affairs is the subject of this book.

---

[1] Goethe, *Faust*, Part I, lines 508–9: 'So schaff' ich am sausenden Webstuhl der Zeit/und wirke der Gottheit lebendiges kleid.'

III

Acceleration in Human History

Mankind's built-in measure of time is the average duration of an individual human being's conscious life. An individual's memory does not reach back—except for a few isolated reminiscences—into the early years of infancy, and senility sometimes overtakes him before his physical death. In most human societies until not much more than a hundred years ago, the average expectation of conscious life was perhaps about forty years, i.e. from the age of five to the age of forty-five. For the technologically and administratively advanced minority of mankind, the average expectation has now been lengthened by perhaps 50 per cent. It now extends from the age of five to about the age of sixty-five years. Yet a span of sixty years, as well as one of forty years, is a very short unit of measurement for expressing the magnitude of the periods of time taken by events in some of the dimensions of the Universe that our curiosity has stimulated us to explore and that our intellect has enabled us to comprehend. Different dimensions prove to have different time-scales, ranging from the scale of an individual human being's conscious life to the scale of events in the stellar cosmos.

The cosmic time-scale is still beyond our knowledge. Even the preliminary question whether the cosmos has had a datable beginning in time or is eternal is still being disputed among present-day astronomers of different schools. There is at any rate a consensus that the planet Earth has had a beginning, and this at a recent date relatively to the age of some other cosmic bodies. Some astronomers seem, at the moment, to hold that our planet is now about 3,000,000,000 years old. If they were to revise this provisional figure, and revise it drastically, before this book was published, that would not be surprising.

The time-scale of the evolution of various forms of life is necessarily of a smaller magnitude than the age of the planet that is life's habitat, and, for the biological series, the current datings are also less indefinite than they are for the cosmic series. They can, in fact, be presented tentatively in the form of the following table:

Age of life on Earth	2,500,000,000—1,500,000,000 years
Age of mammals	150,000,000—125,000,000 years
Age of pre-human australo-pithecus	more than 1,000,000 years
Age of pithecanthropus and some of the other known species of hominid	less than 1,000,000 years

The age of 'homo sapiens', which is the only now surviving species of hominid, is still uncertain. We have no warrant for assuming that 'homo sapiens' is no older than the earliest of the bones attributable to him, and the earliest of the tools associated with these bones, that have been discovered so far.

Technology, as we have noted already, is coeval with Man; and the technological series begins at the date which marks the ending so far of the particular stream of biological evolution of which Man has been the outcome. In the technological series the later datings, at any rate, are sure and indeed precise. The series can be tabulated as follows:

Age of Lower Palaeolithic technology	less than 1,000,000 years
Age of Upper Palaeolithic technology	50,000—30,000 years
Age of Neolithic technology and of agriculture and the domestication of animals	9,000 years
Age of the harnessing of wind-power for driving ships	5,000 years
Age of the harnessing of water-power for driving mills	2,000 years
Age of the application of experimental science to technology	350 years
Age of the harnessing of non-muscular power, other than wind-power and water-power	200 years
Age of the harnessing of electricity	120 years
Age of the harnessing of mineral oil	60 years
Age of the harnessing of atomic energy	20 years

We can also make the following table of a series of stages in the history of religion:

Age of the burial of the dead as a religious rite	earlier than the extinction of homo neandertalensis
Age of the worship of the Upper Palaeolithic hunter's game (and perhaps also of the worship of other non-human natural objects and forces), to guess by inference from the subjects of Upper Palaeolithic Man's cave-art	about 15,000 years
Age of the worship of collective human power	about 5,000 years
Age of higher religions that seek to put individual human beings into direct touch with ultimate spiritual reality, and that address themselves to all mankind	2,500 years

A series of stages in the history of Man's political organization can be tabulated likewise:

Age of bands of nomadic food-gatherers	less than 1,000,000 years
Village communities of sedentary. agriculturists and pastoralists	9,000 years
Local states and would-be world-states	5,000 years
Communities of nomadic pastoralists	4,000 years

When, however, we come to examine Man's works of art, which are not the least impressive of Man's achievements up to the present at any rate, the presentation of these in their chronological order turns out to be unilluminating. The aesthetic value of the cave-paintings made by Upper Palaeolithic Man, which are the oldest specimens of Man's works of art that our modern archaeologists have discovered so far, cannot be appraised on a common scale with the value of, say, the landscape-painting of the Sung Age or of the Italian schools of painting in the fifteenth and sixteenth centuries of the Christian Era. Every great school of art has an absolute value of its own, because it has an incomparable style of its own. The values of the different schools are incommensurable, and it would be fantastic to award to each school so many marks out of the same possible total. All that we can say is that, so far as we know, human beings have been creating works of art only during the last 15,000 years out of the rather less than one million years of human history up to date. But, since the production-date of the oldest surviving works of art, the lapse of time has not brought with it any measurable increase in excellence. The order of time in which the great schools of art have arisen bears no relation to their respective merits. The great schools tower up like mountain-peaks, and each of them can look the others in the face without regard to their chronological sequence. To present them in chronological order gives us no relevant information about them and is of no help towards an aesthetic appreciation of them.

This absoluteness, and consequent incommensurability, of great works of art was recognized in the course of the controversy in the Western World, towards the end of the seventeenth century, over the relative merits of the contemporary Western culture and the Graeco-Roman culture that had been resuscitated and idolized in the fifteenth-century Italian Renaissance. The champions of 'the moderns' were victorious over the champions of 'the ancients' in contending for the superiority of the moderns in the domains of technology and natural science. In this field the champions of 'the ancients' were forced to admit defeat. But, when a contemporary French poet sought to 'cash in' on the moderns' victory by claiming that this proved him to be as good a poet as Homer and Virgil, if not a better one, the victors flinched from trying to follow up their victory to that length. However logical the contemporary poet's contention might seem to be, it manifestly flew in the face of the facts. The champions of the moderns showed their common sense by conceding that their claim did not apply to poetry. They were admitting that the greatness of great poetry is timeless and is not tied to any particular phase of any cultural environment. This is true of poetry because it is true of all forms of art.

Let us now look again at the four series of events, in four different dimensions, that we have presented in chronological order, and let us ask ourselves two questions about them. How far, if at all, in these cases, does the chronological order have, as its counterpart, a corresponding increase in the particular kind of excellence that is the appropriate standard of valuation for each series? And, in so far as any series does display an increase in excellence as time goes on, what are our observations about the pace of its progress? Is the pace erratic, or is it uniform, or has it accelerated?

The purpose of politics is to rid human social life of the violence that is the price of anarchy by substituting for it the peace and security of which the price is law and order. Success in achieving this purpose is the criterion by which the value of a political system has to be judged, and, on this criterion, the would-be world-states stand out as the best of all those on our list. They have provided the greatest amount of internal law and order while committing the least amount of violence in the shape of wars with other communities. If any of them had succeeded in extending its authority over the whole habitable surface of the globe and had also managed to make itself permanent, it would have completely fulfilled the purpose of a political institution, since it would have brought permanent peace and security to the whole human race.

Judged by the same criterion, the local states—exemplified in the 114 present states-members of the United Nations—stand at the bottom of our political marking-list. As compared with the would-be world-states of the past—not to speak of a possible future world-state that might be truly world-wide—the local states have each given peace and security to a smaller fraction of the human race, and even this limited benefit has been conferred by them on their citizens at the cost of incessant wars between them and their neighbours that have inflicted a disproportionate amount of suffering on their own citizens as well as on their neighbours' citizens.

Both the village-communities of the Neolithic stage of culture and the far more ancient bands of food-gatherers have been less maleficent forms of political organization than the local states of the Age of Civilization. It is true that this was due, not to any positive merits of theirs, but to propitious circumstances for which they cannot be given credit. They were not gravely tempted to go to war with each other, partly because they were insulated from each other by wildernesses which, as yet, had no human occupants and partly because, if, nevertheless, they did go to war with each other, they did not have either an advanced enough technology or a big enough surplus of production, beyond what was required for their subsistence, to be able to wage wars of a devastating intensity. This negative merit of being relatively impotent to perpetrate destruction outweighs any superiority over them that the local states of the Age of the

Civilizations may have possessed in point of ability to impose domestic law and order.

As for the nomadic pastoralists, whose form of community is the youngest, their atrocities and their benefactions have both run to extremes. The Mongols in the thirteenth century of the Christian Era committed genocide almost on the scale on which it has been committed by the Nazi in our Western society in our day. On the other side of the balance sheet, we must enter to the Mongols' credit the fact that they succeeded in establishing, and in maintaining thereafter for a century, a would-be world-state that came nearer to being world-wide than any other that has been established either before or since, hitherto.

If the foregoing valuation of the various forms of political organization that have been created up to date carries conviction, we have to conclude from it that in the field of politics, as in the field of art, the chronological series has no value-significance. Unlike the great schools of art, the various forms of political organization can be arranged in an order of their relative value, but this order has no relation to that of their relative ages. The would-be world-states and the local states, to which we have given respectively the highest marks and the lowest, came into existence almost simultaneously. When, round about the turn of the fourth and the third millennium B.C., the curtain rises on the history of the oldest of the civilizations, in the country that is now 'Irāq, we find this Sumerian society fractured politically into a number of local states, as our Western society is fractured today. When, shortly after, the curtain rises, in Egypt, on the history of the second-oldest civilization, we find the Egyptian society in the act of being united politically in the oldest of the would-be world-states. In the course of the 5,000 years that have elapsed since the rise of the Sumerian and Egyptian civilizations, both world-states and clusters of local states have come and gone without any abiding result so far. In the political history of the Age of the Civilizations so far, we can discern no cumulative progress towards the achievement of world-wide and permanent law and order. We can see only chaotic fluctuations, of which the outcome is not yet in sight.

When we turn to the history of religion, we do find both progress and acceleration here. We can distinguish three stages of religious development. The first is the worship of non-human nature, which arose in the course of the long age—by far the longest period of human history so far—during which Man was still at non-human nature's mercy. It is not possible to worship anything that one has mastered; and, therefore, when Man became aware that he had established his ascendancy over Nature, he subordinated the worship of conquered Nature to the worship of the collective human power that had given him his victory. The apotheosis of the community spells slavery for individual human beings, as is illustrated by the experience of the German people under the Nazi régime and by the sacrificial role of the individual in the community life of the social insects. The third stage in the progress of religion has been the advent of higher religions that have liberated the individual human being from his former ant-like enslavement to his community by putting him into direct personal touch with the ultimate spiritual reality behind all the phenomena of the Universe, non-human and human alike. This liberating vision has inspired martyrs to court death by refusing to obey human authorities when they have believed that obeying them would be incompatible with their duty to God.

In this series of stages of religion we can see spiritual progress; for, while we may fail to find in man-worship a spiritually higher form of religion than nature-worship, there can be no doubt that both these forms have been surpassed in spiritual excellence by a form that orients human souls towards ultimate spiritual reality. The series also reveals acceleration. The worship of collective human power began at the dawn of civilization about 5,000 years ago. This was at least 10,000 years after the creation of the Upper Palaeolithic cave-paintings, which are our earliest evidence for the existence of nature-worship. This evidence is only inferential, and it is also tenuous; yet we may guess that nature-worship is not just 15,000 years old but is nearly one million years old, since it seems likely that this form of religion is coeval with mankind itself. If man-worship did not begin till nearly a million years after the beginning of nature-worship, and if the worship of, or striving towards, ultimate spiritual reality began only about 2,500 years after that, there is an unmistakable case of acceleration here.

However, another 2,500 years have now elapsed, and the higher religions—the earliest representatives of which were the

Judaism of the Prophetic Age and Zoroastrianism and Buddhism—have not yet been superseded by any form of religion that is manifestly higher still. So far from that, Christianity, at any rate, which has been losing ground in the West since the later decades of the seventeenth century, has, in our own day, been ousted to a large extent by a set of post-Christian ideologies, of which Nationalism, Communism, and Individualism are the three principal representatives—Nationalism being the most potent of the three. These ideologies are all reversions, in different forms, to the worship of human power which the higher religions appeared to have superseded. Actually, the higher religions have proved merely to have driven man-worship underground—to reappear when a higher religion has lost its hold. At the time of writing it was impossible to foresee what the outcome of the current contest between the historic higher religions and the post-Christian ideologies was going to be.

The ideologies were formidable because they had heightened the intrinsic appeal of man-worship by reinforcing it with a fervour and fanaticism derived from Christianity. The weakness of the ideologies was that they severed the direct contact that the higher religions had established between the individual soul and ultimate spiritual reality. Consequently none of the ideologies had any help to give to individual human beings in their rough passage through life; and two, at least, out of the three, had re-subjected the individual soul to the servitude to its human community from which the higher religions had liberated it. For these reasons it might perhaps be expected, on a long view, that the higher religions would eventually prevail over the ideologies—not, probably, in their traditional outward form, but with their essence stripped of the non-essential accretions by which it had been overlaid in the course of time. The future was uncertain, and the present situation gave no warrant for prognosticating that the spiritual level represented by the historic religions was going to be surpassed, while on the other hand it did indicate clearly that the spurt of acceleration in Man's spiritual progress, which had culminated in the advent of the higher religions, had not been maintained since the seventh century of the Christian Era—the century which had seen the latest of the higher religions, Islam, brought to birth.

When we turn from art and politics and religion to

technology and biology, the course of events is much less obscure and less ambivalent. The technological series and the biological series each reveal a progressive rise in degree of excellence (measured in terms of technological and biological values respectively). They also reveal a progressive acceleration in the rate of this progress.

In the biological series an improvement in biological efficiency is manifestly exhibited in the evolution of mammals, and a further, and still more sensational, improvement, within the mammalian order, in the evolution of Man. There is also here a no less manifest acceleration. It took at least 1,350,000,000 years for mammals to evolve out of the primeval form of life. Possibly this took as much as 2,375,000,000 years. But it took, at most, 149,000,000 years, and possibly no more than 124,000,000 years, for Man to evolve out of the primitive forms of mammal. Moreover, Man has been in existence for less than one million years (probably), so far; and this is a short span of time compared with 149,000,000 years and with 1,350,000,000 years. In contrast to the table of events in the religious dimension, which suggests that, since the advent of the higher religions, Man's progress in this dimension may, temporarily at least, have come to a pause and be experiencing a recession, the table of events in the biological dimension does not indicate that there has been either a pause in progress or even a decline in the acceleration of its pace.

Does this imply that, less—and perhaps considerably less—than 149,000,000 years from now, we may expect that Man will have been surpassed, in his turn, by the evolution of some new species that will be more advanced than Man himself is? Our answer to this question will depend on our analysis of the difference between Man and the other forms of life that have evolved on this planet up to date. In the preceding chapter, we have noted that the primary distinctive feature of human nature is consciousness; and, with the emergence of consciousness, the psycho-physical evolution of life passed beyond its purely biological stage into a 'metabiological' stage. As early as the beginning of the Upper Palaeolithic Age, Man's consciousness had given him an ascendancy over all other species of living creature; and this ascendancy has, long since, become potent enough to enable Man, if he chooses, to arrest the evo-

lution of life on Earth by killing off any animal or human being
that displays a biological mutation out of which a new species
might possibly evolve.

Lusûs naturae (biological 'sports') have, in the past, excited
superstitious fears that have moved people to extirpate these
unfortunate creatures ruthlessly. Livy's annals of Roman history record a number of instances in which the ecclesiastical
authorities of the Roman state condemned to death herma-
phrodite human children or calves with two heads. In some of
the more primitive societies, human twins have been put to
death as a matter of ritual routine. It looks as if, since the emergence of Man, biological evolution can no longer continue to
take its course except with Man's consent. It also looks, as has
been noted in the preceding chapter, as if Man may soon acquire the power to conduct and direct the process of biological
evolution artificially, without having any longer to wait for
Nature to take her course at a pace that, however greatly it may
accelerate, will still be vastly slower than the now dizzily accelerating pace of human science and technology. If this is the
truth, it means that the future of biological evolution will depend on the future of the technological development that
started when 'homo faber' made his entry on to the stage.

In the technological series, both progress and the acceleration of progress leap to the eye. At the present time, both are
in full swing. Their impetus is unprecedented and portentous.
Here, manifestly, we are in the presence of a factor that is confronting Man with a new challenge—the greatest, perhaps, of
any that have yet confronted him. Though technology is man-
made, it is now challenging Man's ability to retain the power of
planning, directing, and controlling his own future by the continuing exercise of the freedom of choice that is one of the distinctive characteristics of human nature. This inanimate apparatus that Man has invented to serve human purposes is now
threatening to make a declaration of its independence of
its inventor. It is threatening to carry Man whither he would
not.[1]

How is it possible for Man to lose the initiative as a result
of his own success in one of the fields of his activity? The
fact is that the present inordinately accelerating progress of

[1] John 21, 19.

technology is now widening, to an alarming degree, the fissure between the conscious and the subconscious layer of the human psyche. This fissure is, of course, as old as consciousness itself is; it is the price that life has had to pay for the evolutionary feat of breaking out into consciousness and thereby achieving humanity.

One of the awkward and painful weaknesses of being human is that this involves being an 'amphibium'[1] who has somehow to contrive to live in two different worlds simultaneously. Ever since our ancestors became human, they have had to drive the conscious and the subconscious components of the human psyche in double harness; and these two steeds—let us call them 'Head' and 'Heart'—give their driver perpetual trouble and anxiety by pulling in two different directions and moving at two different paces. The head's pace has always been faster than the heart's pace; but, throughout by far the greater part of human history till now, this difference of pace has not made the driver's task unmanageable, because the head was dilatory, at first, in gathering speed. After the shaping of the earliest tool by a creature who proved, in the act, that he had become human, the technique of the Lower Palaeolithic Age remained virtually stationary for perhaps more than 900,000 years. It was not till after the beginning of the Upper Palaeolithic Age that technology began to advance fast enough for its development to be perceptible to the layman's eye in a display of stone tools arranged in chronological order. Till then, the head's slower yoke-fellow, the heart, had not been so hard put to it to keep abreast. Though the heart had been under strain ever since the head had been yoked to it, this original strain had at any rate not been appreciably aggravated as yet. What has now made the heart's plight almost intolerable is that the head, besides being faster from the start, has latterly been accelerating its already faster pace, and accelerating each successive degree of acceleration, with an energy that shows no sign of reaching any limits. By contrast, the heart's pace, which has been slower from the first, seems to be a pace that has been fixed by Nature and that cannot be speeded up beyond this natural limit.

[1] 'Thus is Man that great and true amphibium, whose nature is disposed to live, not only like other creatures, in divers elements, but in divided and distinguished worlds' (Sir Thomas Browne, *Religio Medici*, Part I, section 34).

Within this speed-limit, the subconscious emotional irrational layer of the human psyche has shown a capacity—and this, fortunately, a considerable one—for digesting the revolutionary technological and organizational innovations that are constantly being thrust upon it by the restless activity of the consciousness and the will; and, in so far as the subconscious does succeed in digesting this uncongenial fare, it can transmute it into viable modifications of a society's traditional culture. Yet the heart's ability to accelerate its pace is not unlimited, as the head's appears to be; and the consequence has been a greater and greater and faster and faster increase in the differential between the heart's and the head's respective speeds. The mounting tension set up by this widening gap threatens to disintegrate the human psyche.

Previews of this possible psychic catastrophe that is now threatening to overtake the human race can be found in the spectacle of what has happened already, at a number of different times and places, when an expanding culture has impinged on some alien culture that, at the time of the encounter, has been less dynamic and less potent. In the society that is the weaker of the two, the effort required for successful adaptation to the requirements of the intrusive stronger culture may be so severe as to exact a prohibitive psychic price. The pre-Cookian Polynesians had a culture of their own that was remarkable for its success in meeting the exacting challenge of living, with a Neolithic technology, in Oceania. But, just because their culture was in such fine balance and harmony with their existing environment, it was difficult for the Polynesians to modify it to meet the revolutionary environmental change to which they were suddenly exposed when, in the eighteenth century, the subversive Western Civilization burst into their hitherto calm Oceanic World. The experience was so agonizing and so discouraging that, for a time, it even put out of action in the Polynesians the impulse to procreate that is instinctive in every species of living creature. Those North American Indians that were still in the hunting and food-gathering stage of economic development when they were hit by the modern West have found it difficult to submit to the discipline, and to bear the monotony, that are the price of making one's living by agriculture, not to speak of making it by tending industrial machines.

A still more impressive illustration of the adverse effect on psychic health of an excessive pressure from an alien culture is given by the picture, in the Gospels, of the contemporary psychic condition of the Palestinian Jewish society. This case is impressive because the Jews' Canaanite culture was not a primitive or a backward one by comparison with the Hellenic culture that was impinging on it. It was the Hellenic culture's equal in achievement. It was, however, different in êthos; and, because this spiritual difference was great and because the Hellenic culture was, at this date, the more potent of the two, the Palestinian Jewish community in the first generation of the Christian Era was reeling under the Hellenic culture's impact. The psychic effect of this impact is registered in an abnormal prevalance of psychic malady in various forms. What was happening in Palestinian Jewry in Jesus's generation under the impact of Hellenism is happening today to the whole human race under the world-wide impact of the Western Civilization in its modern phase. The whole of mankind is reeling, and not just the non-Western majority of it; for, in this case, the quantity and the pace of the cultural change that is being demanded by the accelerating progress of technology are so great that even the Western authors of this technological revolution are now being carried off their feet by the impetus of the psychic tidal wave that they themselves have set in motion.

If, in our present world-wide psychic crisis, the tension between heart and head were to mount to a degree at which it would disintegrate the psyche, the consequent psychic explosion would be even more devastating than the physical explosion that can be produced by the application of the scientific discovery of the procedure for splitting an atom. In fact, an annihilating atomic world war might be the first consequence if the tension between head and heart were to issue in a schizophrenic divorce between them in our time.

This tension that has been mounting latterly in a steeply rising curve has, as has been noted, been perennial at lesser degrees of intensity, since it is coeval with the human psyche itself; and, even at these lesser degrees, it has caused many moral and material disasters in the past. It has, indeed, been the chief single cause of mankind's failure in the all-important field of a human being's relations with himself and with his fellows—a failure that presents such a melancholy contrast to the brilliance of mankind's success in its dealings with non-human nature through technology, reinforced in recent times by the application, to technology, of systematic scientific exploration and discovery. The misfit between head and heart is bound to cause trouble because the human psyche—fractured though it is into a conscious and a subconscious component—must, nevertheless, act as a unity if it is to have any chance of controlling the situations in which it finds itself or into which it brings itself. This unity in action is necessary because either of the two components has it in its power to frustrate the other —and thereby to incapacitate the psyche as a whole—if the other component tries to act independently, without regard for its yoke-fellow. When new wine is poured into old bottles, there is a risk that the aged leather may have lost its elasticity. It may no longer be capable of stretching in response to the pressure of the new wine's ferment; and, in that event, the bottles may burst and their incongruous new contents may be spilled and lost.

In the head's intellectual realm of science and technology, the head can race forward at a speed that the heart cannot emulate. Consequently the head is constantly taking the heart by surprise by confronting it with revolutionary new situations in the head's realm for which the heart is not prepared. Since all departments of human life are interdependent, a revolutionary change in one department requires adjustments to match, in the rest, in order to keep life in balance and in harmony. The head knows this well enough; and, when it has made some revolution in technology, it can discern, without much difficulty, what answering changes now have to be made in the social and cultural field in order to ensure that the revolutionary technological change shall be beneficial, or at least to prevent it from becoming disastrous. The head is almost as perspicacious in the social field as it is in the technological; but in the social field, unlike the technological, the head cannot translate its knowledge into action unless it can persuade the heart to co-operate with it in taking the action that has now become necessary for their common salvation. So long as the head is dealing with science and technology, it is free to act, because here it is acting within its realm of intellect, and it is, of course, master in its own part of the psyche's house. In the realm of social relations, on the other hand, the last word lies with the heart; for, in this part of the psyche's house, feelings count for more than reason. So the head cannot bring the existing social situation into conformity with the new technological situation that the head has created unless it can persuade the heart, too, to see reason. The heart sometimes does see reason. If it were impervious to reason, the human race would hardly have succeeded in surviving till now. But, even when the heart does eventually reconcile itself to falling in with the head's revolutionary demands, this process of agonizing emotional reappraisal always takes time; and this time-lag is inevitably a source of danger; for this is a time during which the heart may still insist on behaving in some familiar way which the head's revolutionary *fait accompli* has now paradoxically fraught with disaster.

This hazardous play between heart and head is exemplified in the dangerous situation in which mankind finds itself today as a result of two of the most recent revolutionary inventions in the never-ending series of innovations that are constantly being sprung upon the heart by its restlessly active yoke-fellow. In our day the head has harnessed atomic energy for human use and it has applied medical science and business organization to the administration of public health. Technology is a morally neutral force. It can be used, at will, to serve either life and good or death and evil. It need not be used for evil. Atomic energy, for instance, can be put into 'atoms for peace', as well as into atomic war-heads. The application of science and organization to public health has produced a result that is wholly good in itself. It has brought about a notable reduction of the death-rate. Yet the reduction of the death-rate, as well as the misuse of atoms for war, will work havoc unless the technological revolution is followed up in each case by a social one, and here is the rub.

The head sees at once what the necessary changes are. It sees that the harnessing of atomic energy will be used, as all previous technological advances have been used, for making new and deadlier weapons of war if the institution of war is maintained in the Atomic Age. The head therefore sees that, now that it has brought the Atomic Age upon mankind, the institution of war must be abolished, and that this involves also abolishing the institution of local sovereignty, since wars are waged by local sovereign states, and local states are likely to continue to go to war with each other so long as they retain the sovereign right to do so. In the Atomic Age a monopoly of the possession of atomic weapons must be given to a single world-authority invested with an overriding control over the governments of all the local states of the World for the purpose of banning the possession of atomic weapons by these.

This abolition of two old institutions and creation of one new one might give the human race security against genocide through atomic warfare; for, if all atomic weapons were lodged in the hands of a single world-authority, an atomic war would have been made impossible, and the atomic weapon would have been turned into the ultimate sanction for the policing of the World in the interests of the maintenance of world-order. But would not the abolition of war make the maintenance of a world atomic authority superfluous? The head sees that it would not. It sees that, if mankind does not commit mass-suicide by using atoms for war, it is going to use atoms for peace on a massive scale in this age of rapidly accelerating economic expansion. On this scale, atoms for peace could extend the material benefits of civilization (and consequently its spiritual benefits too) to that great majority of the human race that has been 'in' civilized society, but not 'of' it, from the beginning of civilization till now. This would be an enormous social benefit, but every good thing has its proportionate price, and the price of harnessing atomic energy, whether for peace or for war, is the production of poisonous atomic waste. This poison can drift round the globe and cause deaths thousands of miles away from the point at which it was emitted. The problem of sterilizing it cannot be solved within the frontiers of even the largest of the World's 124 sovereign local states. It can be solved only by action on a world-wide scale, and this action can be taken only by a world-authority invested with overriding powers for this purpose.

The head also sees that the immediate effect of the recent reduction in the death-rate has been to set off a population-explosion, and that this will continue until the birth-rate has been reduced proportionately.

The application of modern science to preventive medicine,

and of modern administrative technique to the administration of public health, has already reduced the death-rate notably, and the rate of infant mortality above all—and this not only in the advanced countries but in the backward majority. This is, in itself, one of the most beneficent achievements of modern Western civilization. Far fewer human beings than ever before are now being brought into the World only to die before they have reached maturity—not to speak of their reaching the natural term of a human life. At the same time, the number of human beings who are being born—and born nowadays with this longer expectation of life—has not yet appreciably diminished; for a reduction of the birth-rate, to match the already achieved reduction of the death-rate, cannot be brought about, as the reduction of the death-rate has been, by simple sanitary and administrative measures in which the beneficiaries acquiesce, even if they do nothing actively to further them. They acquiesce because they can hardly fail to appreciate the value of the lengthening of the expectation of life, and they have received this boon without being required to pay for it by making any change in their personal habits. By contrast, a reduction of the birth-rate can be brought about only by tens of thousands of choices on the part of hundreds of millions of pairs of wives and husbands; and for them to make this reduction—and it can be made only by their voluntary action—will require them to break with a habit that is as old as our pre-human ancestors. This habit is the rabbit-like one of breeding up to the maximum in the expectation that one's progeny will be prematurely decimated by the maximum number of casualties.

This expectation no longer holds good; and a recognition of this change in the human situation should bring with it a change of objective. The number of children that parents should now aim at bringing into the World should not be the maximum number; it should be the optimum number. That is to say, it should be the number that, in the particular social and cultural circumstances of the particular time and place, will have the best prospect of enjoying the kind of life that will be the best possible, both materially and spiritually, for the new generation. In the advanced countries, parents have already appreciated this point and have acted on it, with the consequence that, in most of these countries, the movement of population has been brought back into approximate equilibrium by now. On the other hand, the backward majority of mankind has not yet taken the point, and, even if and when it does take it, there may be a considerable time-lag between understanding and action. The head sees that, since no species of living creature can increase its numbers to infinity, the current increase in the World's human population will eventually be curbed by one agency or another. It will be curbed brutally by the traditional scourges of famine, pestilence, and war if it has not previously been curbed humanely by voluntary family-planning. The head foresees that this will take much longer to bring about than the reduction of the death-rate has taken. The sudden reduction of the death-rate has taken the majority of mankind by surprise, and it can be foreseen that this majority will need time to re-educate itself into begetting only the optimum number of children instead of the maximum number. It cannot yet be foreseen how long this process of self-education is going to take; but it can be foreseen that, until it has been completed, the size of the World's population will continue to soar, and that already, by the year 2000, it will have doubled or trebled the figure at which it stood in 1965.

Fortunately, science applied to food-production appears to be equal to the task of feeding two or three times as many people as there are to be fed today, and feeding them all on the standard now enjoyed only by an affluent minority of the human race. Science can increase the fertility of soils by adding missing elements to them; it can make potentially fertile deserts bear crops by irrigating them with desalinated sea-water; and, when the whole land-surface of the Earth that is not smothered by building has been utilized to the full for agriculture, science can start cultivating the sea (a beginning has already been made off the coasts of Japan). Science can perform these feats of food-production, but it can perform them only on one condition, which is a political condition and not a scientific or a technological one. Agricultural science's potential performance will be paralysed unless the whole surface of the globe is administered as a single unit both for the production of food and for the distribution of it; and this will require us to take the determination and execution of food-policy out of the hands of the 124 local states and to vest it in the hands of a world food authority. This will have to be set up beside the world atomic authority, and, like this, the food authority will have to be given overriding powers.

All this can be seen by the head in a trice. Reasoning is quick work. The head also knows that, in this age in which the application of science to technology has 'annihilated distance', there would be no technological or organizational obstacle to the efficient working of public authorities with a world-wide range of operation. In 1965 it would have been an easier logistical task to administer the whole surface and air-envelope of the globe and the whole human race as a unity than it was in the seventeen-eighties to administer the original domain of the United States, or than it was in the fifth century B.C. to administer Attica. In Attica, Sunium was the most distant point from the seat of government at Athens; the distance is forty English miles; and, since an Athenian citizen had no swifter means of conveyance to transport him than his own feet, he would have to spend a full day on his journey if his home was at Sunium and if he wanted to hear and see Pericles make a speech on the Pnyx. In 1965, Washington, D.C., could be reached within the day from points more than half-way round the globe; and, now that supersonic planes were in prospect, a time could be foreseen in which it would have become possible to travel, within the day, from any point on the globe's surface to any other. Meanwhile, by 1965 it had already become unnecessary for people who wished to see and hear the President of the United States to transport their bodies to within seeing and hearing distance of the White House. By radio or by television, they could hear the President's voice and see his face and gestures in their own homes. Through these distance-annihilating means of communication, a world-wide public could now become familiar with the personality of any of the leading figures in the contemporary World. An eminent leader's constituency was no longer just his own country; it was now the World itself. It has been noticed already that, when President Kennedy was assassinated, hundreds of millions of people, all over the World, felt as keen a sense of personal loss as if they had met Kennedy in the flesh.

With this world-encompassing apparatus at its command, the head could have established a world-government in 1965 if it had had a free hand. The way had been shown, by this date, by a number of private commercial and industrial corporations that had organized for themselves world-wide networks of branch offices, subsidiary factories, and local purchasing and marketing agencies. These corporations did have a free hand, because there was no cherished institution or ingrained habit that stood in the way of their operating on the world-wide scale that their business interests required. As soon as they had found that they needed to operate on this scale, they could proceed to set up the requisite organization unopposed. By 1965 there was a more imperative and more urgent need for the establishment of world-wide political authorities with overriding powers. The prompt establishment of them had become a matter of life and death since the advent of atomic weapons, of poisonous atomic waste, and of public hygiene that had achieved a sensational reduction of the death-rate. In this field, however, the task of meeting the need by translating the idea into accomplished fact was going to be slow and arduous. This task could not be accomplished till the head had persuaded the heart to co-operate with it; and this meant persuading the heart to renounce the two cherished institutions of national sovereignty and war, and to break with the ingrained habit of breeding up to the limit.

In 1965 the great majority of mankind was still behaving as if the death-rate had not yet been reduced and as if atomic weapons had not yet been invented.

The indigent two-thirds of mankind were still breeding recklessly, regardless of the revolutionary new fact that their children were now no longer dying like flies. In these indigent countries the population was now increasing so fast that this was threatening to cancel—and perhaps more than cancel—the effect of the increase in their productivity through the application of modern science to their technology. While these peoples were demanding and expecting a rise in their standard of living, they were playing for a fall in it—a fall that would be catastrophic, since they were on the verge of famine, as it was. Yet, so far, this grim prospect had not jolted them out of their traditional rut.

In the field of politics the spectacle was similar. Since the end of the Second World War, the number of the sovereign

independent states among which the land-surface of the globe
was partitioned had almost doubled, and the representatives of
the new ruling class in the recently liberated states were demonstrating, by their actions, that their emancipation from Western
colonial rule had not emancipated them from the Western
ideology of nationalism. As they saw it, nationalism was the
dynamic force from which the West derived the power by
which they had been subjugated. The first use to which they
were putting their newly-gained liberty was to make this
Western talisman their own; and they were resorting to violence
in pursuit of national aims as recklessly as their peoples were
continuing to breed. This nationalist-mindedness in the recently
liberated countries was, of course, understandable. It was a
perhaps inevitable reaction against the political subjection to
foreign rulers from which they had just escaped. It was more
disconcerting to see nationalism still rampant in countries that
had not been under foreign rule and that, in the not distant
past, had met with repeated calamities in the international
arena.

President de Gaulle had set his heart on resuscitating his
country's glorious past, as if he had forgotten that her path of
glory had led to the successive disasters of 1714, 1812, 1815,
1870, 1914–18, and 1940. Undaunted by these death's-head
dates, de Gaulle was straining France's material resources in
order to create an atomic armament that could have no practical effect except to ensure that France would bring on herself
a final irretrievable disaster if an atomic world war ever should
break out. The passion for prestige that was the motive for this
folly was another expression of nationalist-mindedness; and in
a French heart, too, this was understandable; for, in 1965,
French hearts were still suffering from the national humiliation
of 1940. Since, in 1940, Britain had played the beau rôle, there
was not the same excuse for Sir Alec Douglas-Home's insistence
that Britain must maintain her atomic armament on the ground
that this—militarily negligible though it was—would nevertheless ensure for Britain a place at the council-table of the super-
great powers. This British snobbery was an even less defensible
ground than French sensitiveness was for an anti-social policy—
and, in the Atomic Age, it was irresponsibly anti-social to work
for an increase in the number of the atomically-armed coun-

tries, when the necessary first step towards bringing atomic power under unified control was to confine the possession of it to the two atomic super-powers that, between them, had held a virtual monopoly of it so far.

The governments and peoples of the Soviet Union and the United States had been showing some sense of the responsibility that their virtual monopoly of this fearful weapon carried with it. More than once, since the end of the Second World War, they had refrained from going to war with each other in circumstances that would probably have resulted in war in the Pre-Atomic Age. All the same, Russia's post-war conduct was a replica, on a larger scale, of France's. After having suffered, twice in one life-time, devastation such as France had never experienced, Russia was now engaging with America in a hazardous struggle for world-power; and this 'cold war' might engulf the World in an atomic war at any moment, so long as it continued to be waged. The spectacle of the United States rushing out into the world-arena, to confront Russia and China there, was stranger still. This was a complete reversal of the classic policy of isolation that had been practised by the American people assiduously, ever since French military and political power in North America had been liquidated in the Seven Years' War. When the prospect of a second world war had loomed up, the American people had set itself to rule out the possibility of any repetition of the entanglements that had involved America in belligerency in the First World War. If, at the time in 1939 when the neutrality legislation was being enacted by the Congress at Washington, anyone had foretold to the Americans that America, not content with having become the protagonist in the Second World War, would be fighting a colonial war for ascendancy in South-East Asia twenty years after the Second World War's close, this Cassandra would have been written off as a lunatic by almost every American then alive. The incessant warfare of blood-soaked Europe had been one of those endemic evils of the Old World from which the American people's ancestors had been intending to jump clear when they had shaken the dust of their native continent from off their feet and had put the breadth of the Atlantic between the Old World and their transoceanic site for a new earthly paradise.

The American people's re-descent into the international arena was an amazing *volte-face*. But it was not so amazing or so poignant or so ominous as the Chinese people's re-conversion to nationalist-mindedness after it had been consistently world-minded for more than two thousand years. For perhaps a thousand years, ending in the eighth decade of the third century B.C., the Chinese World had been partitioned among a number of contending local states, like the contemporary Hellenic World and like the Western World and the World at large in A.D. 1965. The wars in which these Chinese local states had pursued their rivalries with each other had been as devastating as the fratricidal wars that the Greeks had waged in the same epoch. The Chinese, however, had been singular in the persistence with which they had acted subsequently on the lessons of a common tragic experience. At both ends of the Old World the recurring bouts of havoc-making wars between local states had been arrested, at the eleventh hour, by a knock-out blow that had enabled a sole surviving victor to impose peace by extinguishing all its rivals and thereby converting itself into an empire that was felt by its citizens to be a world-state because it embraced all of the world within their ken that seemed to be of any account. The Chinese world-state at the eastern end of the Old World had had its counterpart, for a time, in the Roman Empire at the western end; but the sequel had not been the same in the two regions. The Chinese world-state had maintained itself, off and on, ever since its establishment in the year 221 B.C. It had occasionally disintegrated, but, each time, it had reconstituted itself. It had occasionally been overrun by foreign invaders, but, each time, it had shaken them off. In the year A.D. 1965 it was still in being, and by A.D. 2000 its citizens would amount to more than half the human race, if the statisticians' forecasts should prove to have been correct. Thus the Chinese world-state was still a going concern at a date when the younger Roman Empire had, long ago, faded away into 'ancient history'.

The Chinese world-state was still on the map, but the Chinese people's political êthos had recently changed as radically as the American people's, and the Chinese *volte-face* was the more portentous of the two. The tradition of isolation with which the Americans had now broken was less than 200 years old; the tradition of world-mindedness, with which the Chinese had now broken, was more than 2,000 years old. The Chinese had not jettisoned their classic tradition readily. This had been their reluctant and tardy reaction to the experience of a century of humiliations that had begun with China's defeat by Britain in the 'opium war' and had culminated in Japan's attempt to conquer China bodily during the years 1931–45. Down to 1840, China, in the Chinese people's estimation, had been co-extensive with the civilized World. The non-Chinese peoples in China's penumbra were tributary barbarians; those beyond, in the outer darkness, did not count. It had required the repeated experience of finding themselves at other peoples' mercy in war to convince the Chinese, at last, that they could no longer afford to behave as if there were no other peoples in the World whom they need take seriously. They had been compelled, by successive blows from foreign fists, to recognize the bitter truth that the Chinese people was now one nation among others—and a weak nation at that. By 1965 the Chinese had become grimly determined to demonstrate that, although China was no longer the world-state of the classic Chinese tradition, she could and would play the novel role of a nation-state with a truculence that would be in scale with her size and her population and her past.

The China of 1965 was, in fact, the France of 1965 written large. Like France, China was kicking against the pricks of a recent humiliation; and, like France again, she had decided that the acquisition of the atomic arm was to be one of the symbols of her recapture of her rightful place in the World. The temper was the same, but the menace was much more serious; for China, now that she had put her heart into making herself into a technologically efficient military power, was capable of becoming more than a match for Russia and America combined. Moreover, the Chinese Government was the only one in the World that was boasting that it could engage in an atomic war and could survive to come out of it victorious. No doubt, this vainglorious boast would be confuted by the event if the boast were ever to be put to the test. Yet, if it was sincere, it was the greatest, though not the most immediate, menace to mankind's prospect of survival of any on the international horizon.

This glance at Atomic-Age Man's persistent follies and crimes raised the question whether Man could survive a revolutionary situation which his head had brought upon him while his heart was still unprepared for it. There was no comfort in the recollection that Man had been committing the same follies and crimes since the dawn of history, and yet was still on the map. He had never sinned with impunity. The wages of sin had always been death. But now mankind had been overtaken by the Atomic Age, and, in this age, the wages of a long-indulged human sin might be the extinction of the human race. The invention of a genocidal weapon could not, of course, make a sin more sinful than it was intrinsically, but it could make the material consequences of committing the sin immensely graver. What, then, in the Atomic Age, were mankind's prospects? Was the human race likely to survive the perilous time-lag between the revolutionary *fait accompli* with which it had now been confronted by its accelerating progress in technology and the obstinacy with which it was clinging to old and familiar habits and institutions that had become mortal dangers to its survival in the revolutionary new circumstances?

For the generation that is facing the challenge of the Atomic Age, there is one consideration that is of crucial importance. Being human, this generation cannot repudiate responsibility by claiming that it is doomed. The social insects would, in truth, be doomed if their behaviour were to become deadly for them; for their behaviour, unlike ours, is built into their psychophysical constitution. It cannot be changed by any deliberate action of theirs. By contrast, human beings have the power, and the responsibility, of choosing. The present generation cannot divest itself of its human power to choose; and, if it were to choose death and evil, this would be its own choice, its own responsibility, its own sin. It has it in its power to make the alternative choice of life and good, if it will make a moral effort to renounce the cherished institutions of national sovereignty and war, and to abandon the ingrained habit of breeding up to the limit.

This effort would be strenuous and painful, but it would be well within human nature's moral power. It would be no more severe than the recent effort that the Chinese people and the American people had each made when they had broken with a traditional policy. In both these cases, unfortunately, the *volte-face* achieved by a mighty effort had been a revulsion towards evil and death. But there had been another contemporary breach with political tradition that was more encouraging. On the eve of the advent of the Atomic Age, the Mahatma Gandhi had demonstrated that it is possible to make a revolutionary political change without recourse to the violence that has customarily been used for making politically revolutionary changes in the past. If the human race refrains from committing mass-suicide, it may come, in retrospect, to recognize, in Gandhi, one of its historic saviours. He may be remembered as the timely prophet of his generation, and the timing of his achievement has surely been providential. In human affairs, change—including revolutionary political change—cannot be arrested or eliminated. In the Atomic Age, as in the Pre-Atomic Age, change is bound to be constantly going on. We have noted already that change is an inevitable accompaniment of a way of life which is transmitted from generation to generation, as our human way of life is, consciously and deliberately, by a process of education, and not biologically, by physical acts of procreation. But this inevitable change need not be brought about by violence, even when the change in question is one of a radical kind that has usually led to bloodshed in the past. There has usually been bloodshed when a subject people has won its freedom from foreign rule and when a subject race has won its emancipation from a dominant race. Yet Gandhi, by his revolutionary new political strategy of non-violent non-co-operation, made it possible for India and Britain to part from each other in peace and friendship, and Martin Luther King is consciously applying Gandhi's method in his leadership of the ex-African citizens of the United States in their struggle to win equality of human rights with their ex-European fellow-citizens. Here is a revolutionary breach with ingrained custom which is making, not for death and evil, but for life and good.

On a more prosaic level the practicability of breaking with the age-old habit of breeding up to the limit has already been demonstrated by the affluent minority of mankind. In the affluent countries the birth-rate has already been reduced, to match the reduction of the death-rate, by a widespread adoption of family-planning. What some human communities have achieved today must be achievable by others tomorrow or the day after; for the power to choose, which the minority has exercised in re-stabilizing the upward movement of their populations, is one of those distinctive faculties of human nature that are possessed by all human beings alike. In the field of population-control the Japanese people's experience is illuminating and encouraging. When, in the seventeenth century, Japan insulated herself from the rest of the World, the size of her population was kept stable by the use of various devices. When, in the nineteenth century, she reopened her doors, these restraints on Japan's population-growth were abandoned, the death-rate was reduced simultaneously by the introduction of Western medicine, and consequently the size of Japan's population soared. Today, this upward movement of Japan's population is being success-fully re-stabilized. The new level will, of course, be much higher than the level of a hundred years ago; but, at this new level, inordinate population-growth will have been arrested for the second time in Japanese history; and in the twentieth century, as in the seventeenth, this will have been brought about by deliberate choices on the part of millions of Japanese wives and husbands.

What, then, are mankind's present prospects, on balance? It looks as if the heart were going to keep the head dancing perilously on the edge of the precipice, but it also looks as if the head may succeed in persuading the heart to allow mankind to change its stance when it is faced with some inescapable, un-mistakable, and immediate choice between plunging over the edge into the abyss and the alternative of recoiling. Though re-coiling may entail the renunciation of cherished institutions and the abandonment of ingrained habits, the heart may re-luctantly recognize the truth that these sacrifices are lesser evils than suicide. It may not only admit this truth; it may consent to act upon it. If this prognosis is convincing, we may expect that, at the eleventh hour of each successive mortal crisis, man-kind will reject the choice of death and evil. Rather than bring mass-destruction on themselves by waging an atomic world war or by contaminating earth, air, and water with the poison from the waste residue of atoms for peace, the nations, we may guess, will agree to transfer sovereign power over the production and use of atomic energy from their own local governments to a new, and novel, world-authority. They will agree only tardily and sulkily, because, in the act, they will be renouncing the institutions of sovereignty and war, and both these institutions are dear to human hearts. Grumbling and growling, they will agree nevertheless, because survival is dearer than any other boon can be. We may also guess that, on the same principle of choosing the lesser evil, they will agree to a second encroachment on the traditional sovereign powers of national states. Rather than bring mass-destruction on themselves by allowing two-thirds of the human race to starve, the nations, we may guess, will agree to transfer sovereign power over the production and distribution of food from their own national governments to another new world-authority that will be still more novel than one with overriding powers in the atomic domain. They will agree to the establishment of a world food authority because they will recognize that this other revolutionary new departure is a political *conditio sine qua non* for enabling science to provide food for two or three times as many people as were alive in 1965, and to feed them all on a standard of nutrition that, in 1965, was the invidious privilege of an affluent minority.

In this debate between head and heart which is also a race between life and death, the head's most telling argument will be that self-preservation overrides all other considerations, and that its requirements must therefore be met, whatever the price. This intellectual exercise in the practice of enlightened self-interest may not, however, be the last word in the dialogue; for appeals to reason are apt to leave the heart cold, even when the reason shown is both evident and urgent. The heart's concurrence in the head's rational but revolutionary plans for salutary action may be won, in the last resort, by an appeal to an emotional urge that Nature has instilled into the heart of every living creature. Every creature has a built-in impulse to provide for the perpetuation of the species of which it is a momentary living representative. This deep concern for the self-preservation of the species overrides, in the heart, the individual's self-centred concern to preserve himself, and, *a fortiori*, it overrides his concern to cling to familiar habits and institutions. The head may succeed in touching and releasing this emotional spring of action that lies in the heart by drawing the

heart's attention to the chart of time-scales that we have un-
folded at an earlier point in this chapter.

At first sight this chart may look like a caricature of a trick
of the head's that the heart finds repulsive. The head has
achieved its dazzling scientific and technological success by
reducing all the phenomena of the Universe to quantitative
terms. It has not shrunk from quantifying the facts of life, and,
as the heart feels it, this is tantamount to denaturing them. In
thrusting upon the heart a set of abstract numerals, will not the
head be giving the heart wanton provocation? Will it not be
going out of its way to alienate it, when its intention is to con-
ciliate it? This might look like an irrational act of folly. Yet the
head has one pair of figures, not yet mentioned in this book, that
does contain a high emotional charge. The first member of this
pair is mankind's age up to date; the second member is its expectation of life on this planet if it does not extirpate itself by its
own action—and no agent except Man himself has the power to
exterminate Man now that Man has established his ascendancy
over bacteria and viruses, as well as over lions and tigers.

If the estimates of our present-day scientists are approximately correct, the human race has been in existence for less
than a million years so far, and this planet will be habitable
for human beings for 2,000,000,000 years more. Mankind's
expectation of life is thus about 2,000 times as long as its present
age. It has also only recently begun to obey effectively the
legendary commandment 'be fruitful, multiply, and replenish
the Earth'.[1] Mankind could be fruitful from the start, but it
could not multiply and replenish the Earth until it had acquired
the medical skill to reduce its specific natural death-rate. These
two facts, taken together, tell us that an overwhelming majority
of the human race is still unborn. Fifty years from now, the
equation of the dead with the majority, which is one of the stock
themes of Roman epitaphs,[2] may have ceased to hold good. The
human beings who will be alive in the year 2015 may be more
numerous than all their predecessors since our ancestors became
human; and, even if, by that date, the Earth has been duly
replenished and the size of the World's population has been
successfully stabilized, this number will have been reproduced
at least 60,000,000 times over, as, in the course of the next

---

[1] Gen. 1, 28; 9, 1.   [2] 'Migravit ad plures.'

2,000,000,000 years, one generation continues to succeed another.

This innumerable host of human beings still unborn has a plea to make to the tiny minority, alive in our day, which holds posterity's destiny in its hands through the accident of happening to be alive at this time. Our unborn potential successors cannot plead their own cause. Their plea to us has to be put to us by ourselves, since we, and only we, out of all those who have departed and all those who are still to come, are now alive and therefore now bear the responsibility of holding the trusteeship for the species of which we are the momentary representatives. The plea is one that has an appeal for head and heart alike.

For the head, the plea is a characteristically numerical one. It would be a monstrously arbitrary and arrogant abuse of power if the minority that happens now to be alive were to decide to prevent an overwhelmingly more numerous potential majority of the human race from ever coming to birth. If the present generation were to liquidate the human race, it would be taking action that would be irrevocable and irreparable; and for this it has no quorum, no prescience, and therefore no mandate. 'Better dead than red' is a value-judgement that a twentieth-century human being is entitled to make only for himself and not for any other human being, either alive or unborn. If 'better dead than red' is his considered judgement, he can act on it, without much inconvenience to his neighbours, by putting his head in a gas-oven after turning on the tap or, Roman fashion, by getting into a hot bath and severing one of his arteries. He is not entitled to carry with him the rest of his present and future fellow human beings. Human sacrifice has been reprobated, long since, by a general consensus; and this would be human sacrifice on a scale that would dwarf any that has been perpetrated by the kings of the first dynasty of Ur or by the kings of the Shang dynasty in China or by Scythian chiefs or by Aztec priests or by Assyrian and Mongol war-lords or by Hitler. Atomic genocide would be total genocide, and the mere thought of committing this abominable atrocity is criminal.

The arrogance of this criminal thought lies in its assumption of a prescience that no human mind can possess. Let us imagine that we are back in the Roman Empire in the last decade of the fourth century of the Christian Era. The fanatical Christian

Emperor Theodosius I has been misusing the power of the
Roman Imperial Government to ban the practice of all current
religions except Christianity, though, in the Roman Empire at
this date, the voluntary Christians are in a minority. Eugenius
has set himself up as a counter-emperor to vindicate the non-
Christian majority's human right to continue to practise its
ancestral religious cults. Eugenius is now losing the war with
his adversary Theodosius; and, if he does lose it, the forcible
imposition of Christianity on the non-Christian majority will be
confirmed without any foreseeable prospect of the issue being
reopened in favour of religious toleration. Eugenius did lose
the war, as a matter of historical fact. But, at this point, let us
insert a piece of historical fiction. Let us suppose that, in the
year 394, the belligerents in the Roman civil war possessed the
atomic weapon (to make this fiction plausible, we have only
to give a slight imaginary additional acceleration to the historical pace of scientific discovery and of its technological application). Let us also suppose that Eugenius, with this genocidal
weapon in his hands, took it upon himself to judge that it is
better for mankind to be dead than to be Christian, and let us
further suppose that, as his last act of state, he also took it upon
himself to act on this personal judgement of his by 'escalating'
his 'conventional' war with Theodosius into an annihilating
atomic war.

There is a point, here and now, in fictionally attributing to a
Roman ruler in 394 the appalling power that is actually possessed by the rulers of the atomically-armed states of the present
day. The point is that the lapse of nearly sixteen centuries has
given us retrospectively, in our time, a knowledge of the sequel
to the forcible imposition of Christianity on the Roman World
which Eugenius did not and could not have, presciently, about
his world's future, and which we ourselves do not and cannot
have about our world's future, either. What is the lesson of the
actual survival, down to the present day, of the world on which
Christianity was imposed by force nearly 1,600 years ago? In
the light of the history of this world between then and now, do
we find that, in our opinion, Eugenius would have been justified
in annihilating this world and bringing its history to an end,
supposing that he had actually possessed the genocidal weapon
that is in the hands of his present-day counterparts?

In trying to answer this question, we have, of course, to accept the assumption that the ideology to which genocide is held to be preferable is in truth as evil as it is held to be by the anti-Communist or anti-Christian who prefers genocide to it. At the least we have to assume that, even if Communism and Christianity are not held to be wholly evil intrinsically, it is held to be an intolerable evil that any ideology, even if it were not wholly bad, should be imposed on an unwilling majority by force. Christianity was successfully imposed by force. As one of the continuing consequences of Theodosius's victory over Eugenius, it became impossible for any Christian under a Christian government's rule to abjure Christianity, or even to subscribe to a version of it that was deemed to be heretical by the civil and ecclesiastical authorities, without being put to death. Judaism was the only non-Christian religion that was now tolerated within the bounds of Christendom, and the Jewish minority was made by the Christian majority to pay for its barely tolerated faithfulness to its ancestral religion by being subjected to outrageous penalization. Moreover, eventually both Judaism and Islam ceased to be tolerated in Christian Spain and Portugal. Without regard to the fact that Muslims and Jews worshipped the same god as the Christians themselves worshipped, the Iberian Christians finally compelled the Jewish and Muslim communities in the Peninsula to choose between embracing Christianity and going into exile. In Western Christendom this monstrous régime of Christian totalitarianism, imposed by force, lasted for 1,300 years, reckoning from the closing decades of the fourth century of the Christian Era to the closing decades of the seventeenth. This reign of totalitarian Christianity in the West was thus longer, by three centuries, than the 'Thousand Years' Reich' that Hitler promised for his totalitarian German nationalism. The disintegration of Western Christendom at the Reformation only aggravated the evil. After that, Western Christians took to persecuting, not only Jews and Muslims, but also fellow Western Christians of the enemy sect. Totalitarian Christianity's 'Thirteen Hundred Years' Reich' culminated, in the West, in the Catholic-Protestant Wars of Religion. Thus its reign was long, and the last phase of it was the worst. But its reign was not eternal. Just because the last phase of it was so bad, this provoked a moral reaction that brought Western Christian totalitarianism to an end. In the Western World by the end of the seventeenth century, the régime of religious toleration, which Constantine had inaugurated and Theodosius had abrogated in the fourth century, had been re-established; and, though three centuries more have elapsed since then, and these centuries have seen Western Man commit further crimes and follies (including, in Nazism, the greatest wickedness ever yet perpetrated anywhere), totalitarianism has not yet been reimposed on the Western society successfully so far.

The lesson of the 1,300-years-long history of Christian totalitarianism in the West is that, so long as the human race allows itself simply to stay alive, it can be confident that it will outlive any of the habits and institutions that it has introduced into its social and cultural heritage. Man's social and cultural heritage is less durable than Man himself is, and that is, indeed, what we should expect, since this heritage is not a built-in part of human nature, but is merely a man-made product which its maker is free to modify if he chooses. This is another way of saying that, while there is life, there is hope. Theodosius's victory over Eugenius condemned forty successive generations in the West to sit in darkness and the shadow of death, but the forty-first generation came out of the end of the tunnel into the daylight again. But what of this generation's forty unfortunate predecessors? Well, forty is only about one in 15,000 out of the 60,000,000 generations and more that will have come and gone by the end of mankind's term of life on Earth if we allow our species to enjoy the full time-span for which the surface of this planet, if left uncontaminated, is expected to continue to be habitable by human beings. Those forty generations did suffer while they were ensuring mankind's survival by staying alive; yet evidently they themselves judged that their suffering did not make life not worth living. Few people in medieval Christendom among those who repined against being compelled to live under a totalitarian Christian régime went so far as to commit suicide as a protest, and equally few people have been committing protest-suicide in states that have been under a totalitarian Communist régime since 1917.

The moral surely is that patience is a better counsellor than intransigence, and endurance a better reaction to evil than suicide.

Odysseus' argument with his heart in favour of endurance holds good for mankind's social life as well as for the personal life of an individual. Recall the past afflictions that you have successfully survived, and the memory of these experiences will hearten you to brave your current trials.[1] Odysseus was rewarded for his endurance by regaining Ithaca at last and recovering his wife and son and kingdom. He earned the title 'god-like' (δῖος) by demonstrating that he was indomitable (πολυτλάς). Mankind's history is an Odyssey; we should be committing an unforgivable sin against the innumerable generations still unborn if we were to act, not like Odysseus, but like Ajax.

[1] *Odyssey*, Book XX, line 18.

IV

Divisive and Unifying Movements
in History

In the preceding chapter it has been suggested that, now
that Man has harnessed atomic energy and has applied medical
science and business organization to the administration of
public health, government on a world-wide scale, for some
purposes at least, has become urgently necessary. The necessity
is urgent because the alternative, in each case, would be an
appalling and perhaps irretrievable catastrophe. A world-authority for the control of atomic energy has become necessary for
saving mankind from either committing mass-suicide in an
atomic world-war or poisoning itself with atomic waste. Another world-authority for the control of the production and
distribution of food is likely to become necessary for saving
mankind from widespread famine. The need for these particular
two world-authorities is already evident; and, since the need for
each of them has arisen from an advance in technology, and
since technology is still advancing at an accelerating pace, we
may expect to find further world-authorities becoming necessary, in increasing numbers and at ever shorter intervals of time,
for solving other human problems to which technology will give
rise. The head can comprehend mankind's present situation and
can also discern its new requirements. Can it persuade the heart
to co-operate with it in making the requisite revolutionary social
and cultural changes that the head is powerless to make by
itself, without its temperamental partner's concurrence? This
perennial question has become one of life and death in the
Atomic Age, and we cannot predict the answer that Man is
going to give to it in this critical case. Today, as often in the
past, a need for unity is having to contend with divisive habits
and institutions. What we can do is to take a look at the history

of past divisive and unifying movements. This may enable us to make some estimate of their respective strengths; and this estimate, tentative though it will inevitably be, may nevertheless throw some light on the prospects of the momentous bout of this perennial struggle in which we are engaged in our time.

The unity and division of mankind must be coeval with Man himself. Since Man is one of those forms of life that propagate themselves by sexual differentiation and reunion, at least two of our pre-human ancestors must have become human simultaneously, and these two must have been of opposite sex. If only one individual at a time had achieved humanity, the newly evolved genus homo would have become extinct at his or her death and would never have been incarnate in more than a single representative. If the minimum possible number of primeval human beings is thus two, there will have been plurality in human affairs from the start; but there will also have been social unity if the primeval two were of opposite sex, since the most intimate form of social union is mating. Plurality, however, had economics on its side during the earliest chapter of human history, which, so far, has been much the longest. For perhaps 99 per cent. of the time during which Man has been in existence so far, he has made his living as a food-gatherer, and food-gathering is such an inefficient form of economy that people who have not yet got beyond it have to live in tiny bands, and these bands have to keep at a great distance from each other; for, if they were to grow larger and to come closer, they would not be able to gather enough berries and roots and grubs to keep them alive. The surviving natives of Australia, who still live by food-gathering, are a living museum of a way of life that has been lived by the ancestors of all human beings now alive for 99 per cent. of the time during which mankind has been in existence.

Accordingly, if there was ever a time in which there was only one band of human beings in existence, and this a band composed of one man and one woman only, that time must have been as short as it is fabled to have been in the story in the Book of Genesis. As soon as food-gathering mankind began to multiply, it must have begun to split and to scatter. There must have been pluralism of communities, as well as pluralism of individuals, since a very early date in human history.

It will be seen that Man's primeval food-gathering economy must have compelled mankind to expand geographically from its place of origin, whether this was in East Africa or Central Africa or somewhere else. The expansion will have been very slow; for primeval Man had no other means of locomotion than his own legs, and the increase in his numbers, which was the force that was driving him to scatter ever more widely over the face of the Earth, will have been gradual at this early stage; for, though Man was providing for the perpetuation of his species by breeding up to the limit, his death-rate was proportionately high so long as he had not yet got the upper hand over other beasts of prey. So far as we know, Man did not establish his ascendency over lions and tigers till he had at least developed his art of tool-making to the Upper Palaeolithic degree of refinement, and that was not more than something between 30,000 and 50,000 years ago. He did not establish his ascendency over bacteria till he had become aware of their existence, and that was only one hundred years ago. Thus, during perhaps more than 96 per cent. of the food-gathering stage of mankind's history—a stage that covers about 99 per cent. of our total history up to date—the pressure on mankind to expand geographically was not great, while its means of locomotion were not good. On the other hand, the time that mankind had at its disposal for occupying the Earth—without yet being able to 'replenish' it—was very long indeed. Since, till recently, the average expectation of life was appreciably shorter than it has now come to be, we may perhaps equate a primeval human generation with about a quarter of a century. This would give about 34,800 generations for the Lower Palaeolithic Age, and about 36,000 for the Palaeolithic Age as a whole. How far could a human family walk, in one generation, over trackless country? The distance would, of course, vary according to the nature of the terrain that homo pedester happened to come across; yet, however low we may set our estimate of a pedestrian generation's average length of trek, this figure, multiplied by the number of the successive trekking generations, will have been amply sufficient to carry mankind to the ends of the Earth before the close of the food-gathering stage of human history.

Food-gathering mankind's geographical expansion would

have been limited only by geographical and climatic barriers. It is still less than 500 years ago that human beings first reached America from the Old World across mid-Atlantic; and, though we can and do now fly over the poles, we have not yet made ourselves at home on either of them. If there was an interval between the time at which our pre-human ancestors shed the greater part of their fur-coverage and the date when their descendants discovered how to kindle fire and keep it alight, the intervening generations' habitat must have been confined to the warm region in which Man is believed to have evolved. But, since we do not know of any species of human being, extant or extinct, that has been ignorant of the art of fire-making, we may guess that Prometheus was identical with primal Man, if he was not his precursor. If we were to mythologize, we might imagine that some near-man was burdened by the gods with a fully awakened human consciousness as the appropriate punishment for his presumption in acquiring a too god-like technological 'know-how'. Anyway, till some human beings had taken, not only to making fire, but also to making and wearing clothes, and this not just for self-adornment but as a utilitarian protection against the elements, human beings could not have made themselves at home in regions with cold winters. However, the distribution of the Palaeolithic tools discovered by modern archaeologists tells us that, before the close of the Palaeolithic Age, human beings of the 'sapiens' species had made their way out of the Old World, over the land-bridge that has now been submerged under the Bering Straits since the end of the most recent of the glaciations, and that they had gone on to occupy the New World right down to the southern tip of South America.

Thus Man had spread a film of humanity over almost the whole of the habitable surface of the Earth while his means of communication had continued to be limited to the same pedestrian means with which he had started at the beginning of his history, when every human being yet alive was still doing his or her food-gathering within easy walking distance of every other. The primeval band of people who were all in touch with each other on foot had split, amoeba-like, into a number of separate bands, each no bigger in numbers than the original one, but numerous enough to occupy the greater part of the Earth's land-surface as densely as is practicable for food-gatherers. Parting and scattering had been inevitable and easy; but, when once this was an accomplished fact, reunion was going to be difficult. To retrace their steps to their first human ancestors' original centre of dispersion would have taken food-gathering human beings as long again as it had taken them to reach the ends of the Earth, since their means of locomotion were still what they had always been. But, long before they could have reassembled, they would either have starved or become engaged in a fratricidal struggle with each other for existence, since the food-supply obtainable by each of the converging bands would have dwindled below the minimum subsistence-point as they drew nearer to each other. Human beings could not live in denser agglomerations than those of the present-day Australian natives until they had discovered more efficient ways of feeding themselves, and they could not communicate with each other, either for co-operation or for conflict, until they had invented better means of communication than those with which they had been endowed by Nature. So long as their means of communication were limited to human feet and human voices, they could not even know of the existence of their fellow human beings in the Antipodes. Indeed, there is a people—and this an agricultural one—in the almost impenetrable interior of Papua whose existence remained unknown to the rest of mankind until within our life-time.

Today the Australian natives' way of life is a rare relic of the long-drawn-out first stage of mankind's history. Within the last 9,000 years the great majority of mankind has changed its way of life so radically, and is continuing still to change it at such a breakneck speed today, that it is difficult for us now to bear in mind the historical truth that, in human history up to date, the Australian natives' way has been the norm, while our way is a very recent exception to it. Yet this truth is not just one of the curiosities of history; it is an important factor in our own present situation. One of the causes of the difficulty that the head is finding in its present attempt to persuade the heart to come into line with it is that the heart of urban and agrarian Man is still captivated by the food-gathering way of life that was being lived by his ancestors, too, till the day before yesterday and had been lived by them for aeons before that, while the head—rational-minded and well-informed though it boasts itself to be—has long ago forgotten the pre-agricultural Garden of Eden in which the heart is still dreamily roaming. Till the head understands the heart, it cannot hope to influence it. One of the hopeful signs of these present anxious times is that our head-made sciences—archaeology, anthropology, and, perhaps above all, psychology—are now informing the head about the nature and origin of those powerful counter-pulls on human heart-strings that are making the head's present tug-o'-war with the heart so arduous for it.

The abiding influence of the age-old food-gathering way of life on our present infant agricultural and industrial society is attested by familiar present-day facts.

One of the present-day facts that are legacies from the Food-gathering Age is the still continuing babel of tongues. Since language, like fire-making, has been a common faculty of all known human societies, extant or extinct, we may conclude that, like fire-making, language is coeval with mankind itself. Indeed, in the second chapter of this book, it has been suggested that the specifically human device of transmitting a social and cultural heritage by education would have been impracticable until the transmitting and the receiving generation had acquired a common language—learnt unconsciously by the children from their elders—as a means of communicating ideas and of inculcating habits and institutions. The members of the primeval band of human beings must have talked to each other, and this in some single language, common to them all. Today, there are hundreds and thousands of living languages whose speakers are unintelligible to each other, and the dead languages, if we could count up them, too, might turn out to be still more numerous. Moreover, besides being mutually unintelligible, most of the living languages are so different from each other in their phonetics and their structure, as well as in their vocabulary, that our present-day scientific students of language cannot trace any affinity between them. Many of these apparently unrelated languages are restricted to small groups of people within a narrow geographical range. Indeed, in some regions, such as the West African forest zone, in which the physical obstacles to communication have been unusually great till recently, a number of mutually unintelligible languages are still being spoken within close range of each other. This extreme diversification of the single language with which mankind may be presumed to have started is one of the consequences of the conditions of life in the Food-gathering Age; and it is also one of the indications of the enduring effect of that 900,000-years-long chapter of history 9,000 years after the majority of us have left it behind us. In this time-perspective, these last 9,000 years are contemporary history, and the preceding 900,000 years are not 'ancient history' but are virtually the whole of history—covering, as they do, everything from our origins down to our very recent past.

Another striking testimony to the lastingness of the Food-gathering Age's influence is to be found in the recreations to which agrarian and urban Man has had recourse for relief from the exacting and irksome conditions of his new-fangled ways of making his living. Down to the present day since the dawn of Civilization about 5,000 years ago, and perhaps since the dawn of the Neolithic Age about 4,000 years before that, human beings have delighted to spend on hunting and fishing the hours of leisure that they have been able to spare from their new avocations of cultivating the soil, tending domesticated animals, manufacturing artificial commodities, selling and buying these man-made goods, as well as food and raw materials, administering states and private businesses, and making war. In contrast to these typical contemporary business activities, hunting and fishing are not recent inventions; they are legacies from the Food-gathering Age; but in that age they were not recreations; they were then Man's staple ways of making his living. The exhilaration that contemporary Man feels when he goes hunting and fishing, or even when he goes picking blueberries, spying mushrooms, or digging up truffles, is an indication of post-food-gathering Man's abiding nostalgia for the life that has been lived by all but the last few generations of his ancestors. He bears unconscious witness to this nostalgia of his in treasuring as forms of recreation for himself those activities that were his food-gathering ancestors' serious business.

These considerations perhaps go some way towards explaining why it is that the political pluralism which, during the first 900,000 years of human history, was inevitable under the then prevailing technological and economic conditions, should have persisted so obstinately during these latest nine thousand years, during which our means of communication have been progressively improving, and this latterly at an accelerating pace. Indeed this legacy from the Food-gathering Age is the key to the paradox that even those present-day peoples that are in the van of modern technological and economic progress are still passionately nationalist in their political feelings in an age in which technology, by annihilating distance, has made mankind's inherited political pluralism not only senseless but also inimical to the survival of the human race.

The first, and, so far, also the greatest, technological and economic revolution in human history has been the invention, some 9,000 years ago, of agriculture and the contemporaneous domestication of several species of non-human animals to serve human purposes. These two major discoveries, together with the arts of pottery-making and spinning and weaving, which followed at their heels, revolutionized the material conditions of human life; but it is not so paradoxical that this first technological and economic revolution should not have produced any appreciable move towards beginning to mend mankind's long since fractured political structure. Man's means of locomotion were improved when he reinforced his own muscle-power with the domesticated donkey's. On the other hand, the practice of agriculture ended his roving in search of Nature's gifts and rooted him in the small patch of soil from which he was now raising his annual crops; and he did not recover his mobility through the domestication of animals—not even when, at a relatively recent date in the present Post-Palaeolithic Age, he invented nomadic pastoralism. The nomadic pastoralist (today on the verge of extinction) has cut loose from his farmer-ancestor's moorings in a Neolithic village. Launching himself, with his family and flocks and herds, on to the sea-like steppe, he has replaced his sedentary ancestor's house with a movable tent that he transports on wheels in his annual migrations between his summer and his winter pastures. These annual migrations, however, do not carry him to the ends of the Earth, as his more remote food-gathering ancestors' continual migrations did eventually carry some of them. The nomadic pastoralist moves in a fixed annual orbit, comparable to the fixed daily orbit of the urban worker who shuttles to and fro between his dormitory and his factory or office. Moreover, the pastoral nomad has never been able to make himself technologically and

economically independent of the sedentary society out of which
he has come. He could not support life on the steppe if he were
not constantly exchanging the surplus products of his animal
husbandry for some of the surplus agricultural and industrial
products of the field and the city; and, if ever the pastoral
nomad, in one of his occasional destructive explosions out of the
desert on to the sown, had succeeded in extirpating all sedentary life within his reach, he would have discovered, too late,
that he had hacked off the branch on which he himself was
perched.

When all but a remnant of the primeval food-gathering
bands were eventually replaced by agricultural village communities—and, more recently, also by nomad pastoral hordes
in regions unfit for agriculture but good for pasture—this was
a revolution that resulted in a great increase in mankind's
numbers, but not in any radical change in human society's
political structure. This is, as has been suggested, not surprising.
But it is, perhaps, surprising that the fractured structure imposed by the conditions of the Food-gathering Age should have
survived the replacement of the Neolithic way of life by civilization, which is the dispensation under which an ever larger
majority of the human race has been living during the last
5,000 years.

The dawn of civilization in the Old World was coeval with
the invention of metallurgy and of writing, but neither of these
two technological and cultural innovations can be taken as a
criterion of the presence of civilization, since neither of them is
a cause of civilization or a distinctive feature of this way of life.
In pre-Columbian America, people succeeded in creating civilizations without inventing either metallurgy or writing simultaneously; and in the Old World, where the invention of these
two arts was concomitant with the creation of civilization, they
can be seen to have been, not civilization's cause, but two of its
consequences.

The practice of metallurgy—and of writing, too, before the
relatively simple alphabetic form of it was invented by a
brilliant feat of analytic thought—was a whole-time occupation
for specialists. To enable smiths and scribes to devote all their
working time to their professions, they had to be released from
the task of producing the food on which they and their families

subsisted. They could not be released from this till the average productivity of an agricultural worker had been raised to a pitch at which a sufficient supply of food to feed the whole community could be raised by the full-time labour of less than the whole of the community's labour-force. In the Neolithic agricultural community, the task of raising food had probably taken up the full working-time of every able-bodied woman, man, and child. A society in process of civilization has been one in which some people—at first, a small minority, though now a great majority—have been released from the daily round and common task of food-producing.

The increase of the food-producer's productivity which has made this possible was first achieved in societies that succeeded in draining and irrigating the potentially ultra-productive alluvial soil of river-valleys—e.g. the lower valleys of the Tigris and Euphrates, the Nile, and the Indus—which had previously been inhospitable jungle-swamps; and the initiation of this new and audacious human enterprise must have set up a chain-reaction, not of diminishing, but of increasing, returns. The increase of productivity made it possible to release some members of the community from agricultural work, and this new class of non-agricultural workers repaid the community for its keep by making technological and organizational inventions and doing industrial and administrative work that, in turn, made it possible to raise the standard of agricultural productivity still higher. The transformation of the former jungle-swamps into drained and irrigated fields would not have been possible if there had not been industrial specialists who could give the community the tools for doing the job, and administrative specialists who could organize the technologically well-equipped labour-force by which the work was accomplished. Conversely, these specialists could not have been released from agricultural work until after the increase in agricultural productivity had been started.

In the lower valley of the Tigris and Euphrates rivers, in the south-eastern part of what is now 'Irāq, there had come into existence, by about the year 3000 B.C., a society whose agriculture was efficient enough to support a non-agricultural minority that was free to use its working time for inventing, planning, manufacturing, and administering. The arts and sciences and institutions of civilization had now been created. Here was a major revolution in human affairs—one that was comparable to the Neolithic revolution in magnitude measured in social and cultural terms. Might not this second revolution, at any rate, reasonably have been expected to produce a turn in the tide of human political affairs? If it is true that the cause of the fracturing of the human race into a large number of small communities had been the technological inefficiency of the Food-gathering Age, might not the human race reunite again now that the technological advance made in the Neolithic revolution had been reinforced by the subsequent advance— this time, an organizational as well as a technological one— that the creation of civilization in 'Irāq had brought with it? Why should not this novel society, called into existence by the Sumerian conquerors of the Tigris-Euphrates jungle-swamp, now reunify the human race by drawing all human beings, all over the World, into itself? The novelty and brilliance of the achievement of civilization in Sumer made Sumer a potent magnet. The job might be a big one, but surely the Sumerians now had the requisite tools and wits.

The Sumerians did do a unifying job which was impressive by contrast with the previous condition of human affairs. Never before had so large a number of human beings shared with each other an identical language, script, technology, economy, religion, ethics, and social structure; and the civilization constituted by these and other elements of culture expanded geographically, beyond the limits of its original home, in the course of its 3,000-years-long history. Expanding north-westwards up the courses of its two harnessed rivers, the civilization incorporated the Sumerians' next-door neighbours, the Akkadians, completely, notwithstanding the obstacle presented by a difference of language (the Akkadians' Semitic tongue has no discernible affinity with Sumerian). Beyond Akkad, civilization in its original Sumerian form captured Assyria, and, farther away still in the same direction, it partially captured first the Hittite World in East Central Anatolia and subsequently Urartu, in what is now the eastern end of Turkey. South-eastward, it partially captured Elam in the adjoining alluvial valley of the Karun River.

This spread of the Sumerian civilization was anticipated and promoted and outdistanced by the journeys of Sumerian, and eventually also Akkadian, commercial travellers. The alluvial homeland of the Sumero-Akkadian civilization was destitute of stone, metallic ores, and timber; these commodities were all indispensable for the civilization's maintenance, so they had to be found and purchased abroad in exchange for Sumer's and Akkad's surplus food and manufactures. The Sumerian and Akkadian commercial travellers set up permanent trading posts, *in partibus barbarorum*, which became so many focal points for the radiation of the Sumero-Akkadian culture.

The Sumerian script, which had been adapted, by a *tour de force*, for conveying the Semitic Akkadian language, and which the Sumerian and Akkadian business men used for keeping their accounts and for writing their records and their correspondence in their own languages, was subsequently adapted for conveying, as well, the Indo-European language of the Hittites, the pre-Hittite languages of East Central Anatolia, and the Hurrian language of Urartu. In the fourteenth century B.C., when the Phoenicians were feeling their way towards the creation of an alphabetic script, a selection from the set of Sumerian cuneiform characters was used, in the Phoenician city at Ras-ash-Shamrah, to stand for letters of an alphabet for conveying the Canaanite language, and, in the sixth century B.C., another selection from the same set of characters was again used alphabetically to convey the Medo-Persian language. This alphabetic use of the Sumerian script was abortive in both cases. However, the Akkadian language, written in the Sumerian script, was the medium of international intercourse in the heart of the Old-World Oikoumenê for more than a thousand years ending at the fall of Assyria in 612 B.C. During that millennium, this medium was used for diplomatic correspondence, not only in South-West Asia, but also in Egypt—devoted though the Egyptians were by that time to the distinctive civilization that they had created for themselves.

The degree of reunification achieved by the civilization created in Sumer was thus considerable, yet, though Sumer had a monopoly of civilization for at least several centuries, her reunifying work fell far short of reunifying the whole human race. She started with a grave initial failure in her homeland, before ever she began to expand beyond its borders.

When the curtain rises on the stage of Sumerian history, we find that the initial unity of the Sumerian World in language, script, technology, economy, ethics, and social structure does not extend to political organization. In its political expression the social structure of the early Sumerian World is the same as that of the Neolithic World and the Food-gathering World. The Sumerian World began life fractured into a number of separate local sovereign states that were alien enough from each other emotionally to feel no scruple about going to war with each other.

This failure, in politics, to take a new departure to meet a new situation was disastrous for the future of the Sumerian civilization and hence for the future of all mankind, since civilization was now mankind's destiny. The reclamation of the Tigris-Euphrates jungle-swamp, and the technology and organization that had made this possible, had endowed each of the Sumerian states with an unprecedented abundance of manpower, surplus production, and leisure for a ruling minority; and this made these states capable of waging war with an intensity that would have been unattainable for the Neolithic villages or for the food-gathering bands. This potential scourge of high-powered warfare became an actual scourge in the Sumero-Akkadian World when the completion of the reclamation of the primeval jungle-swamp brought the Sumero-Akkadian states into immediate contact with each other, with no insulating fringes of unreclaimed swamp left any longer to serve as buffers between them. Land-hunger, now that there was no more swamp-land to reclaim, was a ready-made cause for collisions between them, and a second ready-made cause was a conflict of interests over water-rights. The reclaimed land could not be kept under cultivation unless it were kept drained and irrigated. This required the upkeep of intricate systems of canals and embankments; and the separate systems of the rival local states could not be co-ordinated, and their conflicting local interests could not be adjusted by compromise, so long as there was no single paramount world-authority to impose its fiat on them all. Hence the local states of Sumer and Akkad fell into wars with each other over these contentious questions; and the wars became more frequent and more devastating until, about three-quarters of a millennium after the date of the birth of civilization in Sumer, unity, peace, and order were forced upon the Sumero-Akkadian World by the imposition of one state, Agadé's, political ascendancy on all the rest. It would have been better for Sumer and Akkad if they had achieved this dearly bought political unity at the dawn of civilization there, instead of allowing it to be so long delayed; for, by the time when they did achieve political unity, they had already wrecked their common civilization by the warfare that had been the slow and costly means by which this eventual unity had been brought about.

The Sumerians' second failure, on the road towards reunion, was their failure to maintain the unity of civilization in the course of propagating it beyond the original borders of its and their homeland. We have seen that they did succeed in propagating it in its native Sumerian form to some extent. They did incorporate, or partially incorporate, some neighbouring regions in their own Sumerian World, and they radiated their script and language more widely than that. There were, however, other regions whose inhabitants reacted to encounters with the Sumerians in a different way. These other peoples, too, were stimulated, by contact with the Sumerians, to adopt civilization in the sense of adopting the new way of life that the Sumerians had been the first people to create; but they were stimulated at the same time, not to take over the Sumerian civilization itself ready-made, but to create for themselves a counterpart of it, in which ideas derived from the Sumerians were embodied in new and non-Sumerian forms. The Elamites, for instance, who were the Sumerians' nearest neighbours of all, and whose country was a second Sumer in miniature, were inspired by acquaintance with the Sumerian script to invent a script of their own, constructed on Sumerian principles, but with independently devised non-Sumerian characters; and, though, when, under the Third Dynasty of Ur, Elam was temporarily annexed to the Sumero-Akkadian world-state, she took for a time to using the Sumerian script and language instead of her own, she reverted to her own after she had recovered her political independence.

Elam, like the Hittite World and Urartu, was a satellite of the Sumero-Akkadian World; but Egypt reacted differently when she was inspired, by an encounter with Sumer, to take to civilization on her own account. Egypt insisted on adopting this originally Sumerian way of life in such a decidedly non-Sumerian and distinctively Egyptian style that the civilization of Egypt became a separate second specimen of the new way of life which, till then, had existed in its original Sumerian form exclusively.

Egyptologists nowadays seem to be agreed that it truly was a stimulus, or a set of stimuli, derived from Sumer that brought civilization to birth in Egypt. They note that the Egyptian script, like the Elamite script, is constructed on Sumerian principles, and they also note that the Egyptian script makes its appearance suddenly, full-blown, in contrast to the Sumerian script, whose gradual evolution out of depictive characters that had not originally stood for words or sounds can still be traced, notwithstanding the fragmentariness of the documents of the Proto-Historic Age in Sumer that have been disinterred by our modern archaeologists. This contrast indicates that the Sumerian script was an original creation of the Sumerians' own, but that the Egyptian script was an Egyptian expression of a borrowed Sumerian idea. The Egyptians might never have thought, for themselves, of the idea of devising conventional visual signs to stand for audible words; but, when once they had acquired this idea from seeing specimens of the Sumerian script, or perhaps only from learning of this script by hearsay, they put the idea into effect for themselves, not by adopting the existing Sumerian script, but by devising a counterpart of it. According to the Egyptologists, the Egyptians, at the formative stage of the Egyptian civilization, were also inspired by other creations of the pre-existing Sumerian civilization—for instance, by a Sumerian build of ship, a Sumerian style of architecture in brick, and the artistic motif of two monsters facing each other symmetrically. Acquaintance with these Sumerian models stimulated the Egyptians to produce counterparts of them too, but each of these counterparts embodied the Sumerian idea without adopting the Sumerian expression of it. The Egyptian expression of it was distinctively Egyptian in these fields too, as in the field of writing.

The Indus valley was a third place, besides Egypt and Elam, where civilization was propagated from its original home in Sumer by the adoption of Sumerian ideas without the adoption of the ready-made Sumerian forms of these. The Indus-Culture script has not yet been deciphered, but we may guess that its relation to the Sumerian script was the same as the Egyptian script's was. The discovery, in 'Irāq, of seals inscribed with Indus-Culture characters tells us that the Indus Culture was in commercial contact with the Sumerian World at a date at which the Indus-Culture script was in use in the Indus valley.

Thus the Sumerians did succeed in propagating, far and wide, the new way of life, civilization, of which they were the original creators; but they did not succeed in propagating it, beyond the neighbourhood of Sumer itself, in its original Sumerian form. In creating a new species of society, the Sumerians were the direct creators of only a single specimen of it out of a number of specimens that has risen, in the course of the last 5,000 years, to a figure of something between fifteen and thirty, according to one's choice among the alternative possible criteria for determining whether or not a society is to count as being a separate civilization. All the civilizations, besides the Sumerian civilization itself, that have arisen in the Old World, and possibly, though perhaps not probably, those that have arisen in the Americas as well, are thus indirect products of the Sumerians' initial creative act; but, in creating civilization, the Sumerians failed to make this into a uniform world-wide way of life that could have knit the whole human race together into a single society. There has never been a single world-wide civilization, and consequently never a single world-wide society, yet, though a world-civilization and world-society may be in the making, for the first time, in our day. We have seen that the plurality of human social groups must have arisen soon after the genesis of mankind itself as an originally food-gathering species of creature; and the survival of this plurality into the Age of Civilization shows how strong a human habit it had become in the course of the first 900,000 years of human history. The civilizational way of life, like the food-gathering way of life before it, has not managed to spread over the face of the Earth without fracturing. The number of separate societies in process of civilization has been much smaller than the number of separate bands of food-gatherers, and the average size of the units has been correspondingly greater. Yet, in this species of human society too, the number is still in the plural and has not yet been reduced again to the singular.

Moreover, the original civilization in Sumer was not even a unity in itself on the political plane. Politically it was fractured into a number of sovereign independent local states, and this has been the usual, though not the invariable, political configuration of the other civilizations that have arisen subsequently. The Western civilization has so far been, and still is, politically fractured in the Sumerian style; and, since the West has drawn all the rest of the World into its net, this fractured political configuration is world-wide today. In Sumerian history, an initial political plurality was eventually superseded by political unity, and this unification was achieved at the cost of a series of ever more frequent and devastating wars that had done irreparable damage to the self-lacerating society before they were stopped. This, too, has been the usual course of the history of a civilization that has been politically pluralistic at the start. That is one of the reasons why, in our own politically fractured present-day world, we are asking ourselves whether our society is going to be unified politically, as most politically fractured societies have been in the past. We are also asking ourselves whether, now that we have been overtaken, in this unstable and unsatisfactory configuration of political plurality, by the Atomic Age, it is going to be practicable for us to achieve political unity by peaceful agreement. So far as we know, this has never been achieved peacefully before. At the same time, we are aware that, in the Atomic Age, an attempt to achieve unity by the traditional method of military conquest could result in nothing except the mutual destruction of the foolhardy belligerents. The novel feature of an atomic war would be that all belligerents would be vanquished and none of them would survive as a victor. This has changed not only the nature of war itself but also war's relation to the rest of life. In the Atomic Age it has become impossible to use war as an instrument of policy, as it has been used, though this perhaps seldom effectually, in the past.

The Empire of Sumer and Akkad, in which all the local states of the Sumero-Akkadian World were forcibly welded together, was a would-be world-state. More than half a millennium before it was established, it had been anticipated by the establishment of a would-be world-state in Egypt. When the curtain rises on the stage of Egyptian history, we catch the Egyptian World in the act of being united politically. In Egyptian, as in Sumerian, history the political unification was achieved by military force, but, in Egyptian history, it was achieved at the dawn of civilization—and this, apparently, at a single stroke—and thus the Egyptian civilization saved itself from a series of devastating wars of the kind that wrecked the Sumerian civilization, and so many other civilizations after it, before political unity was achieved eventually in each of these cases. Since the Egyptian World was so prompt in uniting itself politically, and was so successful in thereby saving itself from the exhausting warfare that has so frequently been the price of unification elsewhere, might not the Egyptian would-be world-state have been expected to expand itself into a literally world-wide one? Could the Egyptian society not have used for this constructive purpose in the World at large the energies and resources that it had forborne from squandering on fratricidal warfare at home?

Egypt's opportunity for giving mankind a world-wide political unity came and went in the half-millennium that elapsed between the establishment of the United Empire of Egypt by Narmer of Hieraconpolis and the establishment of the United Empire of Sumer and Akkad that was founded by Sargon of Agadé some 500 or 600 years later. If, in the meantime, one of the Pharaohs of an already united Egypt had intervened in the fratricidal wars of the Sumero-Akkadian local states and had given them peace and order by uniting them with his Egyptian world-state under a single government, this would have been tantamount to a political union of all communities that were already in process of civilization by that date. In that event the united world-government could and would have extended its authority, *pari passu* with the spread of civilization itself, as fast and as far as would have been practicable logistically at each stage.

Some 1,500 years later, about half way through the course of Egyptian history, the Egyptian world-state did expand beyond the borders of the Egyptian civilization's homeland. Southward it expanded up the Nile to Napata, just below the Fourth Cataract. Northward it expanded up the whole length of Syria to the right bank of the Euphrates, at the elbow where the river approaches nearest to the Mediterranean. Here the Egyptian Empire had reached the Sumero-Akkadian World's threshold. This Egyptian 'New Empire' was a large one—the largest that had ever been built yet; but it was not large enough; for, by this time, civilization had already spread beyond the limits of both the Egyptian World, and the Sumero-Akkadian World. The date was more than half way through the second millennium B.C., and by then there was already a third civilization in existence in the Aegean basin, a fourth in Anatolia, and a fifth in the Indus valley, while a sixth was on the point of arising in the far-away valley of the Yellow River in China. Thus, though the Egyptian would-be world-state was the earliest of its kind, and this by at least half a millennium, it failed to ensure that it should be the only one ever to be established. Just as the Sumerian civilization failed to become *the* civilization, so the Egyptian world-state failed to become *the* world-state. Since the date, some 5,000 years ago, at which Narmer gave political unity to the Egyptian World, there have been as many less-than-world-wide world-states as there have been less-than-world-wide civilizations.

All the same, the emergence of these would-be world-states is significant, and is also encouraging, because it is an indication that the divisive movement in human affairs, which is almost as old as mankind itself, is now being opposed, at last, by a counter-movement towards reunification. At the same time, the relative recentness of the earliest would-be world-state reminds us that the counter-movement is still in its infancy, while the number of the representatives of this ambitious new species of polity that have already come and gone gives us a measure of the abiding strength of the divisive movement. This has the momentum of a 900,000-years-old habit; this ancient habit is still in the ascendant; and today, when a literally world-wide world-state has become Man's only alternative to mass-suicide in an atomic war, we still do not know whether Man is going to establish it. The establishment of it would not only make an exacting call on his insight and his willpower. It would also require him to expose himself to a severe emotional ordeal. He would have to pluck out of his social heritage, and to discard, an ancient habit that he cherishes.

If the plurality of the would-be world-states is a striking testimony to the strength of Man's habit of disunity, the plurality of the would-be higher religions is a still more striking testimony to the same effect.

A religion earns the title 'higher' in virtue of its being an attempt to bring human souls into direct touch with the ultimate spiritual presence behind the phenomena of the Universe. The epiphany of the higher religions within the last 2,500 years or thereabouts has been the most important event, and also the most revolutionary one, in human history hitherto since the primordial mutation through which a pre-human being became human. In so far as a higher religion succeeds in putting a human soul in direct touch with the ultimate spiritual presence behind the Universe, it liberates that soul from servitude to the human society to which the human being 'belongs'. Hitherto the society has had a claim on its 'member's' total allegiance. Now the individual is free, at his peril, to obey God rather than Man if he judges that Man's and God's demands on him conflict. This perilous spiritual freedom is the well-spring of freedom in every secular province of life. The higher religions have achieved this saving act of liberation; but they have each achieved it separately from the others and along a different path, though the goal of all these paths is one and the same.

Though all the higher religions have liberated human beings from their imprisoning societies, not every one of them has drawn the logical conclusion that its liberating mission extends beyond the limits of the particular society from which it has broken out, and that its mission-field has no limits short of the whole World. Hinduism, Zoroastrianism, and Judaism are examples of higher religions that have not set out to be world-religions, but have confined their ministry to a single ethnic community. By contrast, Buddhism, Christianity, and Islam in succession have each addressed its gospel to all mankind. In the cases of Christianity and Islam, however, it was not certain from the beginning that the new religion was going to take the World itself for its mission-field. Christianity's mission might have been confined to the Jews if it had not been for Saint Paul, and Islam's might have been confined to the Arabs if converts among the non-Arab peoples whom the Muslim Arabs had conquered had not taken the Kingdom of Islam by storm. On the other hand, the Buddha, unlike Jesus and Muhammad, seems, from the start, to have been a universalist. The Buddha ignored the barriers of caste, by which the Hindu society was already partitioned in his time, and his successors did not halt at the confines of India. He and they were consciously addressing themselves to all human beings everywhere.

Buddhism was not only the most unhesitatingly world-minded of the three missionary higher religions; it was also the earliest of the three. It is 500 years older than Christianity, and 1,100 years older than Islam. Thus it was the only missionary religion in the World for as long a time as the united empire of Egypt was the only would-be world-state yet in existence. Why did Buddhism, like the Egyptian world-state, fail to take advantage of its 500-years-long opportunity? Why did it not forestall the emergence of these other two missionary religions by having already converted all mankind? Buddhism has succeeded in propagating itself throughout Eastern and South-Eastern Asia. At this eastern end of the Old-World Oikoumenê today, most people are adherents of Buddhism, even though a majority of them may also have continued to adhere simultaneously to Confucianism, Taoism, Shinto, or some other pre-Buddhist philosophy or religion. On the other hand, at the western end of the Old World, Buddhism has never struck root, and, in the course of the half-millennium ending in the thirteenth century of the Christian Era, this Indian religion has also receded from India itself.

The cause of Buddhism's failure to convert the whole of mankind cannot have been that the innate temperament and disposition of the population was sympathetic to Buddhism in regions to the east of India, but not in regions to the west of it. Our modern psychologists' investigations do seem to have shown that, in our common human nature, there are variations that constitute so many distinctive 'psychological types'; but the evidence indicates that the representatives of each of these different types are to be found in approximately equal numbers in any sample of mankind. There is no indication that the types are sorted out and segregated from each other geographically. It might, perhaps, be suggested that, though all psychological types may always be equally represented everywhere, one type may be encouraged, and the contrary type may be repressed, by the particular cultural tradition that is prevalent at a particular place and time. This, however, would not account for Buddhism's spread throughout Eastern Asia; for, in Eastern Asia during these last 2,500 years, there has been no uniform culture-configuration. The Chinese and Japanese culture-configurations, for instance, are markedly different; yet Buddhism has succeeded in striking root in Japan, as well as in China.

Nor could it be maintained that Buddhism's failure to strike root to the west of India has been due to its having neglected this half of the Old-World mission-field. *Circa* 260 B.C., rather less than 250 years after the date of the Buddha's enlightenment, Buddhism was embraced by the ruler of the Indian world-state of the day, the Maurya emperor Ashoka. Buddhist missionary enterprise now had behind it, for the rest of Ashoka's reign, the resources of an empire that included all but the southern tip of the Indian sub-continent. Ashoka appointed officials whose duty was to spread the knowledge of Buddhism.[1] Some of these were to concern themselves with Buddhists and non-Buddhists within Ashoka's own dominions.[2] Others were to address themselves to peoples beyond his empire's western frontier, including, among others, the Greeks (Yōnas).[3] At this time, India had closer diplomatic, commercial, and cultural relations with the Greek successor-states of the Persian Empire, extending from the Maurya Empire's western frontier as far to the west as Cyrenaïca, Epirus, and Macedon, than she had with Eastern Asia; and Ashoka did make efforts, that are recorded in inscriptions of his, to propagate Buddhism in this westerly direction. By the year 258 B.C., he had sent missions to the dominions of each of the principal rulers in the Hellenic World of the day. In his inscription recording this, he mentions these rulers by name.[4] Moreover, Ashoka did not limit himself to preaching the word. He has recorded[5] that he also provided medical care—and this for animals as well as for human beings—not only in his own dominions but abroad in the independent states of Southern India, in Ceylon, and in the Seleucid Greek empire and the states that were its neighbours.

We have no corresponding record, from the Greek side, of these missionary activities of Ashoka's in the Hellenic World.

[1] Rock Edict VII.   [2] Ibid.   [3] Rock Edict V.
[4] Rock Edict XIII.   [5] Rock Edict II.

So far as we know, they were abortive. It has been suggested that Buddhism did, nevertheless, eventually have at least one important effect on the religious history of the western end of the Old World. It has been conjectured that Christian monasticism derives from Buddhist monasticism. This is possible, since Buddhist monasticism is older than Christian monasticism by more than seven centuries; Christian monasticism started in the third century in Egypt, in the Thebaid and in the Wadi Natrun; and at this time Egypt was in active commercial relations with India. This trade was sea-borne; its termini, at the Egyptian end, were the harbours that had been built along the Red Sea coast of Egypt in the Ptolemaic Age and the port of Alexandria. The Wadi Natrun lies in the hinterland of Alexandria, and the Thebaid lies in the hinterland of the Red Sea harbours. These chronological and geographical considerations make it credible that Christian monasticism may have been called into existence by the influence of Buddhist monasticism. At the same time, a comparison of the structures and spirits of the two monasticisms suggests that, if Egypt was indebted to India in this case, what she borrowed was not the Indian institution of Buddhist monasticism itself, but only the idea, and that she then proceeded to translate this idea into a new institution that was distinctively Egyptian and Christian. In other words, the relation of Christian monasticism to Buddhist monasticism will have been like the relation of the Egyptian hieroglyphic script to the Sumerian cuneiform script. If something was transmitted from the one society to the other, what was transmitted was not a ready-made product; it was a stimulus to perform an independent act of creation.

If this is the truth, Buddhism's influence on the western end of the Old World will have been as faint as Christianity's influence on the eastern end of it has been. Christianity, like Buddhism, has failed, so far, to convert the whole of mankind; and, like Buddhism again, it has receded from the region in which it originated. It was Islam, the youngest of the three great missionary religions, that gave Buddhism in Northern India its death-blow; and it was Islam, likewise, that supplanted Christianity in South-West Asia and North Africa. Islam has won masses of adherents, not only from Christianity and Buddhism, but from Zoroastrianism and Hinduism as well. Yet

Islam, in its turn, has failed to convert the whole of mankind. Starting, as Christianity started, from the western border of South-West Asia, Islam has captured Central Asia and most of Indonesia from Buddhism and Hinduism, and has gained footholds in Eastern Bengal, Yunnan, Kansu, the Southern Philippines, and South-Eastern Europe; but the ground that Islam has won in Eastern Asia and Russia and Western Europe is small, and it has gained no foothold at all in the Americas. There, Christianity and Judaism are the only Old-World religions that have established themselves.

The coexistence in the present-day world of three missionary religions, each of which has set out to convert the whole of mankind, is perhaps the most impressive testimony of all to the strength of the divisive movement in human affairs. This climax to our survey of this divisive movement's assertion of itself in a number of different fields might incline us to conclude that the unifying movement has no prospect of prevailing against it. This conclusion would, however, be premature; for the unifying movement's achievements have been impressive too.

The unifying movement has been handicapped by the relative lateness of its start. The divisive movement is as old as mankind itself; the unifying movement did not begin till about 5,000 years ago. But it did begin as soon as Man acquired his first new and more effective means of communication, to reinforce his own feet, which had been his sole means of locomotion for the first 900,000 years of his history. At the dawn of civilization, Man reinforced his own muscle-power with animal muscle-power by domesticating the donkey, and he discovered how to travel on water, as well as overland, by inventing boats and learning to harness wind-power to propel them with sails, besides harnessing his own muscle-power to oars. These were the modest first steps towards 'the annihilation of distance' that we have achieved in our time. Since that beginning, there has been progress in moving towards this present-day climax. But the progress has been arrested repeatedly, and this sometimes for centuries on end; and it was not till after the opening of the nineteenth century of the Christian Era that the improvement in Man's means of communication began to gather the speed that is accelerating so sensationally now. The domesticated donkey was reinforced by the domesticated horse and camel; the solid-wheeled cart was superseded by the spoke-wheeled chariot, and the charioteer by the rider. The primitive sailing-ship that may have conveyed some of the seminal ideas of civilization from the Tigris-Euphrates valley to the Nile valley and the Indus valley was gradually developed into the modern three-masted ship, in whose build and rig and rudder and compass the improvements in ship-building and in navigation that had been made in the course of centuries in the Indian Ocean, the Mediterranean, and the Atlantic were combined to produce a craft that could keep the sea for months on end. It was not, however, till after the beginning of the nineteenth century that other inanimate forces, besides wind-power, were harnessed for traction, and that the movement of bodies by steam-power, electric power, oil-power, and atomic power was supplemented by the discovery that people could communicate with each other at a distance from each other, without having to travel to meet each other, if they set waves in motion, in some inanimate medium, to do the travelling for them. In the meantime, the rudimentary pre-nineteenth-century improvements in means of communication had already turned the tide of human affairs.

The last 5,000 years have seen the divisive movement opposed, for the first time in human history, by a counter-movement towards reunification. This counter-movement has not yet prevailed. At this time we cannot foresee whether it is going to prevail or not. All that we can see is that the outcome of the tug-o'-war is being decided, not by impersonal forces beyond Man's control, but by human choices, and that, in the Atomic Age, these choices are momentous. Our only light on the future comes from our knowledge of the choices, on this issue, that our predecessors have made, and the record of these is remarkable and encouraging. We have to keep in mind the shortness of the time since the counter-movement towards re-unification began, and the feebleness of the technological means at Man's command till less than 200 years ago. Considering the greatness of these material handicaps, it is not surprising that world-unity has not yet been achieved; it is surprising, rather, that so much progress towards it should have been made nevertheless. This suggests that the impulse to reunite, though recent, must be strong; and, if it is indeed strong, we may expect it **to** gain impetus now that it has at its disposal the relatively high-powered means of communication that have been created at last by the application of modern science to technology.

Consider what feats of unification Man achieved, between the dawn of civilization and the opening of the nineteenth century of the Christian Era, when his own muscle-power had been reinforced only by the muscle-power of domesticated animals and by wind-power harnessed for propelling ships. With the aid of no more efficient means than these, the Sumerians enlarged the domain of their civilization from its original home and propagated civilization itself to both ends of the Old World by stimulating other societies to create separate civilizations of their own. By the same primitive means the founders of all the would-be world-states, beginning with Narmer in the Egyptian World at the dawn of civilization there, have succeeded, at the political level, in uniting and holding together and reuniting large sections of the human race over long periods of time. The Chinese world-state has given political unity to a whole sub-continent for most of the time from the eighth decade of the second century b.c. down to the present day. The Roman world-state gave political unity to the whole perimeter of the Mediterranean for four centuries, and to the north-eastern sector of it for eight centuries after that, while its avatar the Ottoman Empire was not extinguished till 1922. The missionary religions have not, any of them, yet achieved their common ambition of converting the whole of mankind. Today, some 2,500 years after the birth of the oldest of them, Buddhism, they are coexisting with each other. Yet, short of winning all the World, each of them has won huge tracts of it. The numbers of their respective adherents and the length of time during which even the youngest of these religions, Islam, has lasted up to date surpass the numbers of the citizens and the length of life of the most successful of the would-be world-states. The soldiers who put together and held together the empires, the missionaries who propagated the religions, and the political and ecclesiastical administrators who organized and consolidated the wide domains that the soldiers and the missionaries had won, had only sailing-ships and domesticated animals to transport them, in so far as they did not still depend on their own feet.

The decisive advance towards reunification on a literally world-wide scale was the achievement of oceanic navigation by West Europeans in the fifteenth century of the Christian Era, and this was achieved with the same instrument with which the Sumerians had wafted the idea of civilization from the Tigris and Euphrates to the Indus and the Nile and with which the Pharaohs had established and maintained the Egyptian world-state. The harnessing of wind-power, which had made it possible for the Sumerians to sail out into the Persian Gulf and for the Egyptians to ascend the Nile against the river's current, was also the means that enabled the West Europeans, 4,500 years later, to reach the Americas across the mid-Atlantic, to reach India round the Cape of Good Hope, and to circumnavigate the globe itself. It was still in a sailing-ship that Captain Cook rounded off Western Man's exploration and mastery of the globe-encompassing ocean by discovering Oceania and Australia. This achievement had been completed before the invention of mechanically-propelled ships and before Man's conquest of the air.

The effectiveness of Man's use of his pre-nineteenth-century means of communication can be measured by the wideness of the diffusion of some of Man's almost innumerable local languages. Ships carried the Greek and Punic languages from the Levant to the shores of the western basin of the Mediterranean and the languages of the Malay family to the Philippines in one direction and to Madagascar in the other, while the Polynesians traversed the vast distances between the islands of Oceania not even in ships but in canoes. Till the invention of mechanically-propelled wheeled vehicles, water-transport was far speedier and less arduous than land-transport; yet nomadic pastoralists spread the Indo-European languages to the Bay of Bengal and to the Atlantic coast of Europe (leaving it for ships to carry several of the languages of this family on from the western extremity of the Old World to the Americas). Other nomads carried the Semitic languages out of Arabia into the South-West Asian 'Fertile Crescent' and into North Africa and into Abyssinia. Others again carried the Bantu languages over most of the southern two-thirds of the African continent from some no doubt narrowly circumscribed place of origin.

Unlike the expansion of the would-be world-states and

world-religions, the propagation of these wide-ranging languages was not planned. Even the spread of the Romance languages from tiny Latium to Rumania and Western Europe and Latin America was an unplanned consequence of the expansion of the Roman Empire. This makes the spread of these far-flung languages the more remarkable. It is true that no single one of them has ever yet become the common language, or even the lingua franca, of all mankind. The Greek language, which, at the beginning of the Christian Era, seemed to be on the road towards achieving this role, has receded, since then, to limits that are slightly narrower than those within which it was confined before the beginning of its expansion in the eighth century b.c., and this reversal in its fortunes casts doubts on the prospects of the English language, which might seem to be on the road towards achieving the same role today. Mankind is still divided by the diversity of speech that is an awkward legacy from its dispersion during the long food-gathering stage of its history. Yet, though world-unity in the field of language is not yet in sight, the extent of the areas over which some once merely local languages have already been spread by sail and hoof shows that, in the Age of the Annihilation of Distance, a world-language is not merely a possibility but is a probability.

The most promising of all the portents of reunification is the emergence of a new type of community, the diasporá, which looks as if it may be 'the wave of the future'.

A diasporá, like a local community, is a splinter of mankind; but, unlike a local community, a diasporá does not occupy exclusively any particular patch of the Earth's surface as its domain. A diasporá is in a minority locally, wherever it may be. At the same time, a diasporá, unlike a local community, is ubiquitous. Like a would-be world-state or a would-be world-religion, a diasporá is potentially world-wide. Like these two other oecumenical kinds of society, diasporás are a relatively recent kind, yet they are coeval with the Sumerian city-states. Local sovereign states had no sooner made their appearance than they began to generate a new kind of community that may be going, not, perhaps, to replace them, but to supersede them in the role of serving as the most important type of cell for a coming world-society.

Diasporás first appeared in the region in which civilization itself first appeared. Diasporás appeared first in South-West Asia, and, like civilization, they have been spreading from there in the course of the last 5,000 years. Like the other symptoms of world-mindedness, diasporás are the product of a wish for unity that has translated itself into accomplished facts in so far as it has had the requisite material means of communication at its command. In an age in which the progressive advance of technology has at last succeeded in 'annihilating distance', we may expect to see the number, size, and importance of the World's diasporás increase as never before. Concomitantly, we may expect to see the hold of the World's local states decrease as the hold of the diasporás increases. We may expect—and hope—to see the local states 'de-mythologized'. Instead of being worshipped as gods, perhaps they will come to be just administered as public utilities. Perhaps it will be recognized that their proper function is to provide those public services that are found, by trial and error, to be still provided most conveniently on a local basis, even in an age in which the world-scale has become the only practicable scale for mankind's more important activities.

Three activities that have been of major importance in the past have worked together to generate diasporás. Diasporás have been the product of trade, war, and religion; and, of these three social forces, trade was the first to get to work.

It has been noted already that trade is one of the necessities of urban life, and that urbanism is coeval with civilization. The Sumerian and Akkadian city-states, which radiated their commercial activity so far beyond the frontiers of the territories under their political sovereignty, gave birth to the earliest diasporás of which we have a record. At least as early as the second century of the second millennium B.C. there was an Akkadian commercial colony at Qatna in Central Syria and an Assyrian one in a suburb of Kanesh in Eastern Anatolia. The Assyrians scattered abroad as traders a thousand years before they began to spread themselves as conquerors, and the results of their earlier expansion were more lasting because this earlier expansion was peaceful. These two are the forerunners and the prototypes of all the present-day commercial diasporás: the Jews, Armenians, and Lebanese all over the World; the

Chinese in South-Eastern Asia and in the Americas; the Gujeratis in Africa south of the Sahara; the Hadhramawtis in Indonesia; the Homsis in Brazil; the Parsees and Marwaris and Sikhs in the Indo-Pakistani sub-continent; the Greeks in the Levant; the Nestorians in Chicago. Between the fifth and the twelfth century of the Christian Era, Nestorian missionaries disseminated their religion from 'Irāq eastwards as far as the Pacific coast of Asia. In the twentieth century, emigrants from the surviving Nestorian fastness in Kurdistan made their way westwards to Chicago and captured the house-painting industry there. The Nestorian Patriarch has since followed these enterprising members of his flock to the North American city that has become the largest source of his revenue.

War has created diasporás through the flight, eviction, and deportation of conquered peoples and also through the planting of garrisons of the conqueror's troops at strategic points in the conquered countries. The classic instance of a deported and evicted community is the Jewish one. The Jews were first deported from Palestine by the Babylonians and were afterwards evicted from there by the Romans. A garrison of Jewish troops was also planted by the Persian Imperial Government on Elephantinê Island in Egypt, just below the First Cataract of the Nile, to guard the Persian Empire's south-western frontier there. The classical instances of diasporás generated by garrisons are those of the Chinese garrisons along the Great Wall and the Roman garrisons along the Rhine, the Danube, and the desert borders of North-West Africa and Syria. The Greek cities planted in South-West Asia and Egypt by Alexander and his successors, and the colonial cities planted by Rome, were also garrisons in effect. In the pre-Columbian Andean World the deportation of conquered peoples and the planting of garrisons by Inca empire-builders made the Incas' Quechua language into the lingua franca that it still is today, more than four centuries after the Spanish language began to compete with it for playing this role. The longest deportations, so far, have been those carried out by the Mongols, who conquered a greater extent of territory than any other empire-builders up to date. In the Mongol Empire's capital, Qaraqorum, in the thirteenth century, West European, Russian, Muslim, and Chinese deportees met and mingled with each other. In early modern Western history the outstanding example of a diasporá created by eviction is that of the Huguenots. The Huguenots have enriched the life of Württemburg, Brandenburg, the Netherlands, South Africa, Britain, and South Carolina. But, in sheer scale, the eviction of the Huguenots from France, of the Eastern Christian sectaries from the centre to the fringes of Russia, of the Congregationalists and Quakers and Catholics from England to New England and Pennsylvania and Maryland, and of the United Empire Loyalists (*alias* Tories) from the United States, have been dwarfed by the eviction, during and since the Second World War, of the millions of 'displaced persons' (to use the anodyne euphemistic term) whose plight is a reproach to present-day civilization. In the modern World again, the former British garrisons in India and the present American garrisons all over the World have dwarfed the Chinese and the Roman garrisons in scale. But the British garrisons were ephemeral and the American garrisons may have an even shorter tour of duty.

Religion has created diasporás by preaching as well as by persecution. Instances of religious denominations that have been evicted on account of their religion have been given above. On the whole, preaching has done more to create religious diasporás than persecution has. Preaching, aided by persecution, has spread the Baha'i religion over the World within the last hundred years. The same combination of forces created the Christian diasporá in the Roman Empire. In China the Islamic diasporá is a product of preaching. In the Indo-Pakistani subcontinent it is a product of preaching combined with military conquest; but, here too, peaceful conversion has played a greater part—for instance in Eastern Pakistan—than Hindus and Christians like to admit.

In the past, the diasporá type of community has gone the farthest towards replacing the local type in the heart of the Old-World Oikoumenê, where civilization made its earliest appearance. The political structure of the Ottoman Empire, for instance, was an association of diasporás, each of which was co-extensive with the Empire itself and none of which was in exclusive occupation of any local province. These millets, as they were called in the Ottoman administrative vocabulary, were autonomous ecclesiastical corporations that corresponded more closely to Western occupational groups and social classes than to Western nations.

In the millet organization of the Ottoman world-state in its heyday, we have what may turn out to have been a preview of the structure of a future world-state on a literally world-wide scale. Unhappily for the peace and welfare of mankind, there has been an interlude in which there has been a regression in this part of the World to the older and cruder political ideology of local nationalism. This has been part of the price of the temporary ascendancy of the West over the rest of the World. In the history of civilization the West has been a parvenu on the fringe of the Oikoumenê. The backwardness of the West's prevalent political ideology is therefore not surprising; but it is unfortunate that, because of the West's temporary ascendancy, this backward ideology should have recaptured peoples with a longer tradition of civilization who had been inducted into a more advanced system of political organization by the long-continuing formative effects of religion, war, and trade.

The diasporá structure of Ottoman society was like a shot-silk robe. Under the influence of Western political ideas and ideals, this subtle texture has been shredded to bits and the threads have been re-woven into a patchwork coat, in which the geographically interwoven millets have been sorted out into geographically separate local national states. This reactionary re-segregative work has been done clumsily and roughly, and the new coat of many colours is stained with blood. The same disaster has also overtaken the Ottoman Empire's neighbours and counterparts, the British Raj in the Indian sub-continent and the Habsburg Monarchy in Central Europe. These multi-national empires, too, have been broken up into patchworks of local national states, at the cost of evictions and massacres like those that have accompanied the break-up of the Ottoman Empire. The former British Indian Empire has been partitioned into two successor states, India and Pakistan, and, within each of these, a further disruptive movement has been started by the rise, within each of them, of a local linguistic nationalism of the kind that has been rife in Eastern Europe since the nineteenth century. Eastern and Western Pakistan cherish the Bengali and the Urdu language respectively, while in India the provincial boundaries have been redrawn to make the area of each province coincide, as closely as possible, with the domain of one or other of India's many local languages. These newly introduced linguistic issues have aroused animosities from which the sub-continent had previously been free. Thus the impact of an out-dated, but temporarily potent, Western political ideology has not only interrupted and reversed the course of political de-velopment in the central regions of the Old-World Oikoumenê; it has also inflicted untold loss and suffering on the unfortunate inhabitants; and the agonizing process of political realignment has taken more than 150 years.

The potency of modern Western nationalism can be measured by its captivation of the Jews. Its appeal to some of the other present-day diasporás is comprehensible, however unfortunate; for some of these have never lost hold of a remnant of territory in which they have continued to constitute a majority of the local population, and, for them, it has been a natural tempta-tion to try to build up Greece, the Lebanon, Erivan, Gujerat, or whatever their residual national territory may be, into a national state on the Western pattern. On the other hand the Jews and the Parsees have been only a small minority, even in their former homeland, for centuries past—the Parsees since the seventh century of the Christian Era and the Jews since the second century. The consequence of the conversion of the Jews to Western nationalism has been the establishment of the local Jewish state of Israel, and the consequence of that has been to despoil the Arab inhabitants, whose Aramaic-speaking and Greek-speaking ancestors had been in continuous occupation of this country for more than 1,800 years. They have been de-prived of their homes, land, and property, and have been turned into refugees. This is the worst of all the many injustices that the reversal of the diasporá structure of society has inflicted on any people so far.

Though the Western ideology of nationalism has been potent enough to create the local Jewish state of Israel, it has not been potent enough to liquidate the Jewish diasporá in the World. The Israelis are, and will assuredly continue to be, a minority of the world-wide Jewish community. The majority remains in the diasporá that is scattered through North America and Western Europe. The West, not Israel, is the Jews' true national home; it is here that the Jews' future lies; and we may guess that the other present-day diasporás, too, are going to ride Western nationalism's fleeting wave without being submerged by it. This seems likely because nationalism is not the West's only gift (in the word 'gift's' German meaning). Besides this Danaan gift, the West has given to the World the Promethean gift of modern technology. Western nationalism is a divisive force; Western technology is a unifying force; these two Western gifts are proving incompatible with each other; and, since it is certain that modern technology is not going to be renounced either by the West itself or by its non-Western proselytes, we can predict with some assurance that Western nationalism is going to go to the wall.

We can, in fact, foresee a world, knit ever more closely together by the continuing advance of technology, in which a human being's local state will have, not the first claim on his loyalty, but the third. His paramount political allegiance will be given to mankind as a whole and to the literally world-wide world-state in which this all-embracing human society will be embodied. His secondary allegiance will be given to one or more world-wide diasporás; some world-wide religious communion, perhaps, and some world-wide professional association (the world-society of doctors, lawyers, farmers, engineers, teachers, ministers of religion, undertakers, garment-workers, or what-not). His allegiance to his local community will be subordinate. He will continue to do his duty by his local community, but the local state will not be able to arouse in him a concern of the kind that he will feel for his other social ties. These others will be important, besides being world-wide; his local tie will be not only parochial but relatively trivial.

The tug-o'-war between the unifying and the divisive move-ment in human history has been going on now for some 5,000 years. The strengths of the two contending forces have fluc-tuated. The current vogue of Western nationalism has given the divisive movement a temporary advantage; but, to estimate the significance of this, we have to view it in perspective. Nationalism's recent gains cannot compare with the gains that the unifying movement has been making in the course of these last five millennia; and in the Atomic Age, which has now over-taken us, mankind has a more potent means and a more im-perious motive than it has ever had before for deciding that the unifying movement shall prevail.

IV

Annex: The Genetic and the Comparative Approach

The study of human affairs has to adjust itself to their nature. Human affairs are a part of life, and life has two salient characteristics; it is perpetually on the move through time and space, and it is plural, not singular. The approach to the study of human affairs in the time-dimension is necessarily genetic, and its form of expression is therefore necessarily narrative. But, since, from the beginning, there have been more human beings than one alive simultaneously, the narration of human affairs cannot be unitary. There have to be as many parallel narratives as there are people, communities, societies, religions, states, and ways of life; and a number of separate narratives of contemporaneous events cannot be linked up with each other by being combined in a single narrative. So long as they are each looked at from the narrational standpoint, they will simply run their separate courses. To link them together we have to compare them and then to analyse their likenesses and differences. This approach is, in itself, non-narrational; but, in comparing and analysing a number of parallel life-streams, we must take care still to keep them all moving. If we mentally arrest their movement in order to study them 'in cross section', we shall be denaturing them and consequently distorting our view of them. Life does not stand still to be studied. It has to be studied on the run.

Thus, if we are to take due account of both the flow of life and the plurality of its flowing streams, we have to look at it, all the time, with both an historian's and a sociologist's eyes. The penalty for trying to segregate these two approaches into two mutually insulated 'disciplines' is to forfeit the possibility of seeing life whole. This is true of the study of human affairs at every stage and on every plane. In pre-civilizational societies the pace of historical change is so slow by comparison with the speed that it has been gathering during these last 5,000 years that an anthropologist may be tempted to ignore the historical approach and to treat his subject as if it were static. In so far as he does that, he will be replacing the reality by an abstraction. The indispensability of both approaches is manifest when we are concerned with an advanced society at the economic level. Economic history and economic analysis in mathematical terms are obviously both needed here.

The unifying standpoint is the psychological one. Consciousness of oneself and consciousness of other people seem to be two inseparable facets of one and the same psychic state, while, at the subconscious level, the human psyche is not bound by the categories of thought that the awakened consciousness has to impose on itself as the price of its precocious form of awareness.

The study of human affairs is, in truth, monolithic. The dissection of this mental monolith into the so-called 'disciplines' is, at the best, a convenient operational device, while, at its worst—that is to say, if it is taken as being a reflexion of reality—it is a distortion of the truth. Taken seriously, it provokes academic warfare between sociologists and historians. The champions of each of the two rival 'disciplines' then each maintain that their own 'discipline' is the only legitimate one, and that the other one ought to be banned. This academic quarrel is foolish, perverse, and inimical to true knowledge and understanding.

V

The Pros and Cons of a Fractured Structure of Society

In the preceding chapter it has been contended that, in the Atomic Age, mankind has to choose between political reunification and mass-suicide. If this is, in truth, the choice with which we are now faced, the issue is clear. In the circumstances of this age, prompt political reunification would be good because it would spell life, while persistent political disunity would be evil, because it would spell death. It does not follow that disunity is evil in all circumstances, or even that there is no virtue at all in it now. All that is being contended is that, on our current balance-sheet, any intrinsic good that there may be in disunity is outweighed by the penalty that this now entails for mankind. This penalty must tip the balance, since it is nothing less than self-liquidation, and this penalty is absolute and irretrievable. However, the weights in the two scales of the balance of choice are constantly changing in accordance with the constant changes in the human situation. There have been circumstances in which the advantages of disunity have been conspicuous, while the worst foreseeable penalties for it have looked so relatively light that disunity has been taken to be an absolute good—taken, in fact, to be the sovereign source of creativity and cause of progress.

This was, for instance, the prevailing judgement in the West in the eighteenth century, during the interval between the end of the Western wars of religion and the beginning of the Western wars of nationality. During this chapter of Western history, Western warfare was kept at an unusually low degree of intensity and destructiveness. The degree was low because the Western wars of this period were not fought in the name of conflicting ideologies and were not inflamed by mass-emotion. War had been reduced from being a passionate popular religious exercise to being 'the sport of kings'; and, though going to war for fun was cynical, it was also an insurance that war would not be carried to the lengths of savagery by which the foregoing wars of religion had been disgraced, since a ruler could not mulct his subjects of an inordinate amount of life, wealth, and happiness through engaging, as a sport, in wars that were not his subjects' serious business. This is the social and cultural background to Hume's and Gibbon's eulogies of the fractured political structure of the Western society in their day. Each of these two gifted observers contrasts the dynamism of the divided eighteenth-century Western World with the torpor that, as each of them sees it, is induced by the establishment of a world-religion or a world-state; and, on balance, each opts for disunity unreservedly.

Nothing is more favourable to the rise of politeness and learning than a number of neighbouring and independent states connected together by commerce and policy. The emulation which naturally arises among those neighbouring states is an obvious source of improvement; but what I would chiefly insist on is the stop which such limited territories give both to power and to authority . . . . Where a number of neighbouring states have a great intercourse of arts and commerce, their mutual jealousy keeps them from receiving too lightly the law from each other in matters of taste and reasoning, and makes them examine every work of art with the greatest care and accuracy. The contagion of popular opinion spreads not so easily from one place to another. It readily receives a check in some state or other, where it concurs not with the prevailing prejudices. And nothing but nature and reason, or at least what bears them a strong resemblance, can force its way through all obstacles and unite the most rival nations into an esteem and admiration of it.

Greece was a cluster of little principalities which soon became republics; and, being united both by their near neighbourhood and by the ties of the same language and interest, they entered into the closest intercourse of commerce and learning . . . . Each city produced its several artists and philosophers, who refused to yield the preference to those of the neighbouring republics; their contention and debates sharpened the wits of men; a variety of objects was presented to the judgement, while each challenged the preference to the rest; and the sciences, not being dwarfed by the restraint of authority, were able to make such considerable shoots as are even at this time the objects of our admiration . . . .

Europe is at present a copy at large of what Greece was formerly a pattern in miniature.

After the Roman Christian or Catholic Church had spread itself over the civilized world and had engrossed all the learning of the times—being really one large state within itself, and united under one head—this variety of sects immediately disappeared, and the Peripatetic philosophy was alone admitted into all the schools, to the utter depravation of every kind of learning. But, mankind having at length thrown off this yoke, affairs are now returned nearly to the same situation as before . . . .

In China there seems to be a pretty considerable stock of politeness and science, which in the course of so many centuries might naturally be expected to ripen into something more perfect and finished than what has yet arisen from them. But China is one vast empire, speaking one language, governed by one law, and sympathizing in the same manners. The authority of any teacher, such as Confucius, was propagated easily from one corner of the Empire to the other. None had courage to resist the torrent of popular opinion; and posterity was not bold enough to dispute what had been universally received by their ancestors. This seems to be one natural reason why the sciences have made so slow a progress in that mighty empire.[1]

The empire of Rome was firmly established by the singular and perfect coalition of its members. The subject nations, resigning the hope, and even the wish, of independence, embraced the character of Roman citizens . . . . But this union was purchased by the loss of national freedom and military spirit; and the servile provinces, destitute of life and motion, expected their safety from the mercenary troops and governors who were directed by the orders of a distant court . . . . Europe is now divided into twelve powerful, though unequal, kingdoms, three respectable commonwealths, and a variety of smaller, though independent, states; the chances of royal and ministerial talents are multiplied, at least, by the number of its rulers . . . . The abuses of tyranny are restrained by the mutual influence of fear and shame; republics have acquired order and stability; monarchies have imbibed the principles of freedom, or, at least, of moderation; and some sense of honour and justice is introduced into the most defective constitutions by the general manners of the times. In peace, the progress of knowledge and industry is accelerated by the emulation of so many active rivals; in war, the European forces are exercised by temperate and undecisive contests.[2]

[1] David Hume, *Of the Rise and Progress of the Arts and Sciences* (published in 1742).
[2] Edward Gibbon, *General Observations on the Fall of the Roman Empire in the West* (written between 1772 and 1781).

The case that is being made, in these passages, by Hume and Gibbon could be supported further by additional illustrations which they have neglected to cite or of which they were necessarily unaware, either because, in their time, these other examples still lay hidden in the future or else because they had not yet been retrieved from oblivion by the archaeologist's spade.

They might have cited the dialogue in which Tacitus accounts for the deterioration of the art of public speaking at Rome between Cicero's day and his own by pointing out that the orderliness, and consequent dullness, of life under the régime of the Empire could not provide a speaker with the opportunity that Cicero had enjoyed in the scandalous but exciting turmoil of the last phase of the Republic. Hume and Gibbon might also have seen a second replica, in miniature, of their own world in medieval and renaissance Italy, in which the Greece of the last millennium B.C. had come to life again. They might have noted, too, that the classical Persian poetry had been written in the course of the half-millennium between the break-up of the 'Abbasid Empire and the political reunification of Iran in the Safavi Empire. During this period, Iran had been fractured politically into a host of local states that had been constantly waxing and waning; and they might have explained why it was that, in spite of the consequent insecurity of life and destruction of wealth, a fractured Iran, like a fractured Greece and Italy, excelled in the arts. Iran, too, excelled in these at first sight unpropitious circumstances because the artists found generous patrons and congenial companions in the competing local courts of the 'Abbasids' politically petty successors and the Safavids' politically petty predecessors the *mulūk-at-tawā'if.* Hume and Gibbon could have pointed out that this was also one of the reasons for the artistic excellence of their own eighteenth-century Western World. Their contemporaries the composers of the classical modern Western music were then finding their patrons at the courts of the petty German princes of the day.

Our recent disinterment of the Sumero-Akkadian and the Egyptian civilization enables us to add a particularly telling illustration of Hume's theme. In lively Sumer, with its host of competing local city-states, Hume would have found a forerunner of Greece. In torpid Egypt, united politically in a world-state, he would have found a forerunner of China, and a more perfect specimen for his purpose. The political unity that China was enjoying in Hume's day, and that she is still enjoying in ours, is not coeval with China herself. For at least five and a half centuries, ending in the year 221 B.C., China was as sharply fractured as contemporary Greece or as medieval Italy or as the eighteenth-century Western World, whereas the political uni-fication of Egypt was coeval with the dawn of the Egyptian civilization and lasted as long as the civilization itself lasted, with only two temporary lapses. Consistently, the deadening uniformity with which Hume finds fault in the Chinese world-state is even more conspicuously characteristic of the Egyptian world-state. Unlike Egypt, China had what, from Hume's point of view, was the advantage of having indulged in an orgy of dis-unity at one stage of her history. The establishment of the Chinese world-state had been preceded by the period that the Chinese themselves label 'the Contending States'. This was an age of agony, like the period of Greek history preceding the unification of the Hellenic World in the Roman Empire. At the same time, in China, as in Greece, the age of social agony was also an age of intellectual vigour. The Confucian philosophy that obtained a monopoly after the establishment of the orderly Chinese world-state was the survivor of a number of diverse philosophies that had arisen during the turbulent but stimu-lating previous age and had found patronage at the courts of the contending local princes before the local states had been liqui-dated and the world-state had taken their place.

It does, in fact, seem to be true, in general, that creativity is stimulated by intercourse between communities that are each other's neighbours but are independent of each other and differ from each other to some extent in their ways of life. It seems unlikely to have been an accident that the region in which agriculture was invented and animals were domesticated in the Old World was 'the Fertile Crescent' in South-West Asia. This was a region where, in the Post-Pluvial Age, population came to be concentrated in a number of oases which lay at no great dis-tance from each other and whose inhabitants could communi-cate with each other readily across short and easily traversable spaces of open steppe. It also seems unlikely to have been an accident that, in the next chapter of mankind's history, after civilization had been brought to birth in 'Irāq, the first region, outside 'Irāq, to acquire it should have been Egypt, which was easily accessible from 'Irāq both overland and by sea, while the last region in the World to be penetrated by civilization has been the interior of the southern two-thirds of the African continent. The 5,000-years time-lag in the arrival of civilization here can be accounted for by the formidableness of the physical barriers by which 'the dark continent' was fenced off from the rest of the World before the recent 'annihilation of distance' through the accelerating progress of technology. Between North Africa and Middle Africa there is the double barrier constituted by the desert that extends from the western shore of the Red Sea to the eastern shore of the Middle Atlantic and by the zone ot plateau and fen and forest that runs parallel to the desert, far-ther to the south. It is true that this double barrier can be out-flanked, at both ends, by coastal navigation. But sea-going ships on the Indian Ocean or on the Atlantic that reach the mouths of Tropical Africa's mighty rivers find that the direct water-passage from the ocean up-stream into the interior is blocked, on most of these rivers, by falls only a short distance above the rivers' mouths. This is why the interior of Africa re-mained untrodden by modern Western Man for more than 300 years after he had made his way, by water, into the interior ot America up the courses of the River Plate and the Amazon and the Mississippi and the St. Lawrence. It is also the reason why the native peoples of Tropical Africa, unlike the Egyptians, had not, long since, forestalled the Westerners' arrival by acquir-ing civilization for themselves. Except on the northern fringe between desert and forest, the peoples of Tropical Africa had been debarred by their physical environment from taking part in the stimulating intercourse that had propagated civilization elsewhere after having first called it into existence in 'Irāq.

Thus there is truth in what Hume and Gibbon say—and say so eloquently—in praise of disunity and in comparative dis-paragement of unity. Their contention is valid as far as it goes; but, if they had probed farther into their historical illustrations of their thesis, they would have seen that they must qualify this thesis by making two reservations. They should have noted that intercourse between local communities following different ways of life is stimulating only where the difference in the character and level of the local cultures is not enormous. When the difference is very great, the effect of the encounter on the party which is culturally the weaker will not be stimulating; on the contrary, it will be discouraging and perhaps even paralysing. They should also have noted that the stimulating effect of intercourse between mutually independent local communities will be worth its inevitable cost in terms of conflict only so long as the conflict remains 'temperate', to cite Gibbon's word. If and when the conflict becomes violent, its 'undecisiveness' will become a curse instead of a blessing, since the only way of bringing violent warfare to an end is for one of the belligerents to win a victory that will be decisive enough to enable him to give peace to his self-tormented world by imposing political unity on it.

Why did Hume and Gibbon fail to make these two patent and pertinent points? They must have been aware of the devastating effect of the impact of their own Western Civilization on the native peoples of the Americas and on the African slaves whom the Western settlers there had uprooted from their homes in order to subject them to forced labour on American plantations. They must also have been aware of the ruin that the once creative city-states of Greece had eventually brought on themselves by carrying their conflicts with each other to intemperate lengths. They must have known that the Greeks had paid for this intemperance by inflicting agony on themselves before they were compelled to commute this price for the lesser one of forfeiting their local independence and having peace imposed on them by the Roman world-state. When they had perceived, as they did perceive, the resemblance of their own eighteenth-century Western World to the Greece of the Periclean Age, why did they have no foreboding that Western history might take the tragic turn that Hellenic history had taken in 431 B.C.?

The eighteenth-century Western advocates of disunity may not have been mistaken in reckoning that the balance of advantage was in favour of disunity in the particular circumstances of their own time and place. Their mistake was their unconsidered assumption that these circumstances were normal and permanent. The 'temperate and undecisive' contests of the eighteenth-century Western states were truly a cheap price to pay for the contemporary 'progress of knowledge and industry' that was being gratifyingly 'accelerated by the emulation of so many active rivals'. But Gibbon forgot, when he was writing these words, the main theme of the book of which this passage is a part. The history of the decline and fall of the Roman Empire is an illustration of the truth that change is of the essence of life, and that therefore even a relatively well-ordered and beneficent state of human affairs is not immune from the possibility of deterioration.

Gibbon lived to be shaken out of his complacent appreciation of the merits of eighteenth-century Western civilization and his consequent optimism about the future. He lived to be overtaken by the French Revolution, and he was shattered by this demonic upheaval because he could not reconcile this revolutionary new fact with his *Weltanschauung*, which, by this time, was hard-set. Yet by this time he had written his history of the 'awful revolution' in which the Graeco-Roman World of the Antonine Age—a world which, in Gibbon's view, was a counterpart of his own world—had been overwhelmed by 'the triumph of barbarism and religion'. Gibbon's own life-work had deprived him, in advance, of all excuse for allowing the French Revolution to take him by surprise. The inadequacy of Gibbon's reaction to the most important public event in his life-time surely impugns the validity of his Humean philosophy of history.

The truth seems to be that, in the history of every society, known to us, that has been fractured politically into a number of separate local states, this political configuration has been ephemeral. The warfare that has been its unavoidable consequence has, in every case, become more and more violent with the passage of time. This devastating effect of plurality has then come to outweigh its stimulating effect, and eventually the price of the stimulus has become so exorbitant that the society has had to purchase peace and order by submitting to the imposition of political unity. It has submitted to this though unity, too, has its price in the shape of uniformity, dullness, and torpor. This price, too, is considerable, but it is not so high as the eventual price of disunity has proved to be; and therefore, on balance, the self-tormented society is reconciled to the suppression of local independence, since experience has proved that this is the lesser of the two evils between which society now has to choose.

The history of the last 5,000 years seems to show that, in the Age of Civilization, the question at issue is not whether a fractured political configuration of society or a unitary one is preferable. A fractured configuration is bound to be ephemeral; so the practical question is: At what stage and by what means is political unity going to be brought about?

The Egyptians succeeded in replacing plurality by unity at the dawn of civilization in Egypt—that is to say, at a stage at which the local communities had not yet become capable of waging war devastatingly. Through this achievement the Egyptians saved themselves from the tribulations that the Sumerians inflicted on themselves before they submitted to the liquidation of their local city-states by the unitary Empire of Sumer and Akkad. The Egyptians paid for their political success in cultural coin. At an early date in their history, their civilization became more uniform, more rigid, and more torpid than the Sumero-Akkadian civilization or the Chinese civilization ever became, even after these civilizations, in their turn, had been living for centuries under the Egyptian-like régime of a universal state. The question is whether the Egyptians' experience or the Sumerians' experience is the happier one on balance.

Whatever our judgement on this issue may be, it seems indisputable that the Egyptians' experience has been peculiar. It may not have been unique. It is possible that the Indus Culture, too, may have achieved political unity at the start, and that the Chinese civilization may have had a first chapter of political unity, in the time of the Shang Dynasty and the early Chou Dynasty, before the Chinese World was fractured politically into 'the Contending States'. The archaeological evidence which is our only source of information about the history of the Indus Culture and the early history of China does not answer this political question for us. However, it looks as if the configuration that we find in Sumero-Akkadian history is more usual, and that it is, in fact, the normal one. The Sumero-Akkadian civilization started its life on the political plane as a constellation of mutually independent states; these local states' wars with each other became progressively more violent; and eventually—though not till after the wars had inflicted irreparable damage—the local states were replaced by a unitary world-state that one of their number established by defeating and conquering all the rest.

This archetypal Sumero-Akkadian pattern of history has been reproduced, in the Old World, in Hellenic history and in Chinese history since the time of 'the Contending States', at any rate. It has been reproduced, in pre-Columbian America, in Andean history and in Middle American history. It has also been reproduced in the still unfinished history of the Western Civilization. So far, our Western World has been a politically fractured World ever since it emerged out of the ruins of the Roman Empire; and it, too, has paid for its culturally stimulating political disunity by tormenting itself with devastating wars. The sixteenth-century and seventeenth-century wars of religion have turned out not to be the final bout of those major public crimes, as the eighteenth-century Western optimists naïvely assumed them to have been. Subsequent experience has proved the wars of religion to have been neither the last bout nor the worst. Gibbon lived to see the driving-force of democracy put into war in the *levée en masse* in France in 1792. The driving-force of technology, too, has been put into war since the Industrial Revolution. In our generation we have lived to see this aggravation of the destructiveness of warfare carried to a peak—though this not yet its highest peak, for all that we know —in the manufacture and use of the atomic weapon in 1945.

On the analogy of the histories of perhaps a majority of the other civilizations that have preceded ours, we may guess that, in the history of ours too, the price of political disunity is going to soar to a height at which we shall find it preferable to submit to political unification, however reluctant we may be. Meanwhile, we have been overtaken by our invention of the atomic weapon before we have liberated ourselves from war by establishing our world-state, and this perilous situation in which we have now placed ourselves raises the question of the means by which political unification is going to be brought about, supposing that we do achieve unification in our world.

All the would-be world-states of the past that are known to us have been established by conquest. Each of them has been the sequel to a knock-out blow that has been the finale of a series of rounds of progressively intensified warfare. The literally world-wide world-state that, in our world, is the only alternative to mass-suicide can no longer be established in this barbarous and costly traditional way now that we find ourselves in the Atomic Age. In a world-war fought with the atomic weapon the traditional pattern of war would not recur. This time, all belligerents alike would be defeated and prostrated; there would be no surviving victor to clear up the ruins; and therefore, in the Atomic Age, the traditional use of war as an instrument of policy is no longer practicable. The instrument would produce the mass-suicide that the policy would be intending to avoid. From now onwards a world-state, even in the minimal form of a pair of world-authorities for dealing with the two most pressing world-problems, can be established, if at all, only by peaceful means—that is to say, only by common consent. The emotional resistance to this revolutionary break with ingrained habits and to this painful renunciation of familiar institutions will have to be overcome by self-education; in the Atomic Age it cannot be broken by force. The Gordian Knot has to be untied by patient fingers instead of being cut by the sword. How much patience have we? How much time have we? How strong is the emotional resistance in us that we have to induce ourselves to abandon? The strongest of the feelings that are generating this resistance in us is the feeling of nationalism. Our prospect of coping with nationalism largely depends on our ability to understand it; and, in order to understand it, we have to take its history into account.

VI

The Exacerbation of Divisive Feeling

In a previous chapter it has been noted that it is only within the last 5,000 years that a progressive improvement in Man's means of communication has produced the technological enabling conditions for the reunification of the human race. It has also been noted that, even when these newly acquired facilities were still in a rudimentary stage, they were used with impressive results, long before their recent sensational development to a point at which they have 'annihilated distance'. Already in the Pre-Mechanical Age, the would-be world-empires and world-religions had spread over whole continents, and the local mother-tongues of some of the pastoralists and the navigators had been disseminated by the speakers of them round the shores of the conductive seas and round the shore-like margins of the sea-like steppes. It is a paradox that the same 5,000 years should also have seen an exacerbation of divisive political feeling. It is a greater paradox that this exacerbated divisive feeling should have risen to a still higher pitch in this latest age. In this age mankind has acquired the technological and organizational means for enabling the human race to reunite on a global scale, and at the same time this consummation of the movement towards unity that began 5,000 years ago has been made imperative and urgent by the possibility that a technological virtuosity which can be used for reuniting the human race may actually be used, instead, for destroying it. Technology is a morally neutral force. It can be used, at will, either for good or for evil. Yet, since the Second World War, the number of the local sovereign states on the political map of the World has nearly doubled, and, in each of them, the temperature of nationalist feeling has been rising.

The divisive feeling that has rankled into present-day nationalism must be almost as old as the human race itself. The distinction between 'insiders' and 'outsiders' must have come into consciousness as soon as the primal band of human beings split, and this must have happened soon after Man's pre-human ancestors had become human, since Primitive Man made his living by food-gathering, and food-gatherers would starve if they did not scatter. This economic pressure accounts for the fission and dispersal of mankind into a number of separate bands, and this fractured state of society would account, in turn, for the differentiation of a human being's feelings towards different representatives of the human species. Towards his fellow human beings within his own band he would feel a greater sense of social and moral solidarity than he would feel towards his fellow human beings with whom he had nothing in common beyond his and their common humanity. Since economic necessity compelled mankind to live in disunity so long as it remained in the food-gathering stage, and since this has been the economic dispensation under which the whole of mankind has lived for perhaps 99 per cent. of the length of its history up to date, it is natural that a human being's alienation from fellow human beings who are not his fellow tribesmen should have become an ingrained habit during this relatively immense period of time. It is also natural that this habit should have persisted in societies that have got beyond the food-gathering stage within the latest one per cent. of the length of human history so far—a span of perhaps no more than 9,000 years or thereabouts.

This habit of tribalism that was originally imposed by a food-gathering economy, and that was confirmed by the long duration of this economic régime, is hard to eradicate today, as we know by our experience of our neighbours' tribal feelings and our own. It is hard to eradicate though it has ceased to be an economic necessity. This is hard even now that, since the advent of the Atomic Age, the persistence of tribalism is threatening to lead mankind to self-destruction. Tribalism is a formidable habit; but it is a habit only, and no more than that. It is, in fact, part of the social and cultural heritage that Man has created for himself and that he is therefore free to modify. Tribalism is not a built-in and consequently ineradicable trait of human nature. We have evidence that it is not; for we know that there have been human beings who have felt as great a concern for all other human beings—living, dead, or still unborn—as a tribal-minded human being feels for his fellow tribes-men exclusively. Their attitude has been 'homo sum, humani nihil a me alienum puto'.[1] These souls who have loved mankind at large with a love that a tribal-minded human being feels only for his family and his personal friends must either have never succumbed to the habit of tribal feeling or must have succeeded in breaking with this habit if they did originally inherit it by transmission from their elders.

The outstanding examples of this all-embracing love are the founders of the missionary religions and their successors who have caught their spirit and have carried on their work. Their spirit is expressed in a declaration that was put on record in India in the third century B.C. by the Maurya emperor Ashoka, who was a missionary of the oldest of the world-religions, Bud-dhism, besides being the ruler of one of the would-be world-states. 'All men are my children. Just as I seek the welfare and happiness of my own children in this world and the next, I seek the same things for all men.'[2]

Few of the adherents of the world-religions have attained this spiritual stature. Yet there are also few of them who have not been liberated to some extent from the bonds of tribal feeling by the influence of the spirit of these religions' founders. Citizenship in a would-be world-state has had the same spiritually liberating effect, and this is more remarkable, con-sidering that the would-be world-states have been established by conquest for the aggrandizement of some single local state at the expense of all its rivals. Ashoka himself had set out to round off his empire by extending it up to the 'natural frontiers' of the Indian sub-continent. He had attacked and conquered the nearest of the independent peninsular states, Kalinga; and it was his recognition of the wickedness and cruelty of what he had done that led him to embrace Buddhism and to devote the rest of his life, not to enlarging his empire by further conquests, but to spreading Buddhism by peaceful missionary work.

Forcible incorporation in a would-be world-state was natur-ally resented and resisted by the victims of it. Yet, in the histories of many of the world-states, the descendants of a world-state's unwilling subjects eventually became its loyal citizens. They had come to feel that the world-state did in truth

[1] Terence, *Heauton Timorumenos*, I, i, 25.　　[2] Rock Edict II.

stand for the unity and concord of the human race, and that world-citizenship was a higher form of political association than the citizenship of any of those local states to which their ancestors had obstinately given their allegiance. The earliest of the would-be world-states, the united empire of Egypt, was established not more than 5,000 years ago. The oldest of the would-be world-religions, Buddhism, was founded not more than 2,500 years ago. By contrast, it must be about 900,000 years ago that mankind split into a number of separate fragments. It will be seen that, so far, the new habit of world-mindedness has had a relatively short time for asserting itself against the old habit of tribal feeling. It is remarkable that it should have been able to assert itself at all, considering the length of the start that tribal feeling has had. This indicates that the habit of tribal feeling, old though it is, is eradicable, as all human habits are.

This divisive feeling, which is at so dangerously high a pitch today, must have been at a much lower tension during the earlier and longer stages of human history. In the food-gathering stage the collective power of the tribe had not yet been deified. A tribe's collective power was puny so long as it was living under this ineffective economic régime. Food-gathering Man was impressed, not by his own power, but by the far more powerful forces of non-human nature at whose mercy he still found himself. Human beings are inclined to worship the greatest powers that are within their ken; so Food-gathering Man worshipped earth and water, Sun, Moon, and stars, and the wild animals that preyed on him or that provided him with his livelihood; he was not tempted to worship himself at this stage; his religious feelings attached themselves to objects outside himself; and therefore his feeling for his tribe was not yet heightened by having any religious emotion injected into it.

Food-gathering Man's feeling of alienation from human beings outside his own tribe was also not yet heightened by his becoming engaged in a struggle for existence with them. Though a food-gathering population has to be thinly spread, by contrast with the relative density of a population that makes its living by agriculture or by mechanized industry, the total numbers of mankind, throughout the Food-gathering Age, were so small that, for them, the habitable Earth was still virtually boundless, however many square miles of territory per head a food-gathering band might require. These roving bands did not have to collide with each other; they merely had to continue to scatter ever more widely.

There was a sharp increase in the size of the planet's human population after the invention of agriculture and the domestication of animals, since these revolutionary innovations greatly increased the food-supply of the communities that made them or adopted them. Yet the Earth continued to be still virtually boundless for Agricultural Man, too, during the Neolithic Age— that is to say, the Pre-Civilizational Age—of Man's post-food-gathering economy. The agricultural village communities that were now replacing the food-gathering bands seem still not to have collided seriously either with each other or with their more backward and therefore weaker neighbours who were still lingering in the food-gathering stage. This seems, at least, to be what is indicated by the archaeological evidence. The earliest agriculturists that drifted out of South-West Asia into Europe in search of new lands to till do not seem to have been warriors.

Thus the divisive feeling that had been evoked by the economic conditions of the Food-gathering Age seems to have been more or less innocuous, not only during that age, but also during the subsequent Neolithic Age. The economic revolution that marked the transition, and the increase in the numbers of the human race that this revolution brought with it, seem not to have had the effect of heightening the tension between the local communities into which mankind had, long since, been fractured. By contrast, the transition from the Neolithic Age to the succeeding Age of Civilization does seem to have heightened this tension to a degree at which it began to take the grievous toll of life, wealth, and happiness that it has been taking ever since. This happened at the dawn of the Age of Civilization because two changes in the human situation—a religious change and an economic one—occurred at this point. Man in process of civilization took to worshipping his own collective power, and at the same time he fell into a struggle for existence with his human neighbours for the possession of economic resources in a world that, for him, was no longer boundless, as the World had been for his Palaeolithic and Neolithic predecessors.

Man took to worshipping his own collective power when he had become aware that this collective human power had enabled him, at last, to get the upper hand over non-human nature, at whose mercy he had been during the greater part of his history so far. Probably Man had already gained his ascendancy over Nature by the beginning of the Upper Palaeolithic Age, when he began to improve his previously almost static technology; certainly he had gained this ascendancy by the time when he had taken to cultivating plants and to domesticating animals. But changes, even when momentous, do not always win prompt recognition, and the recognition of them is perhaps particularly slow to express itself in corresponding changes in religion, since religion is a field in which Man is apt to be conservative. Man's immediate reaction to his invention of agriculture was to add to his existing pantheon of nature-gods some divinities representing the plants and trees that he had learnt to cultivate. It was not till after his achievement of civilization that he deified himself as well and gave himself the precedence over all his older gods.

Man was bound to be impressed by his collective power when it had won for him such sensational victories over Nature as the conversion of the once-savage jungle-swamps in the lower Tigris-Euphrates valley and in the lower Nile valley into docile canals and dykes and fields, and when the unprecedented productivity of these reclaimed wildernesses had raised the wealth and populousness of a local community from the level of a Neolithic village to the level of a Sumerian city-state. Accordingly, at the dawn of civilization in Sumer, we find that some of the old nature-gods have now been given a new role, and that this role has come to overshadow their original one. While continuing to be the representatives of natural forces, they have now come to be also the representatives of political communities. Enlil the wind-god is now also the deification of the state of Nippur; Nanna the moon-god is now also the deification of the state of Ur. At the dawn of civilization in Greece and in Canaan, nearly 2,000 years later, we find the same. Athena the olive-goddess is now also the deification of the state of Athens as Athene Poliûchus and the deification of the state of Sparta as Athana Chalcioecus. The water-god Poseidon is now also the deification of the state of Corinth, which had a coastline on two seas and which lived by commerce. The vegetation-god Baal is now also the deification of the state of Tyre. The volcano-god or thunder-god Yahweh is the deification of the states of Israel, Judah, and Edom. The local communities have become divinities, and these divinities that stand for collective human power have become paramount over the divinities that stand for natural forces. The injection of this amount of religious devotion into nationalism has turned nationalism into a religion, and this a fanatical one.

The second ominous change at the dawn of civilization was an economic one. The world that had been boundless for the food-gatherer, and also for the Neolithic cultivator and pastoralist, closed in upon the societies that had created civilization in the process of reclaiming the jungle-swamps. Edible berries and roots could be gathered and edible animals could be hunted almost anywhere on Earth; the range of terrain on which rainfall agriculture and small-scale irrigation agriculture could be practised and on which goats, sheep, and cattle could be pastured was very wide; but the regions that could be reclaimed for large-scale irrigation-agriculture were relatively rare, and their areas were sharply limited. Accordingly, when all of the lower Tigris-Euphrates valley and of the lower Nile valley that it was possible to drain and irrigate had been reclaimed piecemeal by local communities that had penetrated the jungle-swamp from different points on its edge, the states whose domains now marched with each other could not find additional land by turning their backs on each other and dispersing, as their Palaeolithic and Neolithic predecessors had done. If any one of them was to add to its present holding of the reclaimed land that was the source of their wealth and their populousness, it would have to do this at the expense of one or more of its neighbours, and it could do that only if it were powerful enough to rob its neighbours by force. In fact, if either Sumer or Egypt continued to be fractured politically into a number of mutually independent local states after its economic resources had been fully developed, wars between the local states were bound to break out, and this with increasing frequency; and, since the local states in these exceptionally productive regions were high-powered, their wars would be serious.

What happened in Sumer at this stage is depicted on the Vulture Stele of King Eannatum of Lagash. The victorious phalanx is bristling with spear-points; the vultures are feasting on the defeated enemy soldiers' corpses. The only way to put an end to this fratricidal warfare would be to subordinate all the deified local states to a single deified world-government, powerful enough to keep the peace. This was what was done in the end in the Sumero-Akkadian World and in the Hellenic World and in China. In Egypt it was done at the beginning, and this saved posterity in Egypt from the tribulations that the Sumerians and Greeks and Chinese inflicted on themselves. The 'wars to end war' were grim too. The scenes depicted on Narmer's palette and on Naramsin's stele are as ghastly as those depicted on Eannatum's stele. But the wars that resulted in unification had the merit of being conclusive. The world-states represented by the living gods Pharaoh and Divus Caesar and the Chinese Son of Heaven did not exact the blood-tax that the warring local states had exacted from their devoted citizens.

The nationalism that, in the Atomic Age, is threatening to lead mankind to self-destruction is the Sumerian nationalism of the third millennium B.C., intensified and reproduced on a world-wide scale. Though this present-day nationalism has now captivated the whole human race, it is, in origin, a specifically Western form of the Sumerian ideology. The non-Western peoples have been adopting Western nationalism because they have been made to feel the force of it while they have been temporarily under Western domination. They have therefore taken nationalism to be a talisman that can raise the collective power of a local community to its maximum height. The most portentous of these cases of conversion is the Chinese. By the time, in the nineteenth century of the Christian Era, when China began to feel the impact of Western power, she had been world-minded for more than 2,000 years, and she continued, for more than 100 years longer, to remain faithful to her traditional *Weltanschauung* at the cost of being trampled on by one Western or Westernized national state after another. It is only since 1911 that China, too, has capitulated to the ideology of her oppressors. China's reconversion to nationalism has been reluctant and belated, but her *volte-face* has been extreme. China is the most aggressively nationalist-minded country in the World today.

We must review the history of the development of nationalism in the West if we are to understand present-day nationalism's nature and to appreciate its strength. Western nationalism started at a relatively low tension; for, although, in the West, the Roman world-state had broken up into a number of local successor-states, these did not, at first, win their subjects' paramount loyalty. This was given, during the Western Middle Ages, to the Roman Church, which, in Hume's words, quoted in the preceding chapter, was 'really one large state within itself'. It was only when the unifying Roman Church's prestige had been undermined by the 'Babylonish captivity' and the Great Schism, and when its unity had been disrupted by the Reformation, that Western nationalism began to increase its hold on Western hearts. In the Modern Age of Western history, Western nationalism has acquired a demonic dynamism through receiving two stimulating injections.

The first stimulant that was injected into Western nationalism was a dose of Graeco-Roman nationalism, which, in the Western Renaissance, was reanimated in Western hearts and minds, together with Greek and Roman literature, art, architecture, and science. Greek science had been surpassed in the West and been discarded there before the close of the seventeenth century; but the other resuscitated elements of the Hellenic civilization have passed into the Western society's blood-stream, and, of these, Graeco-Roman nationalism has been the most potent, perhaps just because the influence of this resuscitated Graeco-Roman ideology on Western life has not been recognized so clearly as the influence of the Hellenic arts has been. The Greek and Roman patriots who are the heroes of Plutarch's *Lives* inspired the Founding Fathers of the United States and the makers of the French Revolution. This dose of Graeco-Roman nationalism raised Western nationalism to a new pitch of intensity. The modern Western admirers of the Greek and Roman patriots seem to have been blind to the truth that this inordinate divisive-mindedness was the chief cause of the Hellenic civilization's downfall.

The second stimulant that has been injected into Western nationalism is a dose of Christian fanaticism. Christianity, like Islam, derives from Judaism and has inherited the evil in Judaism as well as the good in it. The evil in the Judaic religions is their exclusiveness, intransigence, and proneness to resort to violence in order to impose on other people what their own adherents believe to be true and right. When, at the Reformation, the Western Christian Church broke up, its violence, which had been directed against Jews and Muslims hitherto, turned inwards and found vent in the Catholic-Protestant wars of religion. These wars were waged with such hatred, malice, uncharitableness, and atrociousness that, after a century and a half of them, the more sensitive, humane, and liberal-minded spirits in the West found themselves alienated from a religion that could instigate the perpetration of such crimes. 'Tantum religio potuit suadere malorum.'[1] The closing decades of the seventeenth century saw the beginning of a recession of Christianity in the West. The tide has gone on ebbing till within our lifetime. The first signs of a possible turn in it did not show themselves till after the end of the Second World War.

Meanwhile, this weakening of Christianity's hold on Western hearts was bound to lead these hearts to transfer their devotion to non-Christian objects of worship. This was bound to happen if it is true, as has been suggested in the second chapter of this book, that religion is one of the stable ingredients in human nature. Human nature, like the rest of Nature, abhors a vacuum; and therefore the devotion that, in human hearts, has been progressively withdrawn from Christianity in the course of the last three centuries has had to find substitutes for Christianity to which it can transfer itself. The substitutes that it has found are the post-Christian ideologies. The three principal representatives of these are Nationalism, Individualism, and Communism, and, of these three, Nationalism is the most obsessive. At any rate, Nationalism usually prevails over the others when these come into conflict with it. The devotion that has been transferred from Christianity to Nationalism has detached itself from what is good in Christianity but has clung to what is evil in it. It has repudiated the ideals of love, self-sacrifice, and concern for mankind as a whole that are Christianity's virtues; it has retained the fanaticism that is the common vice of the religions of the Judaic family; and this sour wine, poured into Nationalism's constricting bottle, has fermented there with explosive effects.

Thus the Western Nationalism that has become the world-

---

[1] Lucretius, *De Rerum Naturâ*, Book I, line 101.

wide Nationalism of today is something more than the archaic form of political divisiveness. The double dose of stimulant that has been injected into it has raised it to a previously unknown degree of potency. It is like one of those doctored gasolines that are sometimes offered to car-drivers at filling-stations. A strident advertisement makes this high-powered mixture seductive; but the driver who is rash enough to replenish his tank with it may find himself soon rushing down a steep place into the sea.

Our analysis of the composition of present-day Nationalism gives the measure of its malignity. This Nationalism is a recrudescence of the worship of collective human power from which the higher religions have been seeking to liberate mankind. It is a recrudescence of the more evil of the two historic forms of man-worship. The worship of the collective power embodied in a world-state is at least the worship of an institution that has brought unity—and, with unity, peace and order—to a large section of mankind. Yet the Christian martyrs of the first three centuries sacrificed their lives rather than perform even a merely formal act of worship on the altars of the goddess Rome and the god Caesar. Undoubtedly they would also have refused, and this with even greater vehemence, to worship Athens or Sparta, if these local states of the Hellenic World had still retained their sovereignty and their divinity at that date, instead of having been reduced, as they had been by then, to being little more than public utilities. In our time in Germany there have been Christian martyrs who did give their lives rather than pay homage to the rampant Nationalism represented there by the human god Adolf Hitler. On the other hand it is also possible in our time to see 'the abomination of desolation, spoken of by Daniel the prophet, standing in the place where it ought not'.[1] Enter a church of any denomination in any Western country today. As likely as not, you will find the local national flag planted in the sanctuary side by side with the Cross. Here we are seeing the symbol of collective human pride confronting the symbol of the self-sacrificing lovingness of God. Man-worship has been encroaching on the worship of the ultimate spiritual reality that exists behind and beyond the phenomena of the Universe, and this encroachment has gone

[1] Mark 13, 14.

far. If candid answers could be elicited by an outspoken ques-
tionnaire, it might be found that, today, nationalism is 90 per
cent. of the religion of 90 per cent. of the people of the Western
World and of the rest of the World as well.

In the Atomic Age, Nationalism is a death-wish, and Nationalism is now in the ascendant. The antidote to Nationalism is
world-mindedness; and the two historic institutions in which
this world-mindedness has found expression are the would-be
world-states and world-religions. The wish for reunification
is a wish for life and good. Does this salutary wish have any
chance of prevailing? If we are to try to answer this question,
we must review the histories of the world-states and the world-
religions in their turn.

PART TWO

THE OVERRIDING NEED IN POLITICS FOR ORDER

VII

The Significance of the Would-be
World-States

A literally world-wide world-state would be a state whose government was effective over the whole habitable and traversable surface of this planet, together with its air-envelope and the adjacent reaches of outer space. It would include the whole living generation of the human race among its citizens. No such state has ever been established so far. Until now there have only been would-be world-states. These have succeeded in uniting large parts of the Earth's surface and of the human race, but not yet ever the whole; and most of these incomplete world-states have failed to perpetuate themselves. Out of the many that have arisen in the course of the last 5,000 years, only two— the Chinese and the Russian—are still in existence today; and, for both of these, the price of survival has been a capitulation to an ideology that is the antithesis of world-mindedness.

The present official ideology of both the Chinese and the Russian state is, of course, Communism, and Communism is a missionary ideology, dedicated, like the Christian religion from which it has broken out, to the conversion of the whole of mankind. This adoption of a missionary ideology is consonant with these two would-be world-states' traditional world-mindedness. However, both Russia and China have also both embraced another of the post-Christian ideologies, namely Nationalism; and, though their Nationalism is unavowed, it is, in fact, paramount over their Communism, as has been demonstrated by the choice that they have made whenever the demands of these two ideologies have been in conflict. The issue between Stalin and Trotsky was whether Russia's national power and interests were to be expendable in the cause of Communism or whether Communism was to be made to serve as an instrument of

Russian national policy. Trotsky gave the priority to Communism; Stalin gave it to Nationalism. It is significant that Stalin won, and that the issue has tacitly been decided in the same way in China. This overriding commitment to Nationalism is incompatible with the universalism that both states still profess, but it is consonant with present facts. It is a recognition of the truth that, today, Russia and China are no longer world-states. They have been reduced to being two out of the 124 local states of the present-day world. Each is a giant, but neither of them can any longer make even a pretence of being unique and solitary.

Thus all the would-be world-states of the past have succumbed in the end to the habit of divisive feeling. Those of them that have not broken up have preserved their existence at the cost of abandoning their world-mindedness. This is not surprising, considering how relatively recent the habit of world-mindedness is, by comparison with the habit of divisive feeling that has reasserted itself. It would be a mistake, however, to conclude, from the failure of past would-be world-states to maintain themselves as such, that there is no prospect of our being able to establish a world-state that would not only be literally worldwide but would also be permanent; for, when we look into the history of the past would-be world-states, we find that there have been successes in it, as well as failures. Within the limited periods of their duration, a number of world-states have succeeded in winning the esteem and loyalty of peoples that had originally been subjected to them by force. This indicates that world-mindedness, as well as Nationalism, has its appeal, and that it makes this appeal to people who have had the experience of living, for a number of generations on end, under a régime that is world-minded in spirit and is world-wide in intent, even though its achievements may have fallen short of its ideals.

All the past would-be world-states whose history is known to us have had a bad start. They have all had to overcome the age-old habit of divisive-mindedness which is a legacy from the Food-gathering Age. They have overcome it by resorting to force, in the teeth of violent resistance. The palette of Narmer records the resistance to the establishment of the united empire of Egypt. In this case the resistance was presumably minimal, because the political unification of Egypt was achieved at the dawn of civilization there, at a stage at which the local communities had not yet had time to develop their material power or to tighten their emotional hold on their citizens. The resistance will have been more violent in those cases—and they have been more frequent—in which unification has been achieved belatedly, at the end of a series of bouts of wars between the local states in which local Nationalism has become exacerbated.

Nationalists have not always been cured of their Nationalism even by this harrowing experience. There have been cases in which, after peace and order have been established through the imposition of political unity at this high cost, the forcibly united peoples have taken the earliest opportunity to revolt, though, in revolting, they have been deliberately exposing themselves to a recurrence of the long-drawn-out tribulations from which they have so recently been released.

For instance, within sixteen years of the completion of the establishment of the Persian Empire through the founder Cyrus's conquest and annexation of the Babylonian Empire in 538 B.C., there were widespread revolts in most of the provinces to the east of the River Euphrates. The assassination, by Darius and his companions, of Cambyses' successor, who had claimed, truly or falsely, to be Cyrus's son Smerdis, gave the signal for almost every nation in the eastern two-thirds of the Persian Empire, including half the Persian nation itself, to take up arms in the hope of recovering its national independence. This still unabated eagerness to endure the horrors of war for the sake of indulging a traditional divisive-mindedness is astonishing, considering what the historical background was to the turbulent year 522 B.C. The Persian Empire, which the rebels were seeking to overthrow, was the fourth attempt to restore peace and order in the Sumero-Akkadian World and its annexes since the establishment of the Empire of Agadé nearly 2,000 years back. This Akkadian world-state of Agadé, its Sumerian avatar established by the Third Dynasty of Ur, its Amorite avatar established by Hammurabi of Babylon, and finally its Assyrian avatar, had each come and gone in its turn. The wars through which unity had been established and re-established and the other wars in which it had, each time, been broken up again had all been costly; and the final bout of the Assyrian wars had been the worst tribulation of all. The spells of peace that had been purchased at this price had been shorter in the aggregate than the intervening bouts of turmoil and anarchy, and the havoc made by fratricidal wars had been punctuated and aggravated by havoc-making barbarian invasions. The Gutaeans, Kassites, Mitannians, Phrygians, Aramaeans, Cimmerians, and Scyths had been the most destructive. Yet all this suffering had left the South-West Asian peoples still unchastened.

This South-West Asian story was repeated in China. Within twelve years of the completion of the establishment of the Chinese world-state in 221 B.C. through the founder Ch'in Shih Hwangti's conquest and annexation of Ch'i, which was the last survivor among the warring local states, there was a general revolt in which the peoples of the liquidated states took up arms, as the peoples of South-West Asia had taken them up in 522 B.C., in the hope of recovering their national independence. In this case the deliberate breaking of the recently imposed peace cost, not just one more year of devastating warfare, but eight years of it, before the disrupted world-state was reconstructed. Yet in China, as in South-West Asia, the historical background to this resumption of strife had been so harrowing that the people that had experienced these tribulations might have been expected to have no stomach left for putting themselves through them again. The physical unification of China in 221 B.C. had been the finale in the fratricidal struggle between 'the Contending States', and, by then, this warfare had been going on, with ever increasing intensity, for about 550 years. The second founder of the Chinese world-state, Kao-tsu, the first emperor of the Han Dynasty, took care not to repeat Ch'in Shih Hwangti's mistakes. Ch'in Shih Hwangti had been a revolutionary. He had been reckless in riding roughshod over cherished traditions and institutions and feelings. Kao-tsu was tactful and wily. He saved the local nationalists' face while effectively clipping their claws. Yet, forty-eight years after his adroit reconstruction of the Chinese world-state in 202 B.C., these claws had grown long enough again to draw blood once more. In 154 B.C. the kings of seven of the pared-down local states made a last effort to undo Ch'in Shih Hwangti's and Kao-tsu's work. They jointly took up arms against the central government. These rebel kings were all members of the Han imperial house; Kao-tsu had seen to that; yet they had become so thoroughly imbued with the persistent dissidence of their subjects that they lent themselves to it to their own undoing. After the failure of their rebellion their kingdoms were *gleichgeschaltet*.

At the opposite end of the Old World, Ch'in Shih Hwangti and Kao-tsu have had counterparts in Caesar and Augustus. Caesar's tactful and wily adopted son had to reconstruct the Roman world-state that his adoptive father had constructed with too little regard for the forcibly deposed Roman nobility's outraged susceptibilities. In this Roman case, in contrast to the Chinese and South-West Asian cases, it was not the subjugated peoples who kicked against the pricks. The foregoing age of agony in the Mediterranean World had effectively broken their spirit. The recalcitrants were the subject peoples' former rulers the Roman nobles; yet their recalcitrance, too, is surprising, considering what the historical background was to their assassination of Caesar in 45 B.C. The four years of civil war that had ended only in 46 B.C. had been the last convulsion in a chronic revolution that had been raging for eighty-seven years by then. The Roman nobility had proved themselves unfit to rule the world that they had conquered. They were politically discredited and bankrupt. Yet, rather than resign themselves to Caesar's new order, they inflicted fifteen more years of civil war on the subject peoples, on the Roman people, and on themselves.

These are striking examples of the strength of the resistance that the forcible establishment of a world-state can arouse. The strength of it has varied in accordance with the character of the cultural relation in which the empire-builders have stood to the society on which they have imposed peace. The opposition has been the least violent in cases in which the empire-builders have come, as the Third Dynasty of Ur came, from the heart of the world that they have united. Empire-builders have, however, seldom been metropolitans; they have usually been marchmen, barbarians, or positive aliens in culture or in religion or in both. The people of Ch'in and the Romans were marchmen; the Persians were semi-barbarians; the Greeks who conquered the Persian Empire and the Spaniards who conquered the Aztec and Inca empires and the British who reunified India were aliens in culture; the Arabs and 'Osmanlis and Mughals were barbarians who were also aliens in religion, and this combination of objectionable features has proved to be the most repugnant of all. Yet even the alien and the barbarian empire-builders did acquire some prestige in the eyes of their subjects, while the marchmen empire-builders succeeded, in time, in converting unwilling subjects into loyal citizens of a world-state that had originally been imposed by force and been maintained by it.

In China, long before the Prior Han Dynasty had exhausted its mandate, the peoples of the former 'warring states' had forgotten their differences. They had all identified themselves with the Chinese world-state, which, as they now saw it, was coextensive with the civilized World and was the master institution that gave the World an abiding peace and order; and this continued to be the Chinese *Weltanschauung* until it was made untenable by the impact of the West on China in the nineteenth century of the Christian Era.

The history of the Roman Empire ran the same course. The political structure of the Roman Empire was Roman, but its culture was Greek, and the Romans could not have done their constructive political work if they had not adopted the culture of their Greek subjects. The Greeks, on their side, resented having unity and peace imposed on them by outsiders who owed to the Greeks whatever culture they had managed to acquire. The Greeks' resentment against Roman domination lasted for a quarter of a millennium after the Greeks had fallen into the Romans' toils—as they had fallen, largely through their own fault, in the course of the second century B.C. Yet, by the second century of the Christian Era, the Greeks had come to appreciate the value of the world-state against which they had so long repined. The most eloquent and perceptive eulogy of the Roman Empire that was made by any of its inhabitants in that century was written, not in Latin, but in Greek. Its author was Aelius Aristeides, a Greek man of letters with a semi-Roman name. In the fifth century, when the Roman Empire had declined to a degree at which its fall could be foreboded, its citizens expressed their attachment to it by coining a new name for it. In calling their world-state 'Romania', they were signifying that they had come to feel that they were all Romans, and that the Roman world-state was their common motherland.

Even the history of the Arab Empire followed this Roman and Chinese course to some extent, though here the conditions were less favourable. In the Roman and Chinese world-states the reconciliation between the subjects and their rulers, and the eventual blending of the two parties into a united world-community, were facilitated by the unifying effect of a common culture. In the Arab Empire, on the other hand, subjects and rulers were held apart by a religious cleavage that coincided with the political one. Nevertheless, when the Arab Empire, in its turn, had reached a point in its decline at which its fall was manifestly imminent, there were mass-conversions to Islam that transformed the Empire's religious and political structure. The Muslims in the Empire had hitherto been a minority, and originally they had all been Arabs. Before the Empire fell, its Muslim citizens had become the majority, and they had come to be representative of all nationalities in the population. Hence, when the Empire died, Islam lived on; and this sequel to the mass-conversions possibly explains why these occurred when they did. They occurred when the Empire was being assailed by Central Asian nomads from the one side and by Western Christian crusaders from the other. The house was falling about its inmates' ears; and this catastrophe made them all realize that it had been their common home, though hitherto they had co-existed in it as aliens to each other. The fall of the Empire was going to leave all its inhabitants shelterless, whatever their ancestral religion might be. They must now quickly find some alternative dwelling-place that, unlike the Empire, was strongly enough built to be able to weather the storm. The only sure refuge within sight was Islam; so the falling Empire's non-Muslim subjects now took the Kingdom of Islam by storm *en masse.*

When the subjects of a world-state have eventually rallied to it, they have been accepting the view of it that has been taken from the beginning by its rulers. No doubt the first concern of any government of any kind is to keep itself in power, since this is the only condition on which a government can be effective. A government that has brought itself into power by force will be particularly sensitive to any challenge to its authority. The governments of would-be world-states, among the rest, have been moved by these self-regarding considerations. Yet most of them have also been animated by an idealistic motive that is peculiar to governments of this species. They have felt that they have a mandate to preserve the unity, peace, and order which they have established at so great a cost and which is so great a boon for their subjects, however blind to this their subjects may be.

This characteristic concern for the welfare of the human race explains the severity with which the government of the Roman world-state treated the Christians. From A.D. 63 to A.D. 311 Christianity was, in the Roman Empire, an illegal religion (*religio non licita*). Humane emperors might turn a blind eye to the practice of Christianity so long as the Christians themselves did not give publicity to those tenets of theirs to which the government objected. But the penalty for conviction, if this was not followed by recantation, was death; and the penalty was duly inflicted by the authorities, however reluctantly, if and when a Christian obstinately and defiantly refused to cast a grain of incense on the altars of the god Caesar and the goddess Rome. From the government's point of view, the refusal to do this was both perverse and subversive. It was perverse because this was a formality that did not offend the consciences of any other subjects of the world-state except the Christians and the Jews. The Christians' refusal was also subversive because the performance of this formality was the government's test of a subject's allegiance, and therefore a public and defiant refusal to comply was an example that was too bad to be tolerated. It is true that the Jews had been exempted in deference to their religious scruples. The Jews, however, were a small community which was acquiring few adherents from beyond its own ethnic limits, whereas the Christians were adherents of a missionary religion which avowedly aimed at converting the whole of mankind. The toleration that had been granted to the Jews must be withheld, so the government felt, from a Christian 'fifth column' that was continually increasing its numerical strength by recruiting among the population at large.

Any Roman public officer would have felt that the Roman government's policy was justified if he had come across the passage in the scriptures of the Christian Church in which its founder, Jesus, is reported to have said: 'Think not that I am come to send peace on Earth; I came, not to send peace, but the sword. For I am come to set a man at variance against his father, and the daughter against her mother, and the daughter-in-law against her mother-in-law. And a man's foes shall be they of his own household.'[1]

This passage would read, to Roman eyes, like a declaration of intention to break up the Roman peace that had been established with so much difficulty. Any representative of the government of the world-state would have found this shockingly irresponsible and immoral, and this judgement would have been shared by many of the world-state's subjects. To work for a recrudescence of the pre-Augustan age of anarchy would have seemed criminal to people who had heard their grandparents tell what that nightmare age had been like.

A brilliant reconstruction of the outlook of one of the world-state's responsible officers has been made by Dostoyevski in his famous imaginary indictment of Jesus by 'the Grand Inquisitor'.

Thou mightest have taken . . . the sword of Caesar. Why didst Thou reject that last gift? Hadst Thou accepted that last counsel of the mighty spirit, Thou wouldst have accomplished all that Man seeks on Earth—that is, someone to worship, someone to keep his conscience, and some means of uniting all in one unanimous and harmonious ant-heap; for the craving for universal unity is the third and last anguish of men. Mankind as a whole has always striven to organize a universal state. There have been many great nations with great histories; but, the more highly they were developed, the more unhappy they were, for they felt more acutely than other people the craving for world-wide union. The great conquerors—Timurs and Chingis Khans—whirled like hurricanes over the face of the Earth, striving to subdue its people, and they too were but the unconscious expression of the same craving for universal unity. Hadst Thou taken the World and Caesar's purple, Thou wouldst have founded the universal state and have given universal peace. For who can rule men if not he who holds their conscience and their bread in his hands?[2]

In the end the government of the Roman world-state reversed its policy towards the Christian Church—and this for the reason for which the non-Muslim subjects of the world-state that the Muslim Arabs had established reversed, in the end, their attitude towards Islam. The mass-conversions to Islam in

---

[1] Matt. 10, 34–36.
[2] F. Dostoyevski, *The Brothers Karamazov*, Part II, Book V, Chapter 5: 'The Grand Inquisitor' (trans. Constance Garnett).

the Muslim world-state in the latter days of the 'Abbasid
Dynasty have their parallel in the individual conversion of the
Roman Emperor Constantine to Christianity. In both cases
the motive for conversion was a feeling that the religion to which
the converts were now transferring their allegiance could be
made to serve the cause of unity, peace, and order—a service
that had been the declining world-state's *raison d'être*. By the
fourth century of the Christian Era the Christian Church had
not yet succeeded in converting more than a minority of the
population of the Roman Empire, but it had already become an
authoritarian institution with an efficient administrative structure, modelled on the contemporary structure of the Roman
Empire itself. This was why Constantine gave the Christian
Church not only toleration but privileges, and why Theodosius I
used the world-state's power to impose Christianity by force on
the still non-Christian majority of his subjects.

The Roman imperial government's concern for stability was
not confined to the fields of politics and religion. It extended
to economics as well—as is illustrated by a story that is instruc-
tive, even if, like Dostoyevski's, it is fictitious. It is said to have
been reported to one of the Roman emperors, as a piece of
good news, that one of his subjects had invented a process for
manufacturing unbreakable glass. The emperor gave orders
that the inventor should be put to death and that the records of
his invention should be destroyed. If the invention had been
put on the market, the manufacturers of ordinary glass would
have been put out of business; there would have been un-
employment that would have caused political unrest, and perhaps revolution; and then the World might have been thrown
back into the turmoil from which the Roman world-state had
salvaged it.

In giving priority to stability over vitality and to conser-
vation over creativity, the Roman world-state was behaving in
a way that is characteristic of states of its species. This deadening effect of an oecumenical régime is the fault that Hume found
in the Chinese world-state and in the Roman Catholic Christian
Church, and he had no hesitation in pronouncing that a politically fractured society is preferable. However, Hume was thinking in terms of his own world—the eighteenth-century world in
which the cost of political disunity was exceptionally low. It was

costing no more than those 'temperate and undecisive contests' that Gibbon light-heartedly condoned. Hume and Gibbon were not living in the Western World of our day, and they were not living, either, in one of those 'times of troubles' that have been the antecedents and the causes of the establishment of world-states. It has been noted above that Hume's and Gibbon's view has been taken, and been acted on, by the peoples of 'the contending states' to begin with, and that in many cases they have been surprisingly slow in recognizing that local independence is not worth its ultimate price. However, as has been noted too, they have also, in most cases, been converted, sooner or later, by their subsequent experience of peace and order under a world-government, to appreciate the value of world-unity on the political plane.

The citizens of a world-state have not only rallied to this oecumenical régime in time enough to regret its decline and fall. When it has broken down and broken up, they have felt a nostalgia for it in retrospect. Now that its collapse has left them out in the cold, they have longed to regain its shelter. This explains why, in so many cases, a fallen world-state has been re-erected, and this not just once but a number of times over.

In the Egyptian World's history, for example, the original world-state, which had been 'the Old Empire' established by Narmer, was re-established, first in 'the Middle Empire', then in 'the New Empire', then by a dynasty based on Napata, the capital of what had been 'the New Empire's' colonial domain in the Northern Sudan, and then by a dynasty based on Saïs, in the Delta, which started as a puppet of Egypt's Assyrian conquerors and ended by supplanting them. When the Persian Empire followed suit to the Assyrian Empire by conquering Egypt in its turn, this alien domination was temporarily thrown off, no less than three times, by Egyptian resistance-movements; and each time—from 485 to 484 B.C., from 465 to 449 B.C., and from 404 to 343 B.C.—the Egyptian world-state was set up again. After the final reconquest of Egypt by the Persians in 343/2 B.C., the Egyptians were never again strong enough to expel their alien conquerors, as they had succeeded in expelling them, time and again, since the eviction of the Hyksos from Egypt by the founder of 'the New Empire'. But the Egyptian people's impulse to maintain its political unity had not yet lost its momentum; this impulse remained active so long as the Egyptian civilization preserved its identity; and it continued to make itself effective by making Egypt's alien conquerors serve this Egyptian purpose from now onwards. From the Egyptian standpoint the Ptolemaic Monarchy and the Roman Empire were continuations of the historic Egyptian world-state with some non-Egyptian provinces appended to it; and the Ptolemies and their successors the Roman emperors played up to the *Weltanschauung* of their Egyptian subjects by having themselves portrayed on the walls of Egyptian temples wearing the Pharaonic regalia. In doing this they were consciously playing the part of the deified ruler of the Egyptian world-state in whose person its unity, power, and beneficence were embodied. Thus the Egyptian world-state may be said to have come to an end when the Emperor Aurelian renounced the world-rulers' claim to be a human god and declared himself to be no more than God's human viceregent on Earth.

At the time when the Egyptian world-state was embodied in the Roman Empire, the Sumero-Akkadian world-state was embodied in the Arsacid Empire, which had divided with the Roman Empire the dominion over the section of the Oikoumenê to the west of India; and this phase of the Sumero-Akkadian world-state, like the contemporary phase of its Egyptian counterpart, was one of a number of successive reconstructions of it.

It has been noted already that the Empire of Agadé, which had been the original Sumero-Akkadian world-state, was reproduced successively, after successive collapses, by the Third Dynasty of Ur, by the Babylonian emperor Hammurabi, by the Assyrian Empire, and by the first Persian Empire that was established by Cyrus the Achaemenid. The First Persian Empire was not the last of the Sumero-Akkadian world-state's avatars. After the Achaemenidae had been overthrown by Alexander the Great, their Asian domain was reunited by Alexander's Seleucid successors, and its unity was maintained by the Seleucids' successors the Arsacids, Sasanids, Umayyads, and 'Abbasids. All these régimes, from the Achaemenid Persian onwards, were imposed by empire-builders who, from the Babylonian standpoint, were aliens. Yet, under all of them, Sumer and Akkad continued to be this world-state's economic power-house under

the new names Babylonia and 'Irāq. Under the Arsacid, Sas-
anid, and 'Abbasid régimes, the political capital was also
located in this region that was the Sumero-Akkadian civilization's original homeland. Under the Achaemenid Persian and
the Seleucid régimes, one out of several political capitals was
located here; and, when the principal capital was located in
Syria, as it was under the Seleucid and Umayyad régimes, it
eventually gravitated back to the lower Tigris-Euphrates valley
on each occasion. It was transferred from Antioch in Syria to
Ctesiphon, the east-bank suburb of the Seleucids' secondary
capital Seleucia-on-Tigris, when the Arsacids conquered from
the Seleucids all their provinces to the east of the Euphrates.
The capital was transferred from Damascus to a new world-
capital at Baghdad when the Umayyads were overthrown and
were supplanted by the 'Abbasids.

The Umayyads and 'Abbasids were the successive rulers of
the Muslim empire founded by the Arabs. In this final reconstruction of the Sumero-Akkadian world-state, its domain was
as extensive as it had been under the régime of the Achaemenidae; and the Sumero-Akkadian world-state lasted 1,200 years
longer than the Sumero-Akkadian civilization itself. The civilization became extinct in the first century of the Christian Era,
but its economic power-house in the lower Tigris-Euphrates
valley kept the Sumero-Akkadian world-state going till the
thirteenth century of the Christian Era, when the Mongol
nomad world-conquerors wrecked the irrigation system that
had been the source of this region's productivity since it had
been reclaimed from its virgin state of jungle-swamp at the close
of the fourth millennium B.C.

There are other world-states whose series of successive avatars
has come to an end only within our own lifetime, and there are
others whose latest avatar is still a going concern.

In the Indian sub-continent the world-state that had been
first established by the Maurya Dynasty before the end of the
fourth century B.C. was revived in the fourth century of the
Christian Era by the Gupta Dynasty and was then revived
again successively by the seventh-century-A.D. emperor Harsha
and, after that, in a series of alien régimes: the Muslim Sultanate
of Delhi, the Muslim Mughal Raj, and the Western British Raj.
It was as recently as 1947 that the Indian world-state's latest

avatar broke apart into the British Raj's present two successor-states, the Indian Union and Pakistan.

The Roman Empire was the Hellenic civilization's world-state, and its cultural and economic centre of gravity lay, not in Italy, but in the Levant, to the east of the Straits of Otranto and the Syrtes. After the temporary dissolution of this world-state during the anarchic half-century A.D. 235–84, it was re-constructed, on new lines, by Diocletian; and, in the Levant, the Diocletianic Roman Empire survived into the seventh century. In this region, the world-state was reconstructed again, successively, by the Syrian, Macedonian, Comnenian, and Ottoman dynasties. The Ottoman Turkish Roman Empire did not break up till the years 1912–18, when it was dismembered by the outcome of the First Balkan War and the First World War. It was not formally liquidated till 1922, when the Otto-man Dynasty was deposed to make way for the latest of its successor-states, the present Republic of Turkey. It will be seen that the Hellenic world-state, like the Sumero-Akkadian world-state, long outlasted the civilization on whose account it had originally been called into being. Its Diocletianic avatar saw the Hellenic civilization replaced in the Levant by a set of Christian civilizations: the Eastern Orthodox, the Nestorian, and the Monophysite. The establishment of the Ottoman avatar of the world-state saw the political power in it pass out of Eastern Orthodox Christian Greek hands into Sunni Muslim Turkish hands. Yet the Turks' fellow Muslims recognized that the Otto-man Padishah had stepped into the Roman emperors' shoes. They signified this by styling him 'the Caesar of Rome' (Qaysar-i-Rum).

Russia has been a rival claimant to be the Roman Empire's heir. Russia entered the field of civilization as a satellite of the Eastern Orthodox Christian civilization. In the course of the fourteenth and fifteenth centuries, Russia was given internal peace, and also some protection against the aggressiveness of her Western and her Tatar neighbours, by the forcible unifi-cation of the local Russian states in the Russian world-state of Muscovy. In Russian eyes the Greek Orthodox Christian Roman Empire at Constantinople forfeited its mandate when, in 1439, it recognized the Papacy's supremacy over the Eastern Orthodox Christian churches in the vain hope that, at the cost of this grievous concession in the ecclesiastical field, it might obtain effective Western Christian military support against the ever-advancing Ottoman Turks. When, fourteen years after the ecclesiastical Union of Florence, the Greek Roman Empire was extinguished by the Ottoman conquest of Constantinople, the Russians saw in this a divine retribution for the Greeks' apostasy. Now that the Muslim Ottoman Empire had imposed its rule on all the Orthodox peoples of Anatolia and South-Eastern Europe, Muscovy was the sole surviving independent Orthodox Christian state. What was more, the Russians were the only Orthodox Christian people that had preserved its orthodoxy uncompromised by any concessions to Papal claims. On these grounds a sixteenth-century Russian ecclesiastical publicist asserted that Moscow was 'the Third Rome'. Augustus's Old Rome and Constantine's New Rome had now each fallen in its turn. Moscow was the heir of both, and her dominion, unlike theirs, was to have no end. This doctrine was endorsed by the Muscovite government implicitly when, in 1547, the Grand Duke Ivan IV 'the Terrible' assumed the title 'Czar' (Caesar). The last Russian czar was deposed in 1917, five years before the deposition of the last Ottoman Turkish qaysar-i-Rum, but the fates of the Russian and the Turkish avatar of the Roman Empire have not been the same. The Ottoman Turkish Roman Empire had broken up before the Ottoman Dynasty was dethroned; the Russian Roman Empire has survived the liquidation of the Russian czardom. It survives today, under a new name, in the Union of Soviet Socialist Republics; and, though it has substituted Communism for Eastern Orthodox Christianity as its official religion, it has not renounced its claim to be the unique interpreter and champion of orthodoxy.

The other world-state that is still alive today in one of its avatars is the Chinese world-state that was originally established in 221 B.C. by Ch'in-Shih Hwangti. In the course of the two millennia and more that have elapsed since then, the Chinese world-state has fallen to pieces from time to time, but, each time, it has been put together again sooner or later. It has been reconstructed successively by a long series of dynasties. When one régime's mandate has expired, a new régime has obtained a fresh mandate to carry on. The Prior Han, Posterior Han, United Chin, Sui, T'ang, Sung, Yüan, Ming, Ch'ing, Kuo Min

Tang, and Communists have taken up the mandate, one after another; and, under the present Communist régime, the Chinese world-state is still as full of life as the Russian world-state is.

Like other world-states in which the will to live has been strong, the Chinese world-state has known how to make alien conquerors serve its purpose; Yüan and Ch'ing are Chinese aliases for Mongols and Manchus; and the staying-power of the Chinese world-state has been emulated by the staying-power of the Chinese civilization. The conversion of the Roman Empire to Christianity brought with it a break in cultural continuity. The Hellenic civilization faded out, and four local Christian successor-civilizations replaced it. The conversion of the Chinese world-state to Buddhism did not have a corresponding cultural effect. In China the Chinese civilization was not replaced by a Buddhist one. On the contrary, the Buddhist religion and culture were successfully digested by the Chinese civilization and were absorbed into it. In our time, China has been converted to an alien religion once again. It is still too early for us to be able to guess whether or not, in China, Communism is going to suffer the fate that has been Buddhism's fate there. All that can be said—and this can be said with assurance, in the light of China's past history—is that, in China, Communism has to contend with a pre-Communist social and cultural configuration that has proved itself to be as tough as the Egyptian one was.

Against the background of this survey of the avatars of world-states in a number of non-Western societies, the history of our Western World looks peculiar. Western Christendom, like Eastern Orthodox Christendom, is a successor of the Hellenic World, and its nuclear area was included in the Roman Empire, as the Levant was. Yet the avatars of the Roman Empire in the West have been feeble and ephemeral by comparison with its avatars in the Levant. The Frankish avatar cannot compare with the Syrian, nor the Saxon-Franconian-Swabian with the Macedonian or even with the Comnenian. The Swabian Roman Emperor Frederick II's power was based, not on the avatar of the Roman Empire in the West, but on the Kingdom of Sicily, which lay outside the West Roman Empire's limits. This kingdom was small compared with the size of the area that was nominally under the Empire's sovereignty; but, in the Kingdom of Sicily, Frederick's rule was effective, and this kingdom was better organized than most of the Western states of the time, since it was a successor-state of the East Roman Empire and had inherited some of that empire's administrative traditions. After the defeat of Frederick and his heirs in their struggle with the Papacy, 'the Roman Empire of the German People' fell into an interregnum from which it never truly re-emerged. Nominally it survived till 1806, when the title 'Roman Emperor' was formally renounced by the reigning representative of the Habsburg Dynasty. But, during the preceding five-and-a-half centuries, the power of the holders of the title had been based, as the Emperor Frederick II's had been, on some local state, or cluster of states, of which they had been effective rulers. The Luxembourg Dynasty's power-basis had been the lands of the Bohemian Crown. The Habsburgs' power-basis had been Austria and the adjoining Western states that had placed themselves under Habsburg rule for their common self-protection after the overthrow of the Kingdom of Hungary, and the annexation of the lion's share of its territory, by the Ottoman Empire in 1526.

In the West, the Papacy has been a more effective reproduction of the Roman Empire than any of the successive secular avatars of it that have called themselves by its name. Between Christmas Day A.D. 800, when Charlemagne was crowned Roman Emperor by Pope Leo III, and the years 1266–8, in which the Kingdom of Sicily was conquered from Frederick II's heirs by Charles of Anjou with Pope Urban IV's and Pope Clement IV's blessing, the Papacy's power waxed as the West Roman Empire's power waned.

The Pope's ecclesiastical authority was recognized over the whole of Western Christendom, and its domain expanded *pari passu* with the Western World. Indeed, the pre-Reformation Western World could be defined as being the territory of the Patriarchate of Rome, with which it was, in fact, then coextensive. By contrast, none of the successive Western avatars of the Roman Empire was ever even nominally sovereign over the Western World as a whole. Charlemagne, whose Roman Empire came the nearest to being conterminous with Western Christendom, did not manage to bring the whole of the relatively small Western Christendom of his day under his rule. His writ did not run in the British Isles or in the Spanish Christian principalities west of Catalonia. When the Saxons resuscitated the West Roman Empire, they managed to reunite Germany, Northern Italy, and Burgundy under the imperial crown, but not France, which was the heart of the Western World of the day. The Papacy's range of jurisdiction, however, was comprehensive, as Hume notes in the passage quoted in Chapter V; and Thomas Hobbes hits the mark in calling the Papacy a ghost of the Roman Empire sitting crowned upon its grave.[1] Manifestly the organization of the Papal government of the unitary pre-Reformation Western Church was inspired by memories of the administrative practice of the Roman Empire, and the Justinianean codification of Roman secular law was the rock from which the medieval Western canon law was quarried. Yet, in spite of the Roman solidity of the Papal Church, its victory over the Western avatar of the Roman Empire was a barren one.

The excommunication of Frederick II missed fire. It did not make his hold over his Kingdom of Sicily untenable. To wrench the Kingdom of Sicily out of the hands of Frederick's heirs, the Papacy had to unleash against them the Angevins. It could not win without pitting one local secular state against another; and, when Pope Boniface VIII sought to gather in the fruits of his predecessors' victory by cracking his whip over the back of the King of France, he brought down in ruins the whole political edifice that his predecessors had been building up since the pontificate of Gregory VII. When Boniface VIII put the feelings of the French people to the test by deliberately competing with the King of France for their allegiance, the King betrayed his anxiety by the pains that he took to mobilize support in France for his stand. The ease with which the King won took him as well as the Pope by surprise.

The design for a commonwealth of Western Christian states under the Papacy's auspices was an imaginative and a grand one; but already, in the medieval chapter of Western history, the divisive political forces were too strong to be overcome by a resuscitation of the Roman Empire in the West in either a secular or an ecclesiastical form. The strength of these divisive

---

[1] Thomas Hobbes, *Leviathan*, Part IV, Chapter 47.

forces in the West is indicated by the decisiveness of the failure of the resuscitated Roman Empire and the Papacy, one after the other, to restore the unity that had been lost in the West when the original Roman Empire had dissolved there in the fifth century.

The Papacy's attempt to serve as a substitute for a secular avatar of the Roman Empire is not the only case in which an ecclesiastical institution has been called upon to come to the rescue of a falling or fallen world-state. In the last phase of 'the New Empire' of Egypt, the Pharaoh tried to shore up his tottering authority by combining with his political office the high priesthood, at Thebes and at Napata, of 'the New Empire's' tutelary god, Amun-Re. In the Levantine Roman Empire, when the sceptre had passed out of Greek into Turkish hands, the derelict mantle of the extinguished Greek imperial office was transferred, by an act of Ottoman statesmanship, to the shoulders of the Greek Oecumenical Patriarch of Constantinople. Without losing his ecclesiastical jurisdiction within the geographical limits of his patriarchate, the Oecumenical Patriarch was now invested by the Ottoman Roman Emperor with the political office of millet bashi of the Millet-i-Rum: that is to say, he was made answerable to the Padishah for the conduct of the Padishah's Eastern Orthodox subjects of all nationalities and in all territories over which the Padishah's secular rule extended. To enable the Oecumenical Patriarch to perform this function effectually for the Ottoman imperial government's convenience, he was now given a measure of civil jurisdiction that he had never possessed under the former Greek East Roman imperial régime.

Just in virtue of surviving and reviving, a world-state may accumulate a prestige that will outlive its effective power. Prestige is imponderable, but it is not altogether unsubstantial, and accordingly the predatory founders of a world-state's successor-states have sometimes given some weight to prestige in their hard-headed calculations. Though *de facto* they are in power, *de jure* they are usurpers, and therefore, like King Philip IV of France in his trial of strength with Pope Boniface VIII, they cannot feel sure of their position. They cannot, in fact, feel sure that they could succeed in maintaining the rule that they have usurped if the nominal ruler of the world-state were to set himself to undermine their subjects' loyalty to them. They will try to guard against this risk by professing to rule their successor-state in the nominal world-ruler's name, and they may also try to spike his guns by wheedling or extorting from him a public certificate of legitimization for their régime.

The history of Japan presents a classic example of the survival of this prerogative of certifying a usurper's legitimacy, long after the certifying authority has lost all its other powers. In Japan the Imperial Dynasty made its power effective when, in A.D. 645, it reorganized the administration of the Japanese Empire on the pattern of the administration of the T'ang Empire, which was the contemporary avatar of the Chinese world-state. In the Japan of that age this centralized bureaucratic régime was too exotic to be able to maintain itself; and, within two centuries, the real political power had passed into the hands of usurpers who ruled by commanding the allegiance of the feudal lords in the provinces. For a thousand years, ending in A.D. 1868, the Emperor at Kyoto was a politically powerless pensioner of one dynasty of usurpers after another; yet, throughout this millennium, the usurpers continued to govern in the shadow-emperor's name as his vicegerents (shoguns). The Imperial House was held to be descended from the sun-goddess Amaterasu, who was the Japanese Empire's tutelary divinity. Moreover, the Imperial House was immemorially old. Accordingly, its reservoir of prestige was inexhaustible; and the prudence of the shoguns' outward deference to it was demonstrated in the event. When, in the mid-nineteenth century, the Tokugawa shogun forfeited his mandate, in the Japanese people's judgement, by failing to cope effectively with the rising pressure from the importunate West, the revolution that liquidated the Tokugawa régime was made in the reigning Emperor's name. The Meiji Restoration abolished the shogunate without putting the Emperor back into power *de facto*. Yet, though a Japanese emperor has never governed again since the ninth century, he still reigns. The aura of the sacrosanctity that the Imperial Office has accumulated through the passage of time has survived all the revolutionary experiences through which Japan has passed during the last hundred years.

In the ninth century of the Christian Era, at the time when the Japanese Imperial Dynasty was losing its real political power, the 'Abbasid Dynasty was meeting with similar adversity at the other end of the Old World; and, in this case too, the usurpers who were superseding an historic government *de facto* sought to legitimize their position by exercising their authority in this government's name. In the thirteenth century, four hundred years after the beginning of the 'Abbasids' decline, the Muslim sultans of Delhi, who had carved out a new domain for Islam in Northern India, were obtaining diplomas of investiture from the reigning 'Abbasid Caliph of Baghdad, and they were inscribing his name, not theirs, on their coinage. After the last 'Abbasid caliph at Baghdad, Musta'sim, had been put to death by the Mongols, the Sultans of Delhi ignored his disappearance and continued for the next thirty-seven years to coin in his name. They could think of no better device, and their need for legitimization was continuous and acute; for, in this dynasty, the crown did not descend from father to son; it passed precariously from master to slave. In contemporary Egypt the system of succession was the same. The ruler was a *mamluk*, i.e. a piece of property that had once belonged to the piece of property that had been the preceding ruler. These slave-kings in Egypt were more resourceful than their counterparts in Hindustan. They acquired possession of a refugee member of the 'Abbasid House, planted him in Cairo, and ruled, from then onwards, in the name of an 'Abbasid Caliph who was under their thumb.

This long-lasting prestige of the House of 'Abbas is doubly remarkable. In the first place the 'Abbasids' effective rule over the Islamic world-state, beyond the narrow limits of their metropolitan province 'Iráq, lasted for not more than about a hundred years after they had seized power. In the second place, their right to confer legitimacy was dubious, inasmuch as they were usurpers themselves. The caliph (*khalifah*) was, as his title proclaims, the successor of the Prophet Muhammad in the Prophet's political function of being the temporal ruler of the Islamic state. The first four caliphs had obtained the office, not by descent, but by election. If, however, this precedent was to be set aside in favour of the dynastic principle of succession in virtue of descent, then the family that had a legitimate title to inherit and transmit the Caliphate was, not the House of 'Abbas, but the House of 'Ali. 'Abbas was the prophet Muhammad's uncle, but 'Ali was both his cousin and his son-in-law, and 'Ali's descendants were thus the offspring of the Prophet himself. Since 'Ali was the fourth of the four elected caliphs, his title to the Caliphate was incontestable, whether election or inheritance was to be taken as being the proper method of determining the succession. The 'Abbasids' title was not good on either count. They had acquired the Caliphate in the way in which their predecessors the Umayyads had acquired it. They had seized it by military force, after having prepared the ground by propaganda. Nevertheless, the mere duration of their tenure of the Caliphate after they had usurped it gave the 'Abbasid Dynasty such prestige that, for seven centuries after the beginning of its decline, this usurping dynasty continued to be utilized by other usurpers as a valuable source of legitimization.

The Timurid Mughal Dynasty in India and the Ottoman Turkish Dynasty in the Levant served the same purpose when they, too, were in decline. The eponymous founders of these two dynasties, Timur Lenk and 'Osman the son of Ertoghrul, were Turkish military adventurers whose sole title was their material success; yet the lapse of time gave them, too, something of the prestige that this had once given to the 'Abbasids.

The Mughal Raj went into decline after Awrangzib's death in 1707, but the Mughal Dynasty was not formally deposed till 1857. Meanwhile, both the Maratha and the British usurpers of the Mughals' power found it advisable to rule in their name; and the British East India Company retained the Mughals as its pensioners at Delhi even after they had ceased to find it necessary to use them as cover for the new British Raj. The Mughals' prestige survived a century and a half of impotence and humiliation. When the Company's army mutinied in 1857, the mutineers—Hindus as well as Muslims—marched to Delhi and declared their allegiance to the Mughal emperor of the day. The Hindu soldiery, at any rate, did not revere him any more than their British employers did; but, now that they had revolted against the British Raj, they needed to give their revolutionary act of military insubordination a stamp of political legitimacy, and the Mughal Dynasty was the only fount of legitimization that might have a chance of being recognized as such by contemporary Indian public opinion. Accordingly the mutineers forced the reluctant Mughal emperor's hand, and their subsequent defeat therefore cost him his crown. If, however, the mutineers had been victorious, it is conceivable that their victory might have brought with it, for the Mughal Dynasty in India, the upward turn of fortune that the Meiji Revolution in Japan did bring, ten years later, for the Imperial Dynasty there.

The Ottoman Dynasty's experience during its decline resembled the Mughals'. In the course of the Ottoman Empire's disintegration, the first stage in almost every instance was the same. When the Ottoman imperial government lost its effective control over one of its provinces, it would be allowed by the usurping local governor or insurgent local nationality to retain a nominal suzerainty over the lost province for the time being. The founder or founders of a successor-state might be ambitious to achieve complete independence; they might bear the Ottoman Empire no love, and might chafe at retaining even a nominal connexion with it. All the same, they might still be willing to purchase legitimization at the price of forgoing full sovereignty until they had given themselves time to consolidate their position. Meanwhile, the recognition of the Ottoman imperial government's nominal suzerainty might continue to be useful, or even indispensable, for the ultimate attainment of the independence that was the usurpers' real objective.

The foregoing survey of passages in the histories of some of the would-be world-states of the past will have served its purpose if it has made two points clear. The first point is that a world-state, once established, usually dies hard. The second point is that the temper of the Western World, down to the present moment in Western history, has shown itself exceptionally recalcitrant to any movement towards political unification.

VIII

Is a World-wide World-State Feasible?

In this book it is being contended that, in the Atomic Age, mankind has to choose between political unification and mass-suicide. If this is indeed the truth about our present situation, we have to ask ourselves what the obstacles to unification are, and how difficult to overcome they seem likely to be.

An obstacle that is peculiar to our present-day World has been mentioned at the end of the preceding chapter. The Western society has shown itself exceptionally recalcitrant to any movement towards political unification hitherto, and this Western peculiarity is a handicap to present-day mankind as a whole, since, in our time, the non-Western majority of the human race is adopting Western manners and customs, Western ideas and ideals, and Western likes and dislikes. However, the fashionable Western liking for political disunity and dislike of political unity is no more than a habit that has found its way into the social and cultural heritage of one section of the human race. It is not a built-in trait of human nature even in the West, and, *a fortiori*, not in the rest of the World, where it is being adopted today in its distinctive Western form. Since habits can be acquired and adopted, they can also be modified and abandoned. We do give up even the most cherished habits if and when it becomes clear that it would be disastrous to persist in them; and the accelerating progress of technology has already made it clear that it will be disastrous now not to give up the habit of political disunity in at least two fields in which the only alternative to a catastrophe lies in common action on a world-wide scale. We are going to have to establish one world-authority to control atomic energy and another to administer the production and distribution of food. These unwelcome steps towards the political unification of the World are being forced upon us by the technological revolution that we ourselves have engineered. Technology cannot, of course, dictate human choices. It can, however, produce a situation in which there are two, and only two, alternatives, one of which is death; and this is the situation that our technology has produced for us now. We can refuse to make the social changes that a technological revolution requires if it is to be made to churn out for us, not death and evil, but life and good. We are free. But to make this 'great refusal' would mean choosing death, and human beings seldom do choose death when it comes to the point. It therefore seems probable that, as the lesser evil, we shall submit to at least the minimum of world-government that we see to be immediately necessary for salvation, though we shall submit to this grumbling and growling, and shall hold back till the eleventh hour.

These considerations make it seem reasonable to guess that the customary Western antipathy to political unification is going, in fact, to be overcome. But, supposing that we do decide to set up public authorities with a world-wide range of operations, are we going to find it practicable to carry this decision out? World-government on a literally world-wide scale has never been achieved yet. Is such a thing conceivable? Can we imagine a world-government seeing to the mending of the drains in a suburb of Sarasota, Florida, or sending firemen to put out a fire in a tenement-house in Tomsk, or appointing the cowherd in a village in Uttar Pradesh, or taking police-action to track down a criminal who has committed a burglary in Birmingham (Alabama or England)? Well, this is, in fact, imaginable in the electronic age. Today we have computors; so the centralization of local government in the hands of world-authorities would probably be practicable, and this would certainly be intolerable. But this nightmare vision of a centralized bureaucracy administering the details of local government all over the globe is, of course, beside the point, because it is a vision of something that is not on mankind's agenda.

The functions of the world-authorities that are urgently required today will be, not maximal, but minimal, and this for two good reasons. The first reason is that the peoples of the World are going to accept world-government only reluctantly, and therefore the statesmen are not going to go out of their way to try to persuade the people to swallow larger doses of world-government than are strictly necessary at the moment. The second reason why world-government will be minimal, at least to start with, is that, in the Atomic Age, world-government cannot be imposed by force, which is the way in which the world-states of the past have all been established. Force in the form of the atomic weapon could not be used for any constructive purpose; the effect of its use would be wholly destructive. Therefore, today, the only practicable way of getting any world-authorities established is to win the consent and co-operation of the powers that be. In the present-day world the powers that be are the peoples and governments of the local states; and these are not going to surrender to world-authorities any more of the local states' present sovereign powers and prerogatives than they see the necessity of surrendering for the sake of self-preservation. *A fortiori*, it is certain that the local states are not going to opt for surrendering their powers *in toto* and putting themselves out of business. We may therefore assume that the world-state of the future will not have the structure of the would-be world-states of the past, which have been imposed by conquest. It will have the structure of those states, past and present, that have been brought into being by a voluntary union of a number of previously separate and independent smaller units; and the structure of states that have originated in this peaceful way has usually been, not unitary, but federal. This has been usual because the first concern of any government is to keep itself in being; and a government that has voluntarily surrendered part, or the whole, of its sovereignty will not go to the length of surrendering its existence as well, so long as it is a free agent. It will prefer to retain its identity and its local autonomy and to limit the powers of the union government to fields in which a unitary administration is patently in the constituent states' own interest.

If we may assume that, in the Atomic Age, a world-government would have a federal structure, do we possess the technological equipment for enabling the federal agencies of a world-government to operate over a literally world-wide range? This question can be answered in the affirmative unhesitatingly. It has been suggested above that our present technological equipment would make even a centralized world-government practicable in the almost unthinkable event of mankind's desiring this.

But is a literally world-wide world-government practicable

psychologically? Even if the functions of the world-authorities were severely restricted, would not the individual citizen of the world-state find himself dwarfed and overwhelmed in a polity of this colossal size? The answer to this question is that the individual citizen already finds himself in this uncomfortable position even in the smallest of the local sovereign states on the World's present political map. However small a state's population may be, and however small the smallest units of local government may be, the individual citizen will find himself caught in a network of impersonal relations with fellow-citizens whom he has never met, and a majority of whom he cannot meet, because the majority are either already dead or still unborn. This social situation does dwarf and overwhelm the individual because it implicates him in relations that spread beyond the circle of the fellow human beings whom he knows personally. Relations of this personal kind are the only relations that are fully congenial to human nature. But, if we want to re-confine our social relations within this limit, we must board Wells' time-machine and re-ascend the time-stream as far up as the Neolithic Age at least, and perhaps even back beyond it into the Food-gathering Age. In a food-gathering band, and perhaps still in a Neolithic village, every living member of the community will have been personally acquainted with every other living member of it. This human-size scale of social relations must have been more comfortable than any of those larger scales on which human relations have been conducted since the dawn of civilization; but the price of this primeval social amenity is too high. A community that remains limited in size to the number of people who can know each other personally will be too small and too weak to undertake those collective enterprises that have made the achievement of civilization possible. In a Sumerian city-state the scale of social life had already increased far beyond the range of personal relations. The citizens were associated with each other by a network of impersonal relations, as the citizens of all states always have been ever since.

The invention of institutions that made effective social relations possible beyond the narrow range of personal relations was one of the revolutionary innovations that made civilization itself possible. This advance from societies based on personal relations exclusively to societies based on impersonal relations as well is the biggest and the most difficult leap forward in Man's social progress; but, fortunately for us, this formidable leap is not required in our present enterprise of establishing world-authorities that will be paramount, within their respective functional fields, over the local states in which we are now living. The leap is not required now because it is not ahead of us but is already 5,000 years' time-distance behind us. This revolutionary leap was made by our predecessors who widened the scope of social relations from the scale of the Neolithic village to the scale of the Sumerian city-state and from the scale of the Egyptian nome to the scale of the Egyptian united empire. This has been the crucial leap in mankind's social history. Its price is the dwarfing and overwhelming of the individual citizen by the scale of the polity in which he now finds himself. The price has to be paid in the coin of psychological discomfort; the discomfort is considerable; but we cannot now get this price refunded to us, and we would not choose to if we could.

The pertinent point about the discomfort of impersonal relations is that this discomfort does not increase *pari passu* with successive increases in the scale of politics based on institutions of the impersonal kind. Life in a food-gathering band or in a Neolithic agricultural village may have been more congenial to human nature than life in Ur or in Lagash. But no addition to the discomfort is involved in changing from the scale of a third-millennium-B.C. Sumerian city-state to the larger scale of a present-day Central American republic or from that scale to the present scale of the United States or the Soviet Union or China, or from that scale again to the scale of mankind itself. This psychological point can be expressed symbolically in figures. When once the ratio between the individual citizen and the numerical strength of the citizen-body of his polity has passed beyond the tolerable limit of, say, 1:500 to the already overwhelming ratio 1:5,000, it will not add to the individual's discomfort if the ratio is then raised successively to 1:2,000,000, 1:200,000,000, 1:600,000,000, and finally 1:3,000,000,000. It may be more taxing psychologically to live in Ur than to live in Jericho or in a band of food-gathering Australian natives; but to be a citizen of Ur is not more taxing than to be a citizen of the United States, and to be a citizen of the United States is not more taxing than to be a citizen of the World.

Yet, if there is no psychological obstacle to the transition from local citizenship to world-citizenship, may there not be a physiological one? Mankind is not physiologically homogeneous. In the course of its evolution, it has split into a number of separate races distinguished from each other by physiological differences. Can we imagine the present-day races of Man living together as each others' fellow-citizens, as they would have to do if there was to be an effective world-state? Well, this is not at all difficult to imagine because it is something that is already an accomplished fact in a number of the World's now existing local states.

It is true that, at present, there is acute racial strife in racially non-homogeneous states in which one of the local races is the European race, and where this race has hitherto enjoyed a political and social ascendancy that is now being challenged. This is the present situation in South Africa, Rhodesia, and 'the Old South' of the United States, and also in Britain since the immigration of Pakistanis and West Indian Negroes after the Second World War. In India, where different races have coexisted with each other for at least 3,500 years, open strife between them has been damped down only by the institution of castes—an institution that has perpetuated the ascendancy of a minority descended from invaders who were originally of non-Indian race. However, it has been demonstrated that people of physiologically different races can, not just coexist, but live together in harmony, as each others' fellow-citizens. In Hawaii, which has recently been admitted to statehood in the United States, Hawaiian American citizens of Polynesian, East Asian, and European race are living together amicably; and there is the same absence of racial discord in many Muslim countries and Latin-American Christian countries in whose populations two or more different races are represented. Antipathy towards fellow human beings of alien race is a moral infirmity that seems to be peculiar to three sections of the human race, namely the higher-caste Hindus, the Jews, and the English-speaking, Dutch-speaking, and German-speaking minority of the Western peoples. Moreover, the Teutonic-speaking Western 'whites'' antipathy to 'non-whites' is not physiological; it is social. A 'white' racialist is willing to own a 'non-white' as a slave or to employ him as a menial, though he is not willing to accept him as a colleague; and he is willing to have a 'non-white' woman for his mistress or for his 'all-white' children's nurse, though he is not willing to have her for his wife or to treat the children that he has by her as his mistress as the equals of his children by a 'white' mistress or 'white' wife. Subject to these still continuing social inequalities and injustices, people who differ from each other in race do, nevertheless, coexist with each other today, even in countries in which a racialist-minded element in the local population is in the ascendancy. Why should they find it any more difficult than they find it now to coexist, supposing that the now sovereign local states were to unite with each other in a world-wide federation?

It is not surprising that race-feeling should be a minoritarian psychological ailment, from which the majority of mankind is free; for the physiological differences that excite such violent feelings in the racialist-minded minority are superficial and non-significant. All surviving representatives of the genus homo are also representatives of a single species of hominid, homo sapiens. There have been other species, besides homo sapiens, in the past, but all these others must have become virtually extinct before the occupation of the Americas by human beings from the Old World in the Upper Palaeolithic Age. At any rate, our archaeologists have not found any non-homo-sapiens bones in the Americas so far. Human remains, dating from the Mesolithic Age, that have been found in caves on Mount Carmel in Palestine indicate that, in that age, representatives of the species homo neandertalensis may still have been surviving there and have been living side by side with representatives of homo sapiens. There are, indeed, indications that here these two races may not merely have coexisted but have inter-married. Whether or not homo neandertalensis and homo sapiens were inter-fertile with each other, it is notorious that all varieties of homo sapiens are. This inter-fertility as between all extant varieties of Man is the racialists' chief stumbling-block. It confronts them with the threat (as it is, for them) of miscegenation, and, at the same time, this ever present physiological possibility of inter-breeding proves that the varieties of homo sapiens are not different races in reality.

The racialists' repugnance to interbreeding is a minority's cultural idiosyncrasy. The majority of mankind has always interbred readily. In India the social barriers of caste have not availed to keep the blood of the higher-caste minority unmixed with the blood of the lower-caste majority. There are few Brahman or Kshatriya families in India today that do not have some autochthonous blood in their veins and whose skins are still as deficient in pigment as the skins of the 'white' Aryan invaders of India must have been 3,500 years ago. As for the Muslims and the Latin-American Christians, they do not attempt or pretend to avoid miscegenation. In present-day Mexico, for instance, and in present-day Western Pakistan, the normal Mexican and normal Pakistani is a mestizo, and, of course, normality carries no stigma. What is peculiar, because exceptional, in Mexico or in Western Pakistan today is to be 'pure-blooded'.

This Islamic and Latin American freedom from race-feeling is not only humane; it is also rational. There is no evidence that the differences in amount of skin-pigmentation or in texture of hair that distinguish the different physiological varieties of homo sapiens are correlated with any differences of mental ability or moral sensitivity. Cleverness and stupidity and better character and worse character seem to be even-handedly distributed by Nature. In all samples of mankind, living or dead, the percentages turn out to be uniform. It is the same with the 'psychological types' that our psychologists have recently been identifying. These, too, seem to be evenly distributed in uniform percentages. Our conclusion will be that the visible physiological differences between one variety of homo sapiens and another are not, in themselves, any impediment to the integration of all mankind into a single society, polity, and family. The hindrance to this is race-feeling, and this is not a built-in ingredient in human nature. If it were, the majority of mankind would not be, as it is, indifferent to physiological differences between one human being and another. Race-feeling is not an instinct; it is a habit; this habit has been acquired only by a minority of mankind; and, since habits are not innate, they can be discarded.

Habits are not innate, but one consequence of this is that they are diverse. It has been noted in the second chapter of this book that habits are part of the social and cultural heritage that is handed down in a society by each successive generation to the next, and that a heritage is inevitably modified progressively in the process of being transmitted. There are as many separate heritages—constituting separate ways of life and separate outlooks—as there are separate societies; and, in our present-day world, there are a number of separate societies coexisting side by side with each other. 'The annihilation of distance' through the progress of technology has now brought all the living societies on the face of this planet into direct physical contact with each other. All over the World today we can meet each other in the flesh and can hear and see each other by radio and by television; and this apparatus provides the material means of communication for a meeting of hearts and minds. But it does not necessarily bring this spiritual unison with it. Though our world has been united physically, we are not yet in unison with each other; and it is evident that one of the major causes of our present conflicts is the dissonance between our different social and cultural heritages that have developed independently of each other in the course of the ages during which the different sections of mankind were still insulated. This social and cultural diversity in the present-day world is evidently one of the present facts of life that have a bearing on the question whether a world-state is feasible today. Would world-government be practicable if it were not underpinned by a certain amount of unity and uniformity in the peoples' outlooks and ways of life? What is the minimum amount of homogeneity in this field that would be needed? Has this amount of homogeneity been achieved yet? And, if it has not, what is the prospect of its being achieved in the foreseeable future?

The histories of the less than world-wide political associations of the past indicate that it is difficult for people to cooperate with each other politically if they are divided socially and culturally—particularly if they disagree in their notions of what is right and wrong.

When the Spaniards conquered and annexed Mexico, they were shocked—brutal though they were—at the institution of human sacrifice which was playing so prominent a part in Middle American life and was being practised in so cruel a form. If human sacrifice had ever been a Spanish institution, it had been abolished in Spain at least as far back as the time of the Roman conquest, and this was a millennium and a half ago by now. It would be morally quite impossible for Spaniards and Aztecs to live together as citizens of the same state if the law permitted the Aztecs to continue a practice that the Spaniards felt to be abominable. The Spaniards had the responsibility for laying down the law, because they now held the power; so they banned human sacrifice in Mexico and suppressed it by force. From the Aztec priests' point of view, this use of power by the Spaniards was a shocking abuse of it. In the Aztecs' belief, human sacrifice was an indispensable means of keeping the Universe going. In suppressing human sacrifice the Spaniards were doing their worst to bring the Universe to a full stop, and what could be more wicked than that? The Aztec and Spanish theologies and codes of morality could not be reconciled; but the two people's behaviour could be standardized by the imposition of the conquerors' rulings on the conquered majority; and, on these terms, Spaniards and Aztecs could live together as fellow-subjects of the Spanish Crown.

When the British conquered and annexed India, they were faced with the question that had confronted the Spaniards after their conquest of Mexico. Should they allow or forbid their new non-Western subjects to continue practices that were abominable in Western eyes? Would it be morally possible for the British to condone these practices when the power to suppress them was in their hands? The British were reluctant to act. They had seen the Portuguese get themselves thrown out of Japan and out of Abyssinia as the penalty for their disinterested but incautious zeal in trying to propagate their own religion there. Warned by this Portuguese example, the British and Dutch had concluded that Western missionary activity in non-Western countries was bad for Western trade; and, since trade was the purpose of their presence in these countries, they intended to concentrate on that and to forbear from interfering with local customs. This policy broke down when the British traders in India became the rulers there as well. In Orissa they found devotees throwing themselves under the wheels of the god Juggernaut's car to be crushed to death; in Rajasthan they found infanticide (of female infants only); all over India they found the institution of sati, i.e. the nominally voluntary self-immolation of a widow by burning herself to death on her dead husband's funeral pyre (sati was often virtually enforced, and it was never practised reciprocally by widowers). Eventually the British government in India banned all these Hindu institutions. This was contrary to its policy; yet it found itself morally unable to tolerate the practice of customs so abhorrent to Westerners in a country that was now under Western rule. From the Hindu standpoint, these British vetoes were abuses of power. The widows were being prohibited from performing a sacred duty; the devotees were being prohibited from winning eternal bliss. Yet, unless at least these extreme differences between Western practice and Hindu practice were eliminated, Westerners and Hindus could not coexist in India as fellow-subjects of the British Crown.

Disagreement over another fundamental moral question—the rightness or wrongness of the institution of slavery—led to the temporary break-up of the United States within less than a century after the establishment of the Union. At the time of the making of the Constitution of the United States, slavery was legal in some of the states that were entering into the Union, while in the other states it was illegal. Subsequent experience proved that it was impossible for these two sets of states to remain politically united if their laws continued to differ on the crucial slavery-question; and eventually the disagreement about slavery in the United States was ended by the resort to force which had ended the disagreement about human sacrifice in Mexico. The slave-states seceded in order to salvage their 'peculiar institution'; the non-seceding states made war on the seceding states in order to salvage the Union; the Unionists won, and they used their power to make slavery illegal in the subjugated secessionist states, where slavery had been legal hitherto. The Southern whites' reaction was the same as the Aztecs'. As they saw it, they were the victims of an abuse of force. Even after the lapse of a century, they are not yet reconciled to the victorious North's *Diktat*. Yet the Union could not have been salvaged if the suppression of the secessionist movement had not been accompanied by the suppression of slavery in the re-subjugated secessionist states.

These historical episodes show that differences in manners and customs are politically disruptive when these differences are

extreme and when the moral issues involved in them are fundamental. Conversely, experience has shown that uniformity in
manners and customs and in notions of what is right and wrong
acts as a political cement.

The Roman Empire, for instance, was established by conquest, as the Spanish and British empires, too, were in a later
age. But the Roman Empire could neither have been put together to begin with nor have been held together thereafter by
force of Roman arms alone. The political unification of the whole
perimeter of the Mediterranean basin under Roman rule had
been preceded, and was also followed up, by the social and
cultural unification of this section of the Oikoumenê. The non-
political unifying agency was the Hellenic civilization. Rome
herself had begun to Hellenize herself long before she conquered Greece; and the provinces of the Roman Empire that
lay to the east of the original Greek nucleus of the Hellenic
World had been Hellenized already before Rome conquered
them in their turn. The master-institution of the Hellenic
civilization was the self-governing city-state. The Roman
Empire began as a vast association of Hellenic or Hellenized
city-states, and in each of these the public spirit of the citizens
could be depended upon at that time to provide for the muni-
cipal administration, so that the central government of the
Roman world-state could concentrate on the two tasks of
keeping the peace between the world-state's city-state cells and
shielding them all against aggression from outside. The government of the world-state and of its component city-states alike
was in the hands of an oligarchy that had a common education,
a common outlook on life, and, of course, a common belief in
its own right to enjoy its political and social and economic
privileges. It was this social and cultural cement that held the
Roman Empire together for more than six centuries in its
Levantine core, and for more than four centuries even in its
relatively backward western territories.

The Chinese world-state has been far more successful than
the Roman world-state was in holding together great numbers
of people under a common government over a long period of
time. It is significant that China's social and cultural cement
was superior to Rome's. The Chinese world-state was held together by a land-owning gentry that was, itself, closely knit

together by inter-marriage and that had a strong sense of class solidarity. This Chinese oligarchy, like the one that governed the Roman world-state, had a common education and a common outlook on life which had been given authoritative expression in the Confucian philosophy. This was a moral code which concentrated on the reciprocal obligations of the members of a family and which envisaged the state as being a family on the grand scale. Proficiency in this philosophy, and familiarity with the literature in which the philosophy was embodied, was the avenue to entry into the Chinese world-state's civil service. The key to admission was success in a competitive examination in which the subject-matter was the Confucian classics. Here was a common way of life that was uniquely close-grained. Its solidarity accounts for the durability of the world-state that it has held together.

A way of life is not itself alive. It is not self-propagating and not self-perpetuating. Accordingly, where we find a common way of life holding a world-state together, we must look for the human agents who have been the bearers of this unifying way of life in its spread over the face of the Earth and in its transmission from one generation to another. In the two cases of the Roman world-state and the Chinese world-state, we have already noted who these people were. In both cases they were the members of a cultural and political oligarchy that staffed the public service. This oligarchy had come to be uniform in culture and united in feeling; but this uniformity and unity were not pre-existent; they were the eventual products of a gradual process. The original nucleus of the oligarchy had enlarged itself progressively. The missionaries of the expanding culture had won converts, and, of the two roles, the converts' role had proved the more important in the end. In the greater part of the expanded Hellenic World and the expanded Chinese World, the local bearers of the common culture were descended from ancestors who had not inherited this culture but had adopted it in place of some different cultural heritage of their own. By the time when the Chinese and Roman world-empires were four centuries old, the descendants of the converts were doing more than the descendants of the creators of the culture to keep their common culture alive and to maintain the world-state that was being held together by it. The Roman builders of the Hellenic

World's world-state were all converts by origin. Kao-tsu, the second founder of the Chinese world-state, was a convert by origin likewise. His home in the present-day province of Kiangsu had been beyond the pale of the Chinese civilization as recently as Confucius's day.

A culture can expand only at the expense of other cultures; and, for the adherents of these assaulted cultures, there are two main alternative possible responses to the challenge of cultural aggression. The victims of cultural aggression can respond negatively by clinging more tightly than ever to their own ancestral culture, or they can respond positively by seeking to come to terms with the aggressive alien culture. When this alien culture is expanding, it is presumably more potent at the time than the cultures on whose domains it is intruding; and, if it does have this superior potency, the negative response to its challenge is, of course, self-doomed to fail. Failure was, in fact, the outcome of the Zealot Jewish response to the challenge of Hellenism, of the Wahhabi and Mahdist Muslim response to the challenge of the Western civilization in the Islamic World; and of the ghost-dance religion's response to the same challenge in North America. The alternative policy of coming to terms offers better prospects of preserving at least some of the elements of the culture that is on the defensive. The Jewish Pharisees held aloof from Hellenism as strictly as the Jewish Zealots did, but their tactics of resistance were passive, not militant, and consequently the Pharisaic form of Judaism has survived. The Edomite King of the Jews, Herod the Great, went a long step farther than the Pharisees (he was not a Jew by conviction, any more than he was by origin). Herod preferred a positive response. He was in favour of adopting the secular elements of the Hellenic civilization; and this was also the policy of many other non-Hellenes in other parts of the vast region, extending westward to the Atlantic and eastward into India, through which the Hellenic culture was being propagated by conquest or by trade or just in virtue of Hellenism's intrinsic attractiveness. Almost everywhere the missionaries of Hellenism were met—and this more than half-way—by Herodian-minded converts who voluntarily took it upon themselves to play the part of interpreters of Hellenism to their own people and of their own people's culture to the Hellenes.

A handbook of Egyptian history and culture was written in Greek, for Greek readers, by the Egyptian priest Manetho. The Babylonian priest Berossus wrote a similar handbook to introduce his world's history and culture, likewise, to the Greek-reading public. The Jewish Torah was translated into Greek by Hellenized Jews at Alexandria. The Jewish soldier and scholar Josephus provided a Greek translation of his history of the Romano-Jewish War of A.D. 66–70 which he had written in Aramaic, the pre-Greek lingua franca of South-West Asia. The scriptures of the Christian Church were written in Greek, and so were the tracts, explaining and defending Christianity, that were published in the second century of the Christian Era by philosophically educated non-Jewish converts. The conversion of the Hellenically cultivated ruling oligarchy in the Graeco-Roman World was not completed until the doctrines of Christianity had been systematically transposed from their original Judaic form of expression into the Hellenic rendering that has been given to them in the Creeds.

In presenting Christianity in this Hellenic philosophical dress, the drafters of the Creeds were not merely expounding and commending Christianity; they were also Hellenizing it. A cultural interpreter's activity is, in fact, always a two-way traffic. The interpreter is a go-between. He is introducing the aggressive alien culture to his own people while he is introducing his own people's culture to the aggressor. Since the aggressive culture is, at the time, presumably the more potent of the two, its spread, at the assaulted culture's expense, is, at least to begin with, a more forceful movement than the assaulted culture's counter-attack. The interpreter's role as a disseminator of the aggressive alien culture therefore overshadows his role as his own culture's exponent and defender. The Greeks were, on the whole, singularly incurious about the cultures of the non-Greek societies that had been incorporated politically in the Hellenic World by force of Macedonian and Roman arms. The present-day Western world-conquerors have taken a much more lively interest in the surviving non-Western cultures, and they have made great intellectual exertions in order to satisfy their disinterested curiosity. This is one of the encouraging features of the present situation. It opens up prospects of a *rapprochement* on a basis of mutual understanding and appreciation. Yet, inevitably, the major movement of cultural radiation will be the expansion of the temporarily dominant culture; and in our present Westernizing World, as in the Hellenizing World that was united politically in the Roman Empire, the dissemination of the dominant culture has been the interpreters' principal role.

The Hellenic culture was already being disseminated by non-Hellenic interpreters of it before an Hellenic world-state, cemented by a common adherence to Hellenism, was established in the form of the Roman Empire. Our present-day world has not yet succeeded in achieving political unity; but the cultural unification that was the prelude to political unification in Hellenic history, and in Chinese history too, is already in full swing in cur world today; and, in our case too, the interpreters have been playing a key role.

In our present-day world we have a name for this interpreter-class. We call it 'the intelligentsia', and this word, itself, is symbolic. A French adjective is compounded in it with a Russian substantival termination, and it is significant that it was in Russia that this hybrid compound word was coined. Of all the non-Western societies that have been hit by the expansion of the West in the course of the last five hundred years, the Russian society is the one that, so far, has been hit the hardest and that has reacted with the greatest vigour and greatest originality. The technical meaning of the word 'intelligentsia' is something more than its literal sense. It does not mean just a class that has wits. Its meaning is more precise than that. It means a class of Russians, or any other non-Western nationality, that has had the wit to master the alien culture of the West and to introduce this culture to the intelligentsia's compatriots.

The present-day world-intelligentsia is partly self-made, but it has also partly been fostered, and in some cases deliberately called into existence, by the governments of some of the World's local states. These have been states that have been confronted with 'the Western Question' and have found in the intelligentsia an instrument for helping them to cope with it. The governments that have promoted the rise of the intelligentsia have been of two kinds. Some of them have been the governments of non-Western states that have reacted to Western pressure on

Herodian lines. They have judged that the only effective way of holding one's own against the West is to fight the West with Western weapons in the broadest sense of the word—a sense in which it covers Western ideas and institutions as well as Western makes of guns and bombs. These Herodian statesmen have then recognized that even a partial measure of Westernization will require something more than just the importation of some Western instructors. They have seen that, if you mean to master Western devices, you have to learn to 'do it yourself', and that you must therefore train up a body of native adepts in the alien technique. To serve this purpose, the Russian intelligentsia was not so much 'called' into existence as forced into existence, like chicks in an incubator, by Peter the Great. The Turkish intelligentsia was incubated at still higher speed by Mustafā Kemāl Atatürk. The other kind of government that has created an intelligentsia or, short of creating it, has promoted its rise, is the Western colonial government of a subjugated non-Western country. The pioneer representative of this wing of the modern world-intelligentsia was Cortés' Egeria, Marina. This Spanish-speaking Indian lady did more for Cortés than just to interpret for him in the verbal sense. She explained to him the thoughts and feelings that lay behind his Indian interlocutors' words. Her judgement of persons and situations was acute, and Cortés profited by her advice. The most important single contingent in this colonial wing of the intelligentsia has been the one that has been called into existence by the temporary British régime in India.

Both wings of the intelligentsia have been fostered for the convenience of governments that have needed their services; but both have eventually taken advantage of the political experience and power that they have acquired through playing their key role. In Russia, India, and Turkey—to mention only three conspicuous cases out of a host—the intelligentsia has supplanted its former employers. In all the non-Western countries that have maintained or recovered their independence or that have rid themselves of an indigenous autocratic régime, the intelligentsia is in power today, and it has produced some of the most eminent figures on the stage of modern world-history. Peter the Great, Mehmed 'Ali, Ram Mohan Roy, the makers of the Meiji Revolution in Japan, Tolstoy, Tagore,

Lenin, Mustafā Kemāl Atatürk, the Mahatma Gandhi, Pandit Nehru, Sun Yat-sen: these are, all of them, representatives of the new class that has been called into existence in the non-Western countries in response to the challenge of the West's increasing pressure.

Is this modern intelligentsia now numerous enough and homogeneous enough to do, in our time, for the World as a whole what the Hellenizers once did for the western end of the Old-World Oikoumenê? Is the modern intelligentsia, too, capable of serving as the social and cultural cement for holding together a world-state? The numerical strength of the modern intelligentsia is still small, measured by the size of the lump that has to be leavened. However, the numerical strength of the Hellenizing intelligentsia was also small from first to last. A small minority can move mountains if it has a lever; and the mastery of an aggressive alien culture, with which all the World has to come to terms, is a powerful lever in the intelligentsia's hands for moving the mass of its fellow-countrymen. Moreover, the homogeneity of the contemporary intelligentsia is remarkable. In every liberated country in which the intelligentsia is in power, it is using its new freedom of manœuvre for the pursuit of an identical purpose. It is using it to carry farther the process of Westernization, and it is Westernizing its people's life more rapidly and more radically than the preceding native autocratic or foreign colonial régime ever did. The current policy of the intelligentsia is the same everywhere, and this policy is arriving everywhere at the same result. It is producing nation-states standardized on the Western pattern, and these units are going to be uniform enough to serve as cells for the construction of a world-wide world-state, as the city-states standardized on the Hellenic pattern once served as cells for the construction of the Roman world-state.

Of course, we have to reckon with the possibility of atavistic reactions against the standardizing process—reactions of the kind that occurred in the expanded Hellenic World. Here these reactions took the form of counter-movements on the religious plane. Christianity and its competitors Mithraism and the worships of Isis and Cybele and Iuppiter Dolichenus were followed by Islam; and, though all of them, including Islam, were Hellenized to some extent in the process of winning their

Hellenic converts, there was enough Judaic dynamite left in both Christianity and Islam to make a breach of cultural continuity between the Hellenic civilization and its Christian and Islamic successors. In the Hindu province of our present-day Westernizing World, Ram Mohan Roy and Tagore and Gandhi and Nehru have come and gone, but Benares is still, apparently, what it was. The Maha Sabha is seeking to re-assert the pre-Western Hindu tradition against the modernism of the Congress. Even in the New World, where the pre-Columbian civilizations were relatively frail and where the Spaniards' blows were crushing, we have seen submerged cultures re-emerge through the Western cultural veneer after having lain concealed under this for more than four centuries. The pre-Western cultures have re-emerged unselfconsciously on the Las Casas plateau in South-Eastern Mexico and in the highlands of Guatemala; they have been deliberately revived in the murals of the three great modern Mexican painters and in the decorations of Mexico's new university city.

The final victory of the Westernizing intelligentsia is not a foregone conclusion, and the outcome of this cultural tug-o'-war may be decisive for the prospects of the political enterprise of establishing a world-wide world-state. However, the present-day Westernizing intelligentsia wields one potent cultural weapon that the Hellenizing intelligentsia did not possess. Compulsory universal primary education, administered by the public authorities and financed out of public funds, is a modern Western institution which has no precedents. In the West it has proved to be a very powerful transformative force already during the short time that has passed since its inauguration there. It influences children at their most impressionable age, and it reaches, not just a minority, but the masses. The governments of the newly liberated countries are adopting this Western institution as fast as their means permit. Perhaps even the massive illiteracy and conservatism of the countless Hindu peasantry may yield to this Western solvent in time.

While the cement of a common culture is indispensable for the construction of a world-state, it is not enough by itself. Social and cultural solidarity will not enable a state to stand if the government does not command effective power. A government is no government at all if it is impotent to impose its will on everyone and everything that is under its sovereignty; and, human nature being what it is, any government, whether its domain is a parish or is the whole World, must be in a position to overcome disobedience to its fiat by the use, in the last resort, of overwhelming force. World-authorities for controlling atomic energy and for organizing the production and distribution of food will be ineffective if there is not this overwhelming force behind them.

At the time of writing, perhaps 90 per cent. of the political and military power in the World was held by the United States and the Soviet Union between them. When these two powers took identical action, the effect was decisive even if their action was unco-ordinated. This had been demonstrated when these two powers severally opposed the Anglo-Franco-Israeli attack on the United Arab Republic. Evidently, if Russia and America ever took to working together positively and continuously, they would be able to put the World in order and keep it in order. At the time when these lines were being written, their governments were making an attempt at a *rapprochement* with each other that seemed to be serious and sincere and that was, to that extent, encouraging for mankind. On the other hand, by this time they had been frustrating each other for nearly twenty years; and they were close enough to being a match for each other to make 'the cold war' run out into a stalemate. This mutual frustration was not to the interest of either of them. Indeed, they had one vital interest in common, namely the preservation of their present virtual monopoly of the atomic weapon. All the same, the psychological effects of two decades of mutual hostility would not be easy to overcome. Each of them had come to distrust the other, and the mutual confidence, without which a positive co-operation between them would be impracticable, would be difficult to establish. It was therefore possible that America and Russia would make 'the great refusal', and, if they did, they would be leaving the initiative to China. It would then be China's turn to try her hand, if she chose, at establishing the political world-organization that, in the Atomic Age, was mankind's only alternative to eventual mass-suicide.

In the early months of 1965, China was not in a propitious mood. She was declaring, for instance, that she had no wish to join the United Nations, from which the United States had managed hitherto to keep China excluded. The Chinese world-state that had put down the Chinese World's contending local states in the third century B.C., and that had given China unity, peace, and order for much of the time since then, had now transformed itself into one of the contending local states of the literally world-wide world of the twentieth century of the Christian Era. Indeed, at the moment, China was the most truculent and militant of all these latter-day replicas of the contending Chinese states of a long past epoch of Chinese history. At the moment, China was not concerned to establish world-unity. Her present objective was to recover her traditional status, of which she had been robbed by British, French, Russian, and Japanese aggression since 1840. China was bent on undoing the effects of a century of adversity and humiliation, and it looked as if she would stop at nothing in her determination to reach this goal. However, it also looked as if she would succeed in reaching her goal, and this prospect raised the question whether her mood was likely then to change. If her wounded pride were assuaged and her self-respect were restored to her, might she not revert from her present Westernizing nationalist-mindedness to her own traditional world-mindedness?

If Russia and America did relinquish to China their opportunity for putting the World in order, and if China did then choose to seize her chance, she would have better tools for doing the job than those that a Russo-American consortium could command. China would have unity, she would have numbers (perhaps more than half the World's population by the year A.D. 2000), and above all, she would have history. By the year 1840, China had been, for 2,061 years, 'the Middle Empire' of her own East Asian world, and, in this role, she had given her world long-lasting unity and peace. In the twentieth century of the Christian Era, unity and peace were the crying needs of the global world that had been brought into existence by Western technology's feat of 'annihilating distance'. If a 'Middle Empire' was now needed as a nucleus for political unification on a global scale, China was the country that was designated by history for playing this part of world-unifier once again, this time on a literally world-wide stage.

PART THREE

THE CONTINUING SCOPE
IN RELIGION FOR FREEDOM

IX

The Significance of the Would-be World-Religions

At previous points in this book, it has already been noted that the would-be world-religions have had the same experience, so far, as the would-be world-states in at least one respect. While they, too, have succeeded in uniting large portions of the human race over long periods of time, they, too, have failed to achieve their objective, which is to unite the whole human race. At the present time there are three would-be world-religions—Buddhism, Christianity, and Islam—coexisting side by side. In the history of the would-be world-states, the strength of the divisive movement in human affairs has revealed itself in the plurality of the states of this class, in the shortness of the duration of most of them, and in the strength of the initial opposition to the establishment of them. This opposition has, as we have seen, eventually changed into appreciation and loyalty in many cases, and this has been a symptom of the strength of the unifying movement that has got under way within these last 5,000 years. By contrast, the initial unity of hearts and minds among the adherents of a higher religion has in many cases been disrupted by schisms. There have been schisms in all the higher religions, including those—for example, Zoroastrianism, Judaism, and Hinduism—that have kept themselves within the confines of some single ethnic community or some single civilization. But the schisms in the three missionary higher religions have been more acute, and they have been the most acute of all in the two Judaic missionary religions, Christianity and Islam.

In a would-be world-religion, schism is a betrayal of the religion's principles and a repudiation of its objective. It is a consequence and a symptom of the imperfection that is inherent in all human institutions. Nevertheless, the breakthrough of the higher religions has been, as we have noted already, the most momentous and most revolutionary new departure, so far, in the history of religion and, indeed, in the history of Man. The higher religions have released Man from the social prison-house which he had inherited from his pre-human ancestors.

The way of life that was bequeathed to primitive Man by his pre-human ancestors was monolithic. His religious life was part and parcel of his total social life. The religious and the secular side of life were not separable or even distinguishable from each other at this stage. Each of Man's activities was religious and political and economic and artistic simultaneously.

Agriculture, for instance, was, to begin with, as much a religious activity as an economic one; and this is notable, considering that agriculture is a recent invention. The religious aspect of agriculture is still conspicuous, today, in the life of the American Indian communities in the South-West of the United States. This aspect of it is even discernible still in Japan, though, in Japan, civilization is at least 1,400 years old by now, and though the Japanese have latterly adopted the secular-minded and technologically-oriented modern Western form of civilization. In spite of this, religious tradition counts for more, today, than agricultural science in deciding what crops shall be cultivated in Hokkaido, the northernmost island of the Japanese Archipelago, which the Japanese have opened up and colonized only within the last hundred years. In the climate of Hokkaido, oats and rye, not rice, are the crops that give the highest yield; yet the Japanese settlers there persist in cultivating rice, with the disappointing economic results that are inevitable under the adverse local climatic conditions. When they are asked why they go on doing this, they reply, with some signs of embarrassment, that 'rice is good'. What they are saying is that, for them, rice is still a god as well as a commodity, and that rice-cultivation is an ancestral act of worship which they cannot bring themselves to give up, even though the economic cost of clinging to it is manifestly high. This non-utilitarian attitude towards agriculture would be incomprehensible to an Iowa farmer who has majored in agricultural science at his university and who is making handsome profits by applying his scientific training to agricultural technology. As the Iowa farmer sees his life, there is no connexion between what he does in his fields on weekdays and what he does in his church on Sundays.

The monolithic structure of life in which the Indians of the South-Western United States are still imprisoned, and from which the Japanese settlers in Hokkaido have not yet completely extricated themselves, allows a human being little or no freedom of individual initiative and choice in any field. In his religion it constrains him to make his approach to truth and salvation exclusively through the medium of his society. His society stands between him and the ultimate spiritual reality behind the phenomena of the Universe towards which every human being is groping his way in order to get into touch with it and to live in harmony with it. If he sees this ultimate reality at all, he sees it 'through a glass darkly'.[1] Yet the pursuit of this quest of ultimate spiritual reality is intrinsic to being human. The higher religions have put human beings into direct personal contact with ultimate spiritual reality, and, in doing this, they have made them spiritually independent of the society in which they find themselves implicated as a result of the accident of their having been born at a particular time and place. A human being who has been illuminated and inspired by a higher religion has been given the spiritual strength to stand over against his society as an independent moral power. He has been enabled to look at his society from outside, and to judge it from a spiritually higher standpoint than its own; and this spiritual liberation has laid upon him the moral obligation to criticize his society and, in the last resort, at his peril, to disobey its commands if he judges these to be in conflict with the higher standard of ethics of which he has now become cognizant. Being morally free, he is also morally bound to obey God, rather than his fellow-men, if he is faced with this formidable choice. In defying his society he will, of course, be courting martyrdom; but, if his society does make a martyr of him, it will be courting its own defeat by the principles for which the martyr has given his life. This spiritual freedom at the possible price of martyrdom is, as we have noticed already, the source of freedom in every other sphere—the political, economic, the aesthetic. The religious sphere is the first in which human beings have won their individual freedom, and the higher religions have been the original liberating agencies.

[1] I Cor. 13, 12.

This liberating religious revolution has not been made once for all, only at some single time and place. It has been made at a number of different times and places, separately and independently, over a period of about 1,200 years ending in the year A.D. 632—the date of the death of the Prophet Muhammad, who is the founder of the youngest, so far, of the religions of this kind. Zarathustra, Deutero-Isaiah, and the Buddha all lived in the sixth century B.C.; and Deutero-Isaiah was, in a sense, a founder, as the other two were; for it was in Deutero-Isaiah's vision that the ancestral religion of Israel and Judah finally became completely monotheistic. The centuries that elapsed between Zarathustra's generation and Muhammad's saw the advent of the six higher religions that, between them, command at least the nominal allegiance of a great majority of the human race today. These six higher religions are Zoroastrianism, Judaism, Buddhism, Hinduism, Christianity, and Islam. Any list is, of course, to some extent, arbitrary. This present list of six major higher religions will, no doubt, be lengthened by some students of human affairs and be shortened by others.

In liberating human beings from their primeval social prison-house, the higher religions have conferred an immense boon on mankind; but this boon, like most boons, has been paid for at a price that is proportionate to the boon's own value. The glimpses of truth and the aids for living that each founder of a higher religion has given to his fellow human beings have been dazzlingly novel and beneficent. The founders of the historic higher religions are, in fact, by far the greatest human personalities that have appeared so far; and today, more than 1,300 years after the death of the most recent of them, they are all of them exercising a far greater influence on the lives of a far greater number of people than anyone who has lived before them or since them—including, of course, the people who are making an ephemeral appearance in our current newspaper headlines. The founders of the historic religions have achieved so much that they have been credited by their followers with an achievement that is beyond the powers of even the very greatest man or woman. The founders have been held to have made a discovery—or to have received a revelation—of total and final truth and of total and final means of spiritual salvation.

Buddhists claim that the Buddha gained his insight into the

nature of reality, and found the way out of self-centredness into Nirvana, by his own unaided spiritual exertions. The adherents of the four higher religions of South-West Asian origin— Zoroastrianism, Judaism, Christianity, and Islam—claim for their respective founders that these have received a direct revelation from God. On first thoughts it might seem less presumptuous to claim that one's prophet has been a mere messenger and mouthpiece of God than to claim that he has discovered his insight for himself, by his own human endeavours. The Prophet Muhammad, in the Qur'ān, has put his conviction in the form of a rhetorical question: 'Is aught else laid upon God's messengers but a plain delivery of the message?'[1] This sounds self-effacing. Actually, however, if one speaks in the name of God, one is claiming to have been given a revelation of truth and righteousness that is supra-human and absolute, whereas, if one claims merely to have found some of the truth by oneself, one's claim is more modest, because one cannot then be claiming to have exceeded the limits of human capacity. Even within these human limits, the Buddha did not profess to be giving a comprehensive account of the nature of the Universe and of the reality that lies behind it. Like Zeno and Epicurus, the Buddha was concerned with action first and last, and his interest in knowledge was confined to the minimum required for taking the action that he was prescribing. When his monks asked him metaphysical questions, he always declined to discuss these with them. He condemned metaphysical inquiry as a form of escapism, and he sternly directed the inquirer back to the pursuit of the Buddhist's arduous spiritual quest. The Buddhist monk must devote all his spiritual energies to the endeavour to rid himself of all desire, since desire is both a symptom and a generator of self-centredness, and the Buddhist monk's objective is to attain to the state of extinguishedness (Nirvana), in which all passion is spent. The Buddha refused to give a definition of Nirvana, but we may perhaps see in it one aspect of the ultimate spiritual reality which Hindus call Brahmă and which Zoroastrians, Jews, Christians, and Muslims call God.

Buddhists revere the historical Buddha, Siddārtha Gautama, the son of the king of the city-state Kapilavastu in what is now Nepal, as devoutly as the adherents of the other higher religions

[1] *Fa hal 'alā ar-rusuli 'illā al-balāghu' l-mubīn?* (Qur'ān, Surah xvi, verse 35).

revere their respective founders. But, in consonance with their recognition that his teaching was a human discovery, achieved solely by human effort, they do not hold that either he or his teaching are unique and final. For Jews, the law delivered by Yahweh to Moses on Mount Sinai is definitive; for Muslims, Muhammad is the last, as well as the greatest, of the prophets; for Christians, Jesus is the only begotten Son of God who became incarnate once only and once for all. For Buddhists, on the other hand, the historical Buddha is one—and this neither the first nor the last—in a long series of Buddhas. His human insight into truth and into means of salvation from self-centredness, penetrating though this insight is, is no more than one stage in a long-drawn-out human spiritual progress.

The adherents of the Judaic religions, too, have recognized the fact of spiritual progress, notwithstanding their unanimous belief that their founders were divinely inspired and that their teachings are therefore infallible. The Jews have come to believe in the existence of an oral revelation that was given to Moses by Yahweh, over and above the written law, and that has been handed down from Moses by a continuous chain of oral tradition. This oral law is, in truth, a commentary on the written law which has modified this written law and, on some points, even abrogated it; and, in Islam, the traditions of unwritten sayings attributed to the Prophet Muhammad have performed the same function. They have saved Islamic doctrine from being frozen in the immutable text of the Qur'ān. In the Christian Church the Holy Spirit is deemed to inspire the findings of the Fathers when these meet in a legitimately convened oecumenical council. The younger Judaic religions even recognize the validity of their predecessors within limits. For Christians, the Jewish Torah is still the Word of God, though, as the Old Testament, it has needed the New Testament to complete it. For Muslims, both the Torah and the New Testament are the Word of God as far as they go, though they have needed the Qur'ān to complete them. The Prophet Muhammad showed his sincerity in holding this belief by acting on its political implications. Since Jews and Christians are, like Muslims, 'People of the Book' (*Ahl-al-Kitāb*), it is laid down in the Qur'ān that they are to be, not merely tolerated, but protected by Muslims so long as they submit to Muslim rule and pay a surtax.

These are qualifications of the Muslims', Christians', and Jews' unanimous belief that the revelation that has been given by God to them (whichever of the three they may be) is complete and final and exclusive. Nevertheless, the three Judaic religions have a record of intolerance, hatred, malice, uncharitableness, and persecution that is black by comparison with Buddhism's record. In practice, each of them has opposed the others at all times and has persecuted them whenever it has had the power; and the strife between the three religions has been surpassed in bitterness and ferocity only by the strife, within each of them, between the sects into which each of them has split. 'Heretics' have aroused still greater animosity than 'unbelievers'.

This deplorable conduct of the followers of the three Judaic religions has been a consequence of the fundamental (and fundamentalist) belief that they hold in common and that has been attenuated only, without being changed in essence, by the shy concessions to the hard fact of relativity that each of them has found itself constrained to make. Each of these three religions, and each separate sect within each of them, claims that its own doctrines and precepts are a direct revelation from God and that therefore they, and they alone, are absolutely and exclusively true and right. Every other religion than my own, and every other sect of my own religion than my own sect, is at best partially in error. I know this direct from God Himself, so I know it for certain, and I am under an obligation to God to take action on this certain knowledge that He has revealed to me.

This claim might be impressive if there were only one religion that had ever made it. But three religions in succession have made it in the course of history up to date, and this historical fact makes the claim unconvincing in all three cases. The claim could not be valid for more than one religion out of the three, and it is impossible for any one of the three to vindicate its own claim, because all three claims are made on an identical ground, and this ground is one that is unverifiable. All three religions claim to have received their respective revelations from one and the same God. They believe that this God is unique, omnipotent, and omniscient. If God is what they all believe Him to be, He will not have given mutually incompatible revelations to different prophets. If we are to assume that one of these incompatible teachings is God's genuine revelation, which one is it? The only convincing way of vindicating a claim to have received the uniquely true revelation would be to put God Himself in the witness-box to testify in this particular claim's favour. None of the rival religions can substantiate its claim in this way; yet this would be the only conclusive way of deciding between the three religions' conflicting claims, if we were to accept their unanimous assumption that God is the source of one of their three mutually incompatible sets of tenets. When each religion declares that its own claim to be *the* true revelation is alone valid, and that the other religions' corresponding claims are unfounded and false, one unverifiable human claim is being confronted with others. The debate between the advocates of these conflicting claims was therefore bound, *a priori*, to be inconclusive. How can I prove that my belief that I have received divine revelation is any better founded than your belief that you have received it? I reject your belief as being false, so what defence have I when my own belief is rejected by you?

This inherent inconclusiveness of the debate between the religions that claim to be based on revelation leaves, for these religions, only two alternative ways of conducting their relations with each other. One way is to try to settle by brute force a controversy that cannot be settled by rational argument resulting in a cogent demonstration of the truth and rightness of some one of the competing religions as against the others. This is the way that the adherents of each of the Judaic religions, and of each of the sects within each religion, have followed in the past. The alternative way is for all of them to recognize that they are, all alike, engaged on an identical quest—the quest for truth and salvation—and that the pursuit of this quest is one of the permanent necessities of human life—that it is, in fact, a necessary consequence of being human. If it is recognized that the identity of the quest is more important than the diversity of the paths, then the adherents of the different religions can tolerate, respect, appreciate, value, admire, and love each other's different faiths. They can then, without prejudice, go on to co-operate with each other, in practical ways, for helping human beings to make their passage through life—a passage that is hard for beings that have awakened to consciousness.

This eirenic course has been followed, for the most part, by the adherents of the religions of the Indian family. Since these religions do not claim to be based on revelation, it is not so difficult for them to recognize and admit their relativity and to reconcile themselves to coexistence with each other and with other religions of different origins. Buddhism has accepted a symbiosis with Taoism and Confucianism in China, and with Shinto in Japan. Hinduism has been less tolerant than Buddhism. Hinduism expelled Buddhism from its homeland in India, as Islam expelled Christianity from its homeland in South-Western Asia. Moreover, Hinduism has identified itself with race-feeling; it has institutionalized race-segregation in the form of caste; and, at the present day, the higher-caste Hindus share with the Teutonic-speaking peoples and the Jews the odium of being racialism's 'die-hard' defenders. At the same time it is true that the relations between rival Hindu sects—e.g. between Shaivas and Vaishnavas—have been less hostile than the relations between sects in Christianity and in Islam.

Since the end of the Second World War, a change of heart, towards greater mutual charity, has been manifesting itself among the adherents of the Judaic religions. This change in this quarter is as encouraging as it has been unexpected. The spiritual possibilities that it opens up are discussed below. But we have first to examine one of the consequences of the Judaic religions' traditional militancy. One of the most recent outbreaks of this militancy has been the sixteenth-century and seventeenth-century Catholic-Protestant Christian wars of religion in the Western World. Before the close of the seventeenth century, these wars had evoked, in sensitive Western hearts and minds, a revulsion from the dark side of Judaic religion, of which these wars (and their many predecessors) were horrifying manifestations. In consequence, during these last three centuries the West's ancestral religion, Christianity, has been losing hold progressively in the Western World; and this movement has now become world-wide and has affected all the other living higher religions, because the same three centuries have seen the West acquire a temporary ascendancy over the rest of the World, and this ascendancy has given the West a prestige which has led other societies to follow current Western tendencies. Since Man cannot live without a religion of some

kind or other, the recession of Christianity in the West has been
followed there by the rise of substitute religions in the shape of
the post-Christian ideologies—Nationalism, Individualism, and
Communism. Since the spiritual vacuum left by the recession
of traditional religion has spread from the West into the domains of the other living civilizations, the ideologies, too, have
spread from the West into the rest of the World as well. As has
been suggested already, the three ideologies, taken together,
represent today perhaps as much as 90 per cent. of the actual
(as distinct from the nominal) religion of perhaps as much as
90 per cent. of the human race.

The ideologies thus loom large in mankind's present spiritual
landscape. In what used to be Christendom, the Cross has been
the symbol of God's self-sacrificing love; and the belief that
this love has taken action in the Incarnation and the Crucifixion
is Christianity's central and distinctive tenet. Today the Cross
is confronted, and is challenged, by the symbols of the post-
Christian ideologies: Nationalism's local flag, Communism's
hammer and sickle, Individualism's commercial advertisement.
The religious history of the West and of the whole World
during these last three centuries is conveyed in one of the
parables in the New Testament.[1] When the evil spirit has gone
out of a man, he walketh through dry places, seeking rest, and
findeth none. Returning to his house, he finds it swept and
garnished. He then re-furnishes it by taking to himself seven
devils that are more wicked than the one that he has shaken off;
and the last state of that man is worse than the first. The evil
spirit that modern Man has shaken off is the spirit of the wars
of religion. The dry places through which he has then walked
are a state of mind that has rid itself of all spiritual fervour.
After Western Man had recoiled from the wars of religion, his
first concern was to immunize himself against the virus of
fanaticism in order to save himself from committing more of
the atrocities that had disgraced the fanatics of the preceding
generation. The swept and garnished house is the world of the
eighteenth-century Western Enlightenment. The devils that
the man introduces into his vacant house are the post-Christian
ideologies. We have counted three of these only, not seven, but
three is enough to be an affliction and a menace.

[1] Matt. 12, 43–45; Luke 11, 24–26.

What are the ideologies' prospects? Unless we can make some estimate of these, we cannot estimate the prospects of the higher religions. In our time, a cold war is being waged between all the ideologies on the one side and all the higher religions on the other side. This cold war is more momentous for the future of the human race than the family quarrel between two of the ideologies, Communism and Individualism, that is receiving so much attention today on both sides of 'the Iron Curtain'. In the true cold war, in which all the ideologies are on the same side, which side's prospects are the more promising? If we are seeking the answer to this question, we must try to understand the nature of the ideologies, as well as the nature of the higher religions whose former field the ideologies have now invaded. We have to recognize that the ideologies, too, are religions, though they are religions of a different kind. What is the kind of religion that the ideologies represent? All three of them are regressions to the kind of religion that was prevalent from the dawn of civilization until the rise of the higher religions. All three are forms of Man's worship of his own power.

This man-worship is older than the oldest of the higher religions, but, like these, it is a relatively recent kind of religion on the time-scale of the present age of the human race. During perhaps more than 99 per cent. of Man's history so far, Man's religion has been neither the worship of himself nor the quest of the ultimate spiritual reality behind the phenomena of the Universe. It has, as we have noted, been the worship of the forces of non-human nature: animals, trees, stones, earth, water, winds, rain, storms, Sun, Moon, and stars. Throughout the food-gathering stage of human history—which has been the first stage of it and by far the longest stage so far—mankind was at the mercy of non-human nature; and we worship things in whose power we feel ourselves to be. Conversely, we cannot worship things that we have mastered; and, since Man has mastered Nature, the primeval religion of nature-worship has receded.

The sequel has been touched upon already in Chapter VI. Man began to master Nature at the beginning of the Upper Palaeolithic Age, when the progress of his technology, which had previously been minimal, suddenly accelerated its pace. Man gained a decisive ascendancy over Nature in the Neolithic

Age, with the invention of ground stone tools, agriculture, the domestication of animals, pottery-making, and spinning and weaving. But he seems not to have become conscious of the mastery over Nature that he had already achieved till he had won the first triumphs of organized collective human action on the grand scale. An advance in social organization, not a further advance in technology, was the new achievement that enabled the Sumerians to reclaim the swamps of the lower Tigris-Euphrates valley and the Egyptians to reclaim the swamps of the lower Nile valley. In their state of nature the future lands of Sumer and Egypt had been more inhospitable to Man than any other regions on which he had stumbled. When these former wildernesses had been drained and irrigated by a massive organized human effort, they yielded a surplus of production over and above the day-to-day requirements of bare subsistence. This surplus was a new factor in human history. It made civilization possible, and the creators and beneficiaries of civilization then took to worshipping their own collective power. In this power of theirs they rightly saw the agency that had brought about this astonishing social revolution, but they were wrong—and disastrously wrong, as it turned out—in drawing the conclusion that human power was God.

When the curtain rises on the history of civilization in Sumer, we find the Sumerian World fractured politically into a number of separate sovereign city-states, and in each of these we find that one of the ancient nature-gods has been made to play a new role in addition to his original role. He has been made to serve as a deification of the collective power of the citizens of whichever city-state it may be. When the curtain rises on the history of civilization in Egypt, we find the Egyptian World in the act of being unified politically in a single world-state, and we find this enormous concentration of collective power being deified in the person of the world-unifier and world-ruler, Pharaoh. In the self-deification of the Egyptians, man-worship comes out naked, instead of cloaking itself in nature-worship, as it does in Sumer. In Sumer and in Egypt, we have the prototypes of the two forms in which collective human power has been worshipped. In the Sumerian form the deified collective human power is that of a fraction of mankind;

in Egypt it is the collective power of mankind as a whole. It has been noted in Chapter VI that the Sumerian city-state gods have their counterparts in younger civilizations that began life, as the Sumerian civilization did, as constellations of separate local states. When the Hellenic World was eventually unified politically by Rome, Pharaoh, the human deification of the Egyptian world-state, found his counterpart here in Divus Caesar.

We can see what the post-Christian ideologies are. They are regressions to the various forms of man-worship which Christianity and the other higher religions had replaced. Nationalism is a reversion to the city-state-worship of Sumer and Canaan and Greece; Communism, with its mission to convert and unite the whole human race, is a reversion to the world-state-worship of Egypt and Rome. Individualism is a reversion to the Greek deification of the self-sufficient individual human being— a form of man-worship that was born of a revolt against the Greek city-states' increasingly exorbitant demands on their citizens. The post-Christian ideologies are authentic regressions to man-worship in its various forms, but their adherents are less frank than their predecessors were in acknowledging what their religions are. They have repudiated their ancestral higher religions, but, as ex-adherents of these, they are still shy of admitting that they have relapsed into the idolatry from which the higher religions had liberated their forefathers. The original man-worshippers recognized and acknowledged what they were doing. In Enlil, Athena, Baal, Pharaoh, and Caesar, the city-states Nippur, Athens, Sparta, and Tyre and the Egyptian and Roman world-states were worshipped consciously as the gods that they were. France, Britain, the United States, and Nicaragua are very gods of the same kind as Nippur, Athens, Sparta, and Tyre; the Soviet Union and China are very gods of the same kind as the Egyptian and the Roman world-state; but their worshippers hesitate to hail them as the gods that they truly are. These present-day man-worshippers are hypocritical if they are not blind.

What is the path along which the post-Christian ideologies have regressed to pre-Christian man-worship? Communism and Individualism have deviated from Christianity as heresies, and they are Christian heresies still, however vehemently their adherents may deny their Christian antecedents. Nationalism has nothing Christian about it except the intolerance and fanaticism which, in all three ideologies, is the sad hallmark of their Christian origin.

A heresy is a variation on the orthodox form of a religion in which some particular precept or doctrine of the religion is emphasized at the expense of all the rest. This throws the religion out of balance; but the responsibility for this heretical aberration often lies at orthodoxy's door; for the particular element in a religion that a heresy over-emphasizes is often one that orthodoxy has unduly neglected. Communism has concentrated on the Christian objective of social justice because this objective was pursued by the Christian churches with too little zeal at the time of the Industrial Revolution, when the new industrial working class was being passed pitilessly under the harrow and when Marx was indignantly formulating his philosophy. Communism has erred, not in insisting on justice, but in sacrificing liberty for the sake of it. Individualism has concentrated on the Christian valuation of human souls as being infinitely precious in the sight of God, as God himself has signified by suffering for their redemption. Individualism has erred, not in insisting on the sacrosanctity of human personalities, but in sacrificing social justice to this. The points that these two ideological Christian heresies have in common are at least as striking and as important as their points of difference, about which so much ado is being made on both sides of 'the Iron Curtain'. Not only do they emphasize one precept of Christianity at the expense of another; they also agree in reducing a spiritual issue to economic terms. Communism tends to think of social justice in terms of preventing one person from exploiting another for his personal economic profit; Individualism tends to think of a human personality's sacrosanctity as being a sacred right to freedom of economic enterprise. Since Man shall not live by bread alone,[1] these economic interpretations of justice and freedom are inadequate.

While the major 'cold war' that is being waged in the World today is the one between all the ideologies on the one side and all the higher religions on the other side, the ideologies are also in competition with each other. At the moment, the contest

[1] Matt. 4, 4; Luke 4, 4.

between Communism and Individualism occupies the foreground of the World's political stage, yet it looks as if this contest is going to be a drawn battle, like the former contests between Islam and Christianity and between Protestantism and Catholicism. The Communist and Individualist ways of life are already each adopting elements of the other. It looks as if they are going to approximate towards each other through a process of trial and error in which the determining consideration will be the imperious requirements of the technological revolution that is making a uniform impact on life on both sides of 'the Iron Curtain'. Their militant labels will, no doubt, be preserved piously, but already a stage in their *rapprochement* can be foreseen at which the realities covered by these labels will have become almost indistinguishable. Communism and Individualism also come into conflict with Nationalism, as well as with each other, though this other family quarrel among the ideologies attracts less attention. In this contest the result is never inconclusive. When Nationalism collides with either Communism or Individualism, Nationalism invariably wins.

The victory of Nationalism over Communism in Russia and China has been noticed in Chapter VII. In the United States the corresponding conflict of interests between Individualism and American Nationalism has been decided in American Nationalism's favour. Individualism is America's established ideology, yet today the United States is operating, in her armed forces, the biggest socialist enterprise that the World has seen yet, and even the most doctrinaire American individualists have not proposed that the armed forces of the United States should be transferred from the Government's hands to private enterprise's. American Individualists put up with this massive Socialism in their midst because they are Nationalists first and foremost, and, without the socialization of armaments, there can be no national power. Thus Individualists and Communists alike are Nationalists first. They are Individualists and Communists only secondarily—that is to say, only in so far as these ideologies do not get in Nationalism's way. Of the three post-Christian ideologies, Nationalism has proved itself to be the most potent. It is unfortunate that, of the three, it is also the most potently divisive.

Evidently the higher religions have found formidable com-

petitors in the three post-Christian ideologies, and in Nationalism above all. The ideologies have, however, one common
weakness which may defeat them in their competition with the
higher religions for winning the allegiance of mankind. In re-
gressing to man-worship, the ideologies have re-interned their
followers in the social prison-house from which the higher religions had liberated their ancestors.

It is true that some of the higher religions have constructed
new social prison-houses of their own. Religion is a social
activity as well as a personal one; social action in any field requires some institutional apparatus; and some branches of some
higher religions have built up authoritarian ecclesiastical or-
ganizations that have threatened to intervene, as primeval
human society has intervened, between individual human
beings and ultimate spiritual reality. This authoritarianism is,
however, in contradiction with the higher religions' essential
purpose and *raison d'être*. The higher religions' conscious mission
is to put individual human beings into direct touch with ultimate spiritual reality. They cannot repudiate this mission of
theirs, and human beings can never forget or renounce the
spiritual liberty that the higher religions have brought them,
when once they have enjoyed it. This experience of liberty is an
accomplished fact that cannot be undone, and it is a stumbling-
block for authoritarianism, whether the authority is wielded by
some branch of the Christian Church or by some post-Christian
ideology.

Moreover, even the most authoritarian forms of higher religion offer to their adherents a precious gift that the ideologies
withhold from theirs. All the higher religions, in all their forms,
offer illumination, guidance, and aid to human beings in the or-
deals that beset us all in our passage through this transitory life.
Every human being makes failures, commits sins, suffers bereavements, and eventually meets death. He needs constant spiritual
help, and this is offered to him by the higher religions, but it is
not offered to him by the ideologies. In the social prison-house
in which human beings are re-confined by the ideologies, life is
as tyrannically regimented as it was in primeval human society.
Here, as there, a human being is reduced to being a human ant
in a human ant-heap. This is contrary to human nature. Man is
not a social insect; he is a person. In liberating his personality,

the higher religions have put him, at long last, in possession of his human birth-right. Man does not exist for society's sake. His goal is communion and harmony with ultimate spiritual reality, and society exists for the sake of this personal spiritual quest. The higher religions have taught Man this truth about himself. It seems improbable that the ideologies will be able to make him forget it.

The ideologies are, in fact, inadequate and unsatisfying substitutes for the higher religions. All the same, the ideologies will, no doubt, continue to win and retain the allegiance of former adherents of the higher religions unless and until the higher religions recover their previous hold over human hearts. To recover this, they must once again be true to themselves; and, to be true to themselves, they have to reform their practice in at least three respects. They have to change their attitude and conduct towards each other from hostility and rivalry to love and co-operation; they have to concern themselves, in practical ways, with the crucial issues of the times; and they have to strip off from the permanent essence of their institutions and doctrines and precepts the non-essential accretions with which this essence has been overlaid in the course of their histories.

The first of these three necessary changes has already been started since the end of the Second World War. Symptoms of it are the oecumenical movement in the Protestant Western churches and in some of the Eastern churches; the spirit that Pope John XXIII reanimated in the Roman Church during his brief but historic pontificate; the pronouncements of the Vatican Council that Pope John convened and that his successor, Pope Paul VI, has kept in being; the contemporary *rapprochement* between Northern and Southern Buddhism; and the unprecedented exhibitions of cordiality in the relations between the different religions, as well as within each of them. The Hindus, for instance, are now welcoming Buddhist pilgrims to Bodh Gaya, where the Buddha gained his enlightenment, and to the park at Sārnāth, near Benares, where he taught, and they are encouraging them to build Buddhist hostels and museums in these Buddhist holy places on Hindu ground. There were some Hindus who demurred when Pope Paul VI announced his intention of attending the Eucharistic

Congress that was held at Bombay in 1965. These Hindus suspected the Pope of designing to win converts at Hinduism's expense. This suspicion was a relic of a past phase in the relations between the historic religions. The Government and people of India, however, recognized that the Pope's motive for wishing to visit India was not a design to promote the sectional interests of his church but was a concern for the welfare of all his fellow human beings, Catholic and non-Catholic alike. The warmness of the welcome that the Pope received when he landed showed that a majority of the Hindu community had not only understood what his feelings towards them were but had been moved to respond in kind. Already, on his previous pilgrimage to the Christian holy places in Palestine, Pope Paul VI had been welcomed, with the same enthusiasm, on landing at the airport at 'Ammān. For a Pope to visit countries in which an overwhelming majority of the population was non-Catholic and non-Christian would have been impracticable till within a few years of these two dates. That the Pope should have been welcomed enthusiastically by a Muslim crowd and by a Hindu crowd would have been inconceivable. These two events are historic, and they may mark a turn in the tide of the higher religions' fortunes. These religions' past dissensions have been the main cause of their recession. A union of hearts among their followers could do more than anything else to win back allegiance to each of them.

The second change that is required of the historic religions is that they should concern themselves with the crucial issues of the times, and this change, too, is already taking place. It is, indeed, bound up with the contemporary change in the religions' attitude towards each other. One of the considerations that has inspired this change of heart is that their traditional dissension, besides being wrong in itself, is a trivial pursuit by comparison with the gravity of the present situation of mankind. Now that mankind's survival is again in doubt, the religions' true mission, which is to give counsel, help, and comfort to human beings, takes precedence over the pursuit of each religion's sectional interests. The religions have to be reconciled with each other if they are to co-operate with each other, and they need to co-operate in working for the preservation of peace, for the furtherance of social justice, and for the discovery of ways and means of keeping human life still human in the revolutionary new environment that modern Man has conjured up around himself through his unprecedented technological progress.

The third change that the historic religions have to make is to strip off from their essence the accretions that have overlaid it in the course of time, and this operation is a delicate one. It is not so difficult to identify and remove the outermost layers of the non-essential crust, and some of this cleansing work has already been done. For instance, the Roman Catholic Christian Church no longer treats a belief in the truth of Aristotelian astronomical theories as being an obligatory article of faith. It is not so easy to discriminate between the inner layers of the crust and the outer layers of the quick. Manifestly, when Aristotle's astronomy has been excised from the traditional corpus of Christian doctrine, Christianity itself remains intact. But at what point does the cleaner's knife enter and mutilate the living flesh? What about the Virgin Birth, the Resurrection, the Ascension? Can a Christian still count as a Christian if he ceases to believe all, or even one, of these intimate Christian dogmas? Islam, again, might remain intact if Muslims were to excise from it the veneration of the Black Stone that has been embedded in the Ka'bah at Mecca since the Days of Ignorance. Islam might also survive the abandonment of the institution of the Pilgrimage. As it is, only a minority of Muslims can afford to make the Pilgrimage now that Islam has spread to the ends of the Old World. But what about Muhammad being the last of the prophets? And what about the Jews being the Chosen People of the One True God who is the creator of the Gentiles too? And what about the return of the Jews to Palestine being the goal and consummation of God's plan for human history? And what about the conception of the nature of the spiritual universe that is presupposed in the Buddha's prescription for finding salvation? It has been noted already that the Buddha deliberately confined his metaphysics to the minimum required for his plan of action. Yet this fragment of metaphysics includes assumptions that will not be taken for granted by non-Indian minds. What about the sorrowful round of rebirths? Is this a reality, or is it an imaginary nightmare? And, if it is held to be a reality, is it necessarily also true that the transmission of karma is the force that keeps the wheel of reincarnation turning?

These, and the like, are questions that the ecclesiastical authorities are shy of raising. The impulse to try to elude such explosive questions is understandable. At the same time, the price of ignoring them would, in the long run, be prohibitive. The religions would lose touch with life, and then the whole of their heritage, its essence as well as the accretions, would be likely to be rejected. This would be a tragedy for mankind; for the essence of the higher religions is a spiritual treasure that we cannot afford to lose.

If the higher religions are to continue to do what they have the power to do for mankind, both their dogma and their ecclesiastical organization will, one may guess, have to be made more flexible than they have been hitherto.

In pre-Christian Greek parlance the word 'dogma' meant an opinion put forward tentatively by a philosopher for being tried out in discussion with other minds. In the vocabulary of the Christian Church, 'dogma' has come to mean truth that has been revealed by God and that is therefore certain, unquestionable, and absolute. The attraction of dogma, in the Christian meaning of the word, has been the definiteness and confidence of the answers that dogma has given to ultimate metaphysical questions; but this self-assurance is also a weakness. The human heart longs for certain knowledge about what lies behind the mysterious Universe in which we find ourselves; and the human intelligence knows that it is not capable of meeting the heart's demand. The higher religions claim that they can supplement the intelligence, and can fill in the missing parts of the picture, which are the key parts, by drawing upon revelation from God or upon enlightenment that has been won by a human sage's efforts. The findings of enlightenment and the pronouncements of revelation have to be taken on faith. But the human intellect, which knows that it is a limited instrument and an imperfect one, also knows that it has the capacity to think for itself. Thinking for oneself is always arduous and is sometimes painful. The temptation to stop thinking and to take dogma on faith is strong. Yet, since the intellect does possess the capacity to think for itself, it also has the impulse and feels the obligation. We may therefore feel sure that the intellect will always refuse, sooner or later, to take traditional doctrines on trust. It refused in the Hellenic World from the sixth to the second century B.C.; it refused in the Islamic World in the ninth century of the Christian Era; it has refused in the Western World since the seventeenth century. Since that century, the modern Western outlook has become the outlook of a world-wide Westernizing intelligentsia; and what the intelligentsia thinks today, the masses will think tomorrow. The modern Western mind's insistence on thinking for itself and on putting traditional doctrines to the test thus seems to be 'the wave of the future' for the World.

Non-Western minds were actually quicker to revolt against Western Christian dogma than Western minds were. When, in the sixteenth and seventeenth centuries, the Spaniards and Portuguese tried to impose dogmatic Western Christianity on the non-Western World, this was rejected everywhere except in the Americas, where the Spaniards had an overwhelming superiority in military force over the heirs of the pre-Columbian civilizations. After seeing what had happened to the Portuguese in Japan and in Abyssinia, the Dutch and British, who followed at the Iberian Christians' heels, took care to be more politic. They propagated the secular elements in the modern Western way of life, but they discouraged missionary enterprise and refrained from putting their military and political power at its disposal. It is their secularized version of the Western Civilization, with the Christian dogma deliberately left out, that has captivated the rest of the World.

This recalcitrance to dogma is surely a healthy feature of human nature; for open-mindedness and independent-mindedness are manifestly the right responses to our specific human condition. 'We know in part and we prophesy in part.'[1] At the cost of unceasing mental strife, we are constantly changing—and perhaps sometimes improving—our dim vision of ultimate spiritual reality; but we cannot expect to attain a vision that will be definitive in the sense of being proof against the possibility of its ever being modified by future findings of experience. Present-day scientists estimate that mankind has about 2,000,000,000 years of future experience to add to its present stock (always supposing that mankind does not liquidate itself in our time). It is not credible that any doctrine that claims to

[1] 1 Cor. 13, 9.

give a certain, comprehensive, and definitive knowledge of ultimate spiritual reality will be borne out by all the future findings of human experience—notwithstanding the patent feebleness of our intellectual power of interpreting our experience when we have it. The longing for certainty seems unlikely ever to extinguish the determination to exercise such mental powers as we have. Faith always provokes reason to challenge faith's pronouncements; and this obstinate intellectual contrariness is the rock on which dogma will always break unless its traditional claim to absoluteness is abated and its traditional rigidity is relaxed.

A relaxation of the rigidity of the historic religions' ecclesiastical organization is also required. The present extremes of authoritarianism and spontaneity are represented in different denominations of the Christian Church—authoritarianism in the Roman hierarchy and spontaneity in the Society of Friends, which has found ways of maintaining unity and taking action effectively with a minimum of institutional structure. Though, from the organizational standpoint, the Society of Friends and the Roman Church are at opposite ends of the ecclesiastical gamut, a Friends' meeting and a Catholic oecumenical council hold that their insights are inspired by the same Holy Spirit. An oecumenical council's conclusions are reached by a majority vote, a Friends' meeting's conclusions by an informal consensus. A consensus that is also informal, though the parties to it are the recognized doctors of the religious law, is the method by which doctrine is established and modified in Judaism and in Islam. Consensus is a middle course between authoritarianism and individualism, and its flexibility makes it an appropriate method for developing the doctrines and constitutions of religious communions that are seeking to survive in a world which, being human, is constantly changing.

At any rate, the extremes of both authoritarianism and individualism have evoked vehement opposition in the past. The Papal monarchy has drawn upon itself the fifteenth-century Conciliar Movement and the sixteenth-century Protestant Reformation before beginning, as it has begun in the Vatican Council convoked by Pope John XXIII, to transform itself, on its own initiative, into a limited monarchy from having been an absolute one. On the other hand, Jesus was denounced by the

Jewish rabbis of his time because 'he taught as one having authority, and not as the scribes'.[1] His offence was that he ignored the rabbinical convention that a rabbi, however original-minded and however eminent, must submit any new findings of his to his brethren's judgement, and must not proclaim them to be valid unless and until they have been ratified by a consensus. Jesus's personal pronouncements, in which the principle of consensus was either ignored or was even rejected, cost him his place in Judaism and his life. Instead of becoming the most highly revered rabbi in all Jewish history, he became, through his death, the founder of a new religious communion which maintained that the Christian Church had now entered into the Chosen People's heritage. In contemporary rabbinic eyes, Jesus's offence was aggravated by his assertion that the authority which he assumed had been conferred on him personally by God. As the rabbis saw it, this was blasphemy. Yet, if it was, the prophets of Israel and Judah stood convicted of having committed the same sin; for the prophets had brought the higher religion of Judaism into being by breaking out of a traditional monolithic society into a personal communion with God himself.

[1] Matt. 7, 29; Mark 1, 22.

X

Is a Fusion of the Higher Religions Desirable?

In a previous chapter it has been suggested, on the evidence of past experience, that some minimum amount of unity and uniformity in the outlooks and the ways of life of the peoples of the World may be one of the necessary conditions for the establishment of world-government. In the past, it has proved impossible, in certain historic cases, to hold even a local state together when different sections of its population have held different views about the rightness or wrongness of, for example, such controversial institutions as human sacrifice and slavery. A common moral standard, at least on fundamental moral questions, seems to be an indispensable basis for social and political solidarity. Morality is closely bound up with religion; and religion is the heart of human life. We therefore have to ask ourselves whether the need for homogeneity in a world-state extends to the religious plane. If we are to establish and maintain a world-state that will be literally world-wide, shall we have to underpin this political structure by fusing together the different higher religions, philosophies, and ideologies that are co-existing with each other in the World today?

The founders of would-be world-states, and these founders' successors, have, in some cases, held that some measure of religious as well as political unity is requisite, and they have accordingly created or adapted or adopted religious institutions to serve their purpose of unifying their world politically. In the Egyptian, Roman, Chinese, and Andean world-states, the worship of the world-community's collective power was deified in the person of its ruler. In the Inca world-state, the virtual deification of the Inca Emperor himself was accompanied by the dissemination of the worship of the Incaic supreme god,

Viracocha. Another expedient of the empire-builders has been to elevate the local god who is the deification of the empire-building local state to the headship of a pantheon in which the gods of the subjected local states are reduced to a subordinate position. When the Egyptian world-state was re-established by the Theban founders of the Middle Empire, Amun, the local god of Thebes, was identified with the Pan-Egyptian sun-god Re and was elevated, as Amun-Re, to the headship of the Egyptian pantheon. When the Sumero-Akkadian world-state was re-established by the King of Babylon, Hammurabi, Marduk, the local god of Babylon, was elevated, as Marduk-Bel, to the headship of the Sumero-Akkadian pantheon.

The Inca empire-builders did not only disseminate the worship of the creator god Viracocha of Tiahuanaco; they also carried the Inca sun-god of Corichanca with them to a position of supremacy over the gods of the Andean states that the Incas had subjugated. The history of the Roman imperial government's religious policy followed a parallel course. After having instituted the worship of Divus Caesar and Dea Roma as the religious symbol of the world-unity for which the Roman Empire stood, the Roman government followed this up, three hundred years later, by adopting a syncretistic religion, devised by the Neoplatonic philosopher Iamblichus, which was a combination of all the religions then current at the western end of the Old-World Oikoumenê with the single exception of Christianity. The Emperor Maximinus Daia, and, after him, the Emperor Julian, gave this Neoplatonic religion an ecclesiastical organization modelled on that of the Christian Church. This was, indeed, an *union sacré* directed against Christianity but armed with Christian weapons. It was a confession that all the non-Christian religions had their backs to the wall. The Emperor Theodosius I therefore resorted to a more practical expedient. Christianity had proved its vitality by refusing to accept co-existence either with the worship of Divus Caesar and Dea Roma or with the subsequent Neoplatonic counter-church. Theodosius followed out his predecessor Constantine's policy of tolerating Christianity, and personally embracing it, to its logical conclusion. Theodosius adopted Christianity as the Roman Empire's officially established religion.

This is neither the only nor the earliest case in which a

would-be world-state has sought to underpin its political structure by giving official status to a higher religion that has previously had an independent life and a separate history of its
own. Already, in the third century of the Christian Era, Zoroastrianism had been made the official religion of the Roman
Empire's rival the Sasanian Persian Empire. In the second century B.C., Confucianism had been made the official philosophy
of the Chinese world-state, some three hundred years after Confucius himself had lived and died without having succeeded in
obtaining employment in the service of any of the local Chinese
states of his day.

Thus a number of different forms and degrees of religious
unification have been promoted by rulers of world-states in the
belief that some measure of religious uniformity is required as
a basis for political unity. Is this belief borne out by experience?
There have been other world-states that have deliberately
followed the opposite policy of tolerating, and even encouraging, religious pluralism. This was the policy of the Achaemenian
Persian Empire. Cyrus, like Constantine, gave liberal toleration
to the religions of all the peoples under his rule, without attempt-
ing to impose on his subjects the particular religion that happened to be his own; and this policy of his largely accounts for
the willingness with which the Achaemenian régime was accepted until Darius's assassination of Smerdis made it evident
that Cyrus's line was now extinct (whether the murdered
Smerdis was an impostor or was Cyrus's genuine son). As for the
religious pluralism of the original Islamic state and of its successor-states, this has been made obligatory on all Islamic states
by the ruling in the Qur'ān that Jews and Christians share with
Muslims the distinction of being 'People of the Book'. In virtue
of this, Jews and Christians are, as has been noted, entitled,
according to the Islamic religious law, to remain faithful to
their own respective religions and to be protected, besides being
tolerated, by the Islamic government, so long as they submit to
the Islamic government's authority and pay a surtax. This
toleration and protection, to which Jews and Christians are
entitled, has been extended, by analogy, to cover the adherents
of other higher religions, e.g. Zoroastrians and Hindus. In the
Ottoman Empire this religious pluralism was, as we have noticed, made into a basis for the structure of a world-state. The

Ottoman Empire was organized as an association of ecclesiastical corporations (millets). The Ottoman Imperial Government's policy was to give the ecclesiastical authorities in each millet the maximum amount of civil jurisdiction over their respective flocks, subject to the Imperial Government's paramountcy in the fields of criminal justice, police, and defence. The Muslim millet was politically dominant, but the various Christian millets and the Jewish millet did enjoy a communal autonomy that was not only genuine but was extensive.

Since the break-up of the Ottoman Empire, some Turkish students of its history have contended that the cause of its break-up was its institutionalization of religious pluralism. They have suggested that the Ottoman Empire might have had greater staying power if, at the time of its creation in the fourteenth and fifteenth centuries of the Christian Era, its builders, instead of behaving like good Muslims, had behaved, instead, like their Castilian, Aragonese, and Portuguese Christian contemporaries. These had massacred, evicted, or forcibly converted the Muslim and Jewish population of the Islamic territories that they had conquered. If only the contemporary 'Osmanli Muslims had done the same, in the Christian territories conquered by them, to the Christian population there, might not Muslim Turkey have survived intact, like Christian Spain and Portugal? This comparison between Hispanic history and Ottoman history is specious, but there are other possible comparisons that invalidate it. The forcible imposition of religious uniformity has not invariably been a talisman for ensuring the survival of the intolerant state. When the population of the Roman Empire had been forcibly converted to Christianity by Theodosius I, the Empire went to pieces in its western provinces immediately after the intolerant emperor's death; and, when the Mughal Emperor Awrangzib departed from the Islamic law and from the previous Mughal practice by persecuting Hinduism, which was the religion of a great majority of his subjects, he aroused a Hindu reaction which brought the Muslim Mughal Empire in India to ruin as swiftly as the Christian Western Roman Empire dissolved after Theodosius I's death. As for the break-up of the Ottoman Empire, the main cause of this was not, in reality, the preservation of the non-Muslim millets thanks to the Ottoman Government's faithfulness to the Islamic tradition of religious toleration. One main cause was the breakdown of the remarkable Ottoman institution under which the rulers of the Ottoman Empire were recruited from among the children of the Empire's non-Muslim subjects. Another main cause was the temporary ascendancy of the neighbouring Western civilization over the Islamic and the Eastern Orthodox Christian civilization alike. The Ottoman Empire was disrupted by the magnetism of the Western ideology of Nationalism, which captivated first the Empire's Christian millets and eventually the once dominant Muslim Turkish and Arab millet itself.

The historical evidence does not suggest that religious unification is a necessary condition for the maintenance of political unity. *A fortiori*, it does not suggest that religious uniformity is a politically unifying factor when it is imposed by force. Thus the historical precedents need not deter us from giving a free rein to religious plurality and diversity in a World that, in the Atomic Age, has to be unified politically, at least for certain purposes, as the only alternative to self-destruction. There are a number of reasons why religious variety and liberty are desirable in all circumstances, and why they would be especially desirable in a literally world-wide world-state.

The first and most obvious reason for allowing religious liberty is that it is morally wrong to try to bring about by force a conversion which can be genuine only if it springs from a spontaneous conviction. The forcible conversion of an adult human being is, in fact, impossible. The most that can be extorted from him is an insincere outward conformity under threat of penalization or martyrdom. A child, on the other hand, can be genuinely converted to a new religion by educating him in it from an early age. The Christian children who were recruited by the Ottoman Government and were educated to become the Ottoman Empire's rulers were not forcibly converted from Christianity to Islam; yet there seems to be no known instance of any of them not spontaneously becoming a Muslim before his education was over. From the moment at which they were taken from their Christian homes, these children were brought up in an exclusively Muslim environment and atmosphere. Naturally Islam came to seem to them to be the only conceivable religion for a human being to embrace. Their adoption of Islam was inevitable, not because they were coerced, but because no alternative religion was any longer left within their mental horizon. This lack of opportunities for making a choice between alternative religions in childhood has been the rule hitherto, not only for the Ottoman 'tribute children', but for all children in all societies at all times. A child has grown up, as a matter of course, in the religion of the adults, whether parents or preceptors, who have had the child's education in their hands. Whatever the older generation's educational policy may be, an inability to choose one's religion for oneself may be one of the inherent disabilities of childhood; but it may be hoped that, in the new oecumenical society into which all sections of mankind are moving in our time, it may become increasingly possible to choose one's religion for one-self after one has reached the age of discretion.

Another reason for allowing religious liberty is that one of our human rights is the right to learn, without restriction, about all the diverse concepts of truth and prescriptions for salvation. Each one of us has a right to make himself acquainted with each of these and to accept or reject any of them, according to his personal judgement. This human right to hear and learn presupposes the reciprocal right to preach and teach. If one is convinced that one has become possessed, whether through discovery or through revelation, of even a glimpse of the truth and a shred of the means of salvation, one would be inhuman if one did not feel an impulse, and an obligation, to share this spiritual treasure with one's fellow human beings. The wish to convert someone is evidence that one feels a concern for his welfare; and the person to whom the missionary addresses him-self ought to bear it in mind that the missionary's intentions are benevolent, even if his attentions are annoying.

The least annoying of all the missionary religions and ideo-logies that have been launched so far is the oldest of them, Buddhism. Buddhist missionary work has been tactful because Buddhism itself is tolerant. Buddhism has not set itself to extirpate all the other religions that it has found in occupation of its mission-field. It has been ready to come to terms with them and to enter, not into a mere coexistence with them, but into a symbiosis. In virtue of this eirenic êthos, Buddhism has spread without arousing violent opposition. The missionary re-ligions and ideologies of South-West Asian origin—Christianity,

Islam, and the three post-Christian ideologies, Communism, Individualism, and Nationalism—have been more militant, and the opposition that they have aroused has been correspondingly lively. Christian missionary work in present-day India, for instance, has been criticized sharply, as being vexatious, by an acute and able Hindu statesman and publicist, K. M. Panikkar.[1] His reaction to Christian missionary work today is the same as the reaction of cultivated Greeks and Romans to Christianity during the early centuries of the Christian Era. It is also amusingly and illuminatingly similar to the present-day reaction to Communist missionary work in well-to-do conservative-minded quarters in the contemporary Western World.

This indignant reaction to Communism in Christian or ex-Christian Western countries is comic, considering that Communism is a Western product and export and is, moreover, one that could have been produced only in a Christian environment. The mission to preach the Gospel to every creature[2] has been of the essence of Christianity from the start. The word 'propaganda' is a Christian term of art. It is derived from the title of the Roman Congregatio de Propagandâ Fidê. This originally Christian missionary spirit is the parent of all Western missionary activities, whether laudable or deplorable. It is the parent of societies for the abolition of slavery and for the prevention of cruelty to children and to animals; it is the parent of the Communist International and of the John Birch Society; and it is the parent of all the commercial advertising firms that operate on Madison Avenue and elsewhere. When Marx and Engels had worked out the Communist concept of truth and prescription for salvation, they took it for granted—being the Westerners that they were—that they would preach this new gospel to all mankind. It did not occur to them to ask themselves whether missionary work is or is not a good activity, any more than it occurred to the Buddha to ask himself whether karma and rebirth are or are not facts of life. In both cases, debatable assumptions were taken for granted because they were so deeply embedded in Marx's and the Buddha's respective cultural heritages.

---

[1] K. M. Panikkar, *Asia and Western Dominance* (London, Allen & Unwin, 1953).
[2] Mark 16, 15.

The writer of this book holds, rightly or wrongly, that the Christian belief in Man's duty to share his spiritual treasure with his fellows reflects an impulse that is innate in human nature. Yet, even if one is justified in being zealous to propagate one's gospel, whatever one's gospel may be, the right to preach has limits, as all human rights have. The right to preach is valid only on condition that the motive is the disinterested desire to share truth and the means of salvation with other human beings. The right loses its validity if and when the preaching of a religion or an ideology is misused for the pursuit of some ulterior political or commercial purpose. The art of propaganda may be misused, for instance, for cajoling or browbeating people into buying goods or services that they do not want or that they cannot afford, or it may be misused for building up a 'fifth column' in one country for the purpose of assisting the people of another country to bring the propaganded country under their political control. Missionary work ceases to be legitimate when it is not performed simply for its own sake.

Subject to this limitation of the human right to preach, it is surely desirable that there should be a plurality and variety of religions and philosophies and ideologies. This is desirable, for instance, if it is true, as has been suggested in Chapter IV, that our common human nature, uniform though it is fundamentally, is differentiated at a more superficial level into a number of different temperaments or dispositions or psychological types. This vein of variety in human nature bears in it a variety of religious experiences and needs, and these, in turn, call for a variety of presentations of the truth and of the means of salvation.

Each of the historic higher religions probably owes part of its success in winning converts to its special capacity for meeting the spiritual needs of one or other of the principal psychological types. If this is the fact, it follows that, so far, the religions have had only a partial opportunity of performing the service that each of them is capable of performing for human beings. Considering the inadequacy of the means of communication that have been at the missionaries' disposal hitherto, the missionary religions have done wonders; they have converted whole continents; but not one of them has propagated itself over the whole World. The adherents of each of them have been confined, so far, to some particular geographical region; and one can draw and paint a map of the distribution of the religions in which their respective geographical domains are distinguished by more or less clearly demarcated local blocks of this colour or of that. The diverse psychological types or temperaments or dispositions of human nature are not, however, sorted out from each other into any such segregated geographical provinces. In any sample of human society, however small in numbers, all the divers varieties of human nature will be found to be represented, as has been noted already.

In consequence, up till now, a human being's religion has usually been determined, not by a personal choice of his in accordance with his temperament, but by the accident of his having happened to be born in this or that time and place. He has, in fact, usually inherited the religion of his ancestors, without regard to the question whether this particular religion is the one that would have been the most helpful to a person of his particular temperament. If the religion that he has inherited is one that meets his personal needs, this will have been a fortunate accident. If the religion that would have suited him best happens to be one whose geographical domain is in the Antipodes, he will have been virtually debarred from obtaining access to it owing to the inadequacy of our means of communication so far. Now, however, that we have 'annihilated distance', it will become possible for any individual, born and brought up at any place in the World, to make himself acquainted with any of the current religions, philosophies, and ideologies and eventually to choose for himself, from among them, whichever appeals to him the most. Individual choice at the age of discretion will replace, in more and more cases, the unquestioning and almost automatic inheritance of the religion of one's family and one's homeland; and, as this change in the way in which people get their religion proceeds, there will be a concomitant change in the religious map of the World. The solid but local blocks of the adherents of this religion and that will dissolve into so many world-wide diaspórás, none of which will be in a majority at any point, because all will be intermingled with each other everywhere.

If and when the adherents of the various religions come to be recruited by individual choice, instead of being conscripted by the accident of geographical location, the higher religions will, for the first time, have it in their power fully to fulfil their *raison d'être*. Their common mission is to liberate the individual from his community by putting him into direct touch with the spiritual reality behind the phenomena of the Universe and helping him to live in harmony with it. This is a mission that the post-Christian ideologies have not taken over. They have no help to offer to human beings in the personal trials and troubles, sins, failures, and bereavements that beset every one of us in the course of his life. Notwithstanding the ideologies' meteoric rise and progress, this field—which, for human beings, is the most important field of all—still continues to be the historic higher religions' and philosophies' domain.

At the same time it has been the higher religions' misfortune, and also mankind's, that, after liberating Man from his ancient social prison-house, they have been constrained to re-confine him in new prison-houses built by the higher religions themselves. This has been inevitable for a reason that we have already noticed. Religion is a social as well as a personal activity; and social activities require institutional frameworks. Even the Society of Friends is an institution, though Friends do their utmost to keep a Friend's encounter with God untrammelled by human social organization. Since Man is a social animal, he cannot be freed entirely from the social toils in which his nature involves him. However, his social trammels can be of different degrees of oppressiveness. His personal freedom is at its minimum when he finds himself in a social prison-house which has been pre-ordained for him by his having been born into it. A choice between alternative prison-houses is the next best thing to freedom itself, and this is the choice that he will have if he becomes free to choose the religion to which he will give his adherence.

We may also hope that the walls of these ecclesiastical prison-houses will become progressively less constricting and less opaque than they have been in the past. One cause of the past rigidity of the higher religions' social structures has been their rivalry with each other. Each of them has been standing on the defensive and has been keeping a tight hand over its flock for fear of desertions to some rival fold. The change of heart that has come over the ecclesiastical authorities and their followers since the Second World War has opened up a new and happier prospect. Instead of continuing to compete with each other for winning and retaining adherents, perhaps the higher religions will begin to co-operate with each other for giving the utmost possible aid to mankind as a whole and to each of mankind's constituent human beings. The greatest spiritual service that a religion can perform for a human soul is to help it in its quest for truth and salvation, even if this quest is leading this soul out of its ancestral religion's fold into another fold of the soul's own choice. The true measure of a religion's success is not the number of its adherents; it is the amount of spiritual help that it has succeeded in giving to human beings without regard to their ecclesiastical allegiance.

Another reason why a plurality and variety of religions is desirable is that this will make for open-mindedness and will be some safeguard against the human mind's constant proneness to lapse into dogma. The level of being with which the higher religions are concerned is incomparably more important for human souls than the level of science and technology. But, just because of their relative unimportance and triviality, science and technology are able to give precise answers to the relatively petty questions that they raise. By contrast, the higher religions are so many attempts to probe the mystery of the Universe and to bring the soul into touch and into harmony with the ultimate spiritual reality behind the phenomena, and the questions that these religions raise are of a kind that human beings will never cease to ask but will also never succeed in answering with scientific precision. The language of religion is not the language of science and technology; it is the language of poetry and prophecy. This wells up from a deeper level of the psyche, and its findings are inevitably tentative and provisional, because its subject is ineffable and infinite. Dogma is an ill-conceived attempt to express religious truth in scientific terms. The diversity of the voices with which the different religions speak is a warning that none of them ought to be taken dogmatically. The danger that mankind might fall into a dogmatic spiritual paralysis would be still greater than it is if all the current religions, philosophies, and ideologies were to be fused into one; for this amalgam would almost inevitably come to be consecrated as an exclusive orthodoxy. This point is made convincingly by Hume, apropos of the medieval Western Christian Church's virtual canonization of Aristotle's philosophy, in a passage that has been quoted in Chapter V.

Another reason why a plurality and variety of religions will be desirable in a politically unified world is that a world-state will be afflicted with dullness. A world-state is the necessary alternative to mass-suicide; but every boon has its price; and dullness will be part of the price that the boon of security will bring with it. We are living still, today, in a world that is almost unmanageably diversified and almost agonizingly interesting. It requires an effort of imagination to picture to ourselves the very different world that we shall have created for ourselves if we succeed in abolishing war and in stabilizing the World's population and in feeding it adequately when it has trebled or quadrupled its numbers. In this novel world there will be a reversal of values. Today the premium is on security, and therefore on unity and uniformity. But, if and when these three objectives have been safely achieved, the premium will be on the variety that, today, is our bane. This coming reversal of values is the subject of the fourth and last part of this book.

PART FOUR

THE IMPACT OF TECHNOLOGY
ON LIFE

XI

Population, Urbanization, Congestion

Let us assume that we are going to succeed in solving the most urgent and most dangerous of the problems that confront us today. Let us suppose that the institution of war has been abolished, that the global problem of disposing of poisonous waste from 'atoms for peace' has been solved, and that science has not been inhibited by Nationalism from feeding the World's population—and feeding it adequately—when it has increased to three or four times its present size. These suppositions are, of course, optimistic, but they are not utopian. The administrative and technological means for translating them into accomplished facts are already at our command. The crux is, as has been emphasized, a political one. These objectives, which have to be achieved if mankind is not to commit mass-suicide, will be practicable only if the achievement of them is entrusted to world-authorities empowered, in their respective fields, to give orders to the hitherto sovereign local governments and, in case of conflict, to override them; and these steps towards the establishment of a world-government will be feasible only if the Nationalism that is now prevalent among all peoples recognizes, and bows to, the stark truth that, in the Atomic Age, a voluntary renunciation of national sovereignty is the only condition on which the nations can survive. It is not unreasonable to hope that mankind will be reasonable to this extent.

If this hope is fulfilled, human history will continue. But under what conditions will it continue? If our immediate problems are duly solved in this not 'impossible way, can mankind look forward to living happily ever after? Surely not—or, at least, not without continuing and constant effort; for change is of the essence of life, and the pace of change in human life in our time is being speeded up, to an unprecedented degree, by the accelerating progress of technology. No doubt it would be unwarrantable to forecast that technology's current progress, at its current rate of acceleration, is going to continue *ad infinitum*. In the past there have been other spurts of technological progress; and, each time, these have run out into subsequent periods of comparative technological stagnation. The Neolithic Revolution was one such temporary spurt; the invention of metallurgy, writing, and large-scale water-control at the dawn of civilization was another. Our present spurt, in its turn, may peter out eventually. At present, however, it shows no sign of slackening its pace; it would be imprudent not to reckon that its present accelerating advance is going to continue for as far into the future as we can see ahead; and, so long as this revolutionary technological change does continue, it is going to go on bringing revolutionary social change with it, as it is bringing this now.

The only way for us to arrest our social revolution would be to arrest our technological revolution, and, theoretically, this choice is open to us. Technological progress is not an automatic process; it is a deliberate and a consciously designed human activity; and Man is free to reverse this man-made movement; we are free to choose technological regress instead. However, our freedom of choice in this sphere is most unlikely to be exercised in favour of economic regress, as has been indicated by the Mahatma Gandhi's experience.

Gandhi wanted to extricate India from the trammels of the world-encompassing civilization of the modern West; he realized that this would require the severing of the nexus between India and the West that had been created by India's adoption of modern Western technology; he therefore advocated a return to hand-spinning and hand-weaving; and he set a personal example by doing a daily stint of this himself. Here, however, Gandhi met with his only big rebuff. On this technological issue the Indian people proved unwilling to follow his lead. It was natural, of course, that his policy did not commend itself to the Indian textile manufacturers in Bombay and in Gandhi's own home-city, Ahmadabad. These Indian industrialists had succeeded, under the shield of a tariff, in capturing from Lancashire the Indian market for machine-made cotton goods. They were not going to go out of business, even for Gandhi's sake; and it was they who were financing Gandhi's political campaign. It is more significant that the line taken by the Indian cotton-goods-manufacturers was also taken by the Indian people at large. The price of adopting Gandhi's technological policy would have been a reduction in the Indian people's already almost intolerably low standard of living on the material plane; and this was a sacrifice that the Indian people were unwilling to make. They could not bear to buy liberation from Western-style technology at this cost; and, when the Indians have refused to do this, it is certain that the same refusal to adopt Gandhi's technological policy will be made by all other sections of the human race. Traditionally, India has been perhaps the least technological-minded of all the seats of a spiritually high civilization; and, when India has hung back, it is inconceivable that America will take the plunge. The Americans are still revolutionaries in the technological field; they eagerly welcome any technological innovation as being something that is intrinsically good in itself; and, though they have not yet acknowledged the truth that it is impossible to combine technological radicalism with social conservatism, they will undoubtedly opt for technological progress, even at the price of social revolution, when the march of events compels them to face, and make, the choice. Technology is the magic mill that grinds out wealth and power; and human beings rush to buy wealth and power at almost any price.

Thus it is highly improbable that Man will deliberately arrest his technological advance; and, meanwhile, technology is already producing revolutionary social effects. It is producing a population explosion, global urbanization, and consequent congestion; it is producing mechanization, regimentation, and consequent boredom; and it is producing an affluence that is going to bring with it a dearth of amenities combined with an abundance of leisure. The social and spiritual effects of these consequences of technological progress are the subject of the present part of this book.

The cause of the current population explosion has been considered in Chapter III, and it has been noted there that the explosion will inevitably continue till the backward majority of mankind has adopted family-planning to offset the already achieved reduction in its death-rate. We do not know how long the process of self-re-education is going to take among the backward majority. We may forecast that they will eventually give up the habit of breeding up to the limit—ancient and intimate though this habit is. After all, any habit can be given up, and this particular habit has been given up already by the advanced minority, as has already been noted. What we cannot forecast is the length of time that it will take for the majority to make the change that the minority has made already. While the majority is in process of changing its habit, the World's population will continue to soar. We must reckon with the possibility that it will have trebled or quadrupled in size before its movement is brought into equilibrium again all over the World.

This huge prospective increase in the World's population raises two questions: How are the additional mouths to be fed and where are the planet's additional inhabitants to go?

The first question is the easier to answer. It has been suggested in Chapter III that science will be capable of feeding a world-population of this vastly increased size, and of feeding it up to the standard attained by the minority of the World's present population that is adequately fed today, if only Nationalism permits science to deal with the whole surface of the planet as a single unit for the purposes of producing food and distributing it. This global scale of operation will be indispensable, because the areas of maximum food-production will be those in which population-growth will be at its minimum. Already, since the Second World War, the application of science to agriculture in the advanced countries has enabled these to produce much greater quantities of food per acre by the work of many fewer hands than ever before. Moreover, these particular acres are above the World's average in natural fertility; for most of the advanced countries lie in the temperate zones, and it is there that the best soils are to be found. At the same time, these are the countries that have been the first to bring the movement of their population back into equilibrium through a reduction of their birth-rate. In consequence, these countries are now producing a great and growing surplus of food, over and above their own requirements, for which there is not, at present, any effective economic demand.

This inability to sell their food surplus at a profit is a present embarrassment for these countries, but it is a piece of good fortune for the World, for this unmarketable food is desperately needed to fill the mouths of the hungry majority of mankind.

This already hungry majority is the part of mankind in which the population explosion is at its maximum and in which a recovery of equilibrium is still beyond the horizon. Moreover, this now rapidly increasing hungry majority lives largely in the tropics, where the soils are poorer, on the average, than they are in the temperate zones, so that, even if and when science is eventually applied systematically to agriculture here too, the consequent increase in the yield per acre will not be so great as it has been in Iowa and in France. The surplus produced in France and Iowa will have to be conveyed to Indian and Chinese mouths, and this humanitarian transaction will create a financial problem which will call for the mobilization of the united financial resources of mankind. Even if the financial as well as the political problem is solved, science will still have a formidable food-deficit to make up; but, so long as it is not baffled by political impediments, we may expect, as has been suggested in Chapter III, to see science rise to the occasion. It is less difficult to foresee how these additional thousands of millions of human beings are going to be fed than it is to foresee where they are to go. Agricultural science is already equal to feeding them if it is given the chance, but the disposal of them will be a matter of social engineering, and this human art is still in its infancy. We can foresee that these new thousands of millions are going to pour into the cities. There will be nowhere else for them to go. But what is going to happen to them there?

In all quarters of the World, advanced and backward alike, the cities are now growing on a scale and at a pace that already foreshadow a future in which the now still separate cities will all have coalesced into one global megalopolis. This world-wide process of urbanization is the effect of several causes, some of them technological, some economic, some psychological.

The technological cause of urbanization is operating the most powerfully in the advanced countries. As a result of technological progress, the labour of a smaller and smaller percentage of the population in these countries is now required for feeding the rest and producing a local surplus into the bargain. In the United States, for example, only 5 per cent. of the population is engaged in agriculture today. The other 95 per cent. are not wanted on the land and must seek their livelihood in some urban occupation. If one travels about the countryside in Iowa, one receives an ocular demonstration of what has been happening. On the farms that are still going concerns, the workshops and hangars that surround the farm-house look more like an industrial plant than like an old-fashioned farmer's barns and stables, and one is astonished to see this equipment making it possible for one man, single-handed, to cultivate from 450 to 600 acres. Perhaps half, or even two-thirds, of these acres that are now being cultivated by one of the surviving farmers constituted separate farms a generation ago, when the average size of an Iowa farm was only 260 acres. This antediluvian age has left memorials of itself in the abandoned farmhouses of the farmers who had not the capital or the education or the enterprise or the energy to stay the course when the minimum economic size for an Iowa farm shot up and when success in farming came to require elaborate and expensive equipment and the technical skill for using it. The children of those former farmers are now growing up in the towns—to lead a less happy life there than the rural life that had been lived by their ancestors since the dawn of the Neolithic Age. The Iowa countryside is a stricken field today. If the surviving farmers' workshops are trophies of victory, the eliminated farmers' derelict houses are the casualities of defeat. The same spectacle confronts one in Australia. The 'outback', which produces the wool and wheat that are Australia's riches, is today an almost empty land. An overwhelming majority of the population of Australia is huddled together in five big cities.

The economic cause of urbanization is operating the most powerfully in the backward countries. The subsistence farming that is still prevalent here could not adequately support the rural population even at the figure at which it stood before the population explosion began. If the additional millions in this part of the World were to remain on the land, they would starve for certain, so they are flocking into the cities, though there is no guarantee that they will not starve there too. In these backward countries, urbanization and industrialization are running a grim race with each other, in which the survival of an ever increasing percentage of the population is at stake.

The psychological cause of urbanization is operating in all

parts of the World; for the city exercises an attraction on the sophisticated and the unsophisticated alike.

One receives an ocular demonstration of the lure of the city at Arequipa in South-Eastern Peru, half way up from the coast towards the top of the Andean plateau. Arequipa stands in an oasis which has been created by irrigation and which is cultivable only so far as the water-supply suffices. Where the water gives out, the desert begins, and the supply is strictly limited; there is not water for irrigating even one field more. Moreover, Arequipa has no non-agricultural resources of any consequence except the workshops of the Southern Railway. The city itself is in scale with its irrigated countryside, but today this city is besieged by an encircling shanty-town. The squatters here have no prospect of finding any remunerative employment in Arequipa; yet they squat on in the blind conviction that, now that they have reached the dazzling city, an earthly paradise is just round the corner. The local authorities beg them to return to their farms on the high plateau. Many of them own land there which could and did support them in the past. Many of them have not alienated their highland property, and they could, if they chose, go back, any day, to live on it again. Nevertheless, the authorities' representations fall on deaf ears. The squatters' golden dream eclipses the sordid reality of the slum-life that they have voluntarily embraced.

A similar shanty-town surrounds Baghdad. Here, as at Arequipa, the squatters come from the countryside; and the flight of these 'Irāqī peasants from the land is still more perverse than the flight of the Quechuas. The Andean plateau is bleak, and the farmer's life there is arduous. On the other hand, the 'Irāqī peasant is heir to a countryside that, during its first four thousand years of utilization, has been as productive as Egypt, and that is capable of becoming a second Egypt once again if and when its irrigation system is fully restored. The rural population of 'Irāq has a golden future ahead of it, if only it would hold on to its heritage and reap the benefits of the redevelopment of it that has already been put in train; for, in present-day 'Irāq, in contrast to present-day Egypt, the rural population is still sparse in proportion to the countryside's potential productivity. Yet, rather than wait to gather in this ripening harvest, the 'Irāqī peasants are crowding into a shanty-town whose occupants have no future. They have sold their birthright for a will-o'-the-wisp. Like moths, they have been hypnotized by the city's garish lights.

In Baghdad and Arequipa and Chicago and the five big cities of Australia we have so many local nuclei of the future world-city, and we can already find previews of megalopolis itself. The north-eastern section of the United States is fast coagulating into one ward of megalopolis in which soon there will be no open country left between Boston, Mass., and Washington, D.C. At the opposite corner of the country, Los Angeles is swelling to the dimensions of a sub-continent. The immensity of the change of scale to megalopolis from a city-state can be measured in present-day Greece at Athens. The Acropolis, that once dominated the city and the countryside beyond, is now smothered in another ward of megalopolis that has surged over the surrounding mountains, and on over other ranges farther afield, and that is threatening to catch the whole of Greece in the tentacles of the speedways that radiate out from modern Athens, northward and westward. It is an awesome and a desolating sight to see the noble features of Greece being obliterated by the proliferation of puny Man. The skylines of the mountains of Greece, and the lights and shadows that play on hill and plain, have given this country a beauty that has been all its own from time immemorial and that has seemed inviolable in the past. This beauty is being violated today.

Megalopolis's devastation of Greece has been surpassed by its devastation of Japan. In the cultivable and habitable part of Japan (which is, of course, the smaller part), megalopolis is already an accomplished fact. In the Japanese lowlands today, streets and houses are the rule and fields are the exception. This inversion of the relative extent of the components of the historic landscape has been brought about at high speed. In 1956 I did not recognize the landscape at the Shimonoseki Straits, which I had seen previously in 1929. Streets and houses and power-lines had obliterated the winding foot-paths and flowery hedges with which I had fallen in love there only twenty-seven years back. Since the date of the building of the first city of Jericho the exceptionalness of the city has been symbolized by the city wall, which has marked off this singular huddle of human beings from the normal open country consisting of the surrounding fields and of the endless wilderness beyond. Today the exceptional patch of the Earth's surface is not the city; it is the park or green belt; and this now has to be fenced in to prevent the boundless megalopolis from engulfing it.

Though a majority of mankind still consists, even now, of subsistence-farming peasants, a time can be foreseen at which even an industrialized farmer of the up-to-date Iowa kind will have become as rare as the artisan and trader of Ur or Nippur was 5,000 years ago. For mankind as a whole, urban life is now going to become the rule, and this revolutionary change of social environment is going to require a no less revolutionary psychological adjustment on the part of human nature. By now, we human beings have been farmers and shepherds for about 9,000 years; we have been food-gatherers and hunters for about 900,000 years before that; but, for the rest of the time during which this planet will continue to be habitable by Man, we are going to have to live in megalopolis; and this urban stage of human history is going to be by far the longest; the scientists estimate that mankind, if it does not liquidate itself, has 2,000,000,000 years of life on Earth ahead of it. Two thousand million years of life in megalopolis! Is it possible to make this ordeal endurable?

To be waifs and strays in megalopolis is a bewildering and terrifying experience for all of us. On the night of Hallowe'en, 1964, my wife and I were having our dinner with friends in Denver, Colorado, and, according to custom, children came knocking at the door for 'tricks and treats'. One seven-year-old child came in tears. His misery was pathetic. It turned out that his family had driven in to Denver that day from a small country town in Wyoming. They had parked their car, and had thoughtlessly sent the child out to knock at the doors round the block. This was the first time in his life that the child had ever found himself in a big city. He had lost touch with the car, and here he was in megalopolis, alone. The effect on him of this experience was shattering. For me, he symbolizes a whole generation of foundlings in a city that is going to be world-wide. If God is going to be as compassionate towards us, in this plight, as my hosts were that evening towards that poor child, we shall be lucky.

To be catapulted into megalopolis straight out of Arcadia is to be given a shock that may turn an innocent countryman into an urban criminal lunatic. This was borne in on me when I was once hovering, in a helicopter, over the interior of Puerto Rico. From only a few hundred feet up, I was looking down at a choppy sea of jungle-covered hills with, here and there, a tiny clearing, containing just one cottage and one corn-patch. If I had been born and brought up in one of these secluded tropical homesteads, out of sight and hearing of the rush and roar of the modern urban world, how should I have felt if, under the spur of economic pressure, I had suddenly been transported to the East Side of New York City? Might I not have lost my moral bearings when, like a palm tree caught in a hurricane, I had been torn up from my social roots? I now understood why, in New York, some of the Puerto Rican immigrants make awkward neighbours for the better-acclimatized older inhabitants. I also appreciated the wisdom of the Puerto Rican Government's policy of seeking to create industrial employment at home for the redundant rural population of the island by offering to United States corporations attractive financial inducements to set up branch-factories in Puerto Rico. It might not be easy for a Puerto Rican peasant to accustom himself to living and working in San Juan; but the transition from agricultural to industrial work would at least be less upsetting for him if he were given the opportunity of making it without having to leave his native shores.

But how is the Puerto Rican peasant, and how are we, to make urban life tolerable for ourselves when San Juan, as well as Princeton, N.J., and Los Angeles and Athens, has been engulfed in the world-wide city of the future? Our most urgent task is to rescue mankind from the shanty-towns, like those now encompassing Arequipa and Baghdad, in which more and more millions of human beings are being dumped like worn-out cars on a mammoth-size rubbish heap. Happily, this sordid menace to life, liberty, and the pursuit of happiness has already evoked some creative planning and building which gives hope for the future.

On my first visit to Calcutta and Karachi after the partition of the former British Indian Empire, I was horrified at the misery in which the millions of 'displaced persons' were living (if such existence can be called life) in the slums of these two cities. On my next visit to Karachi, not many years later, I found that the shanty-towns among the mangrove swamps had been cleared away and that their former occupants had been re-housed. The site of this rehousing had been, in its virgin state, a bare dry desert which, in its own way, had been as forbidding to look at as the swamps, though it was, of course, not pestilential but salubrious. I now found this former desert clothed, as far as the eye could see, in a cluster of new satellite cities. The brick-work was simple (Pakistan has no money to spare for luxury building), but the result that had been achieved at a minimum cost in terms of money was satisfying in terms of human needs. Each of the new cities had been articulated into a number of distinct hamlets, and each of these hamlets had been kept within a human size—that is to say, within a size that would allow the inhabitants to be personally acquainted with their neighbours. Each hamlet had its own store, school, mosque, and wash-house, and all these public facilities were within walking dis-tance of the people's new homes. As a result, the displaced per-sons' lives had been re-humanized. They had not, it is true, been repatriated to their original homes, but they had been rescued from the shanty-town and had been rehoused in circumstances in which they were evidently striking new roots.

Who, I asked, had planned these inspiriting new cities for the Pakistani Government? The designer, I was told, was Mr. C. A. Doxiadis of Athens, Greece. I was eager to meet the man who had done so human a service for so many human beings in distress; and, when I did meet him in Athens, later on, my first question to him was: 'Mr. Doxiadis, how did you discover what the living-conditions are that give displaced persons a chance of making a new start in life?'—'I did not have to discover this,' Mr. Doxiadis replied; 'I knew it by experience, because I grew up with the problem. I and my family are displaced persons our-selves. My father was a doctor in the former Greek community in the town of Stanimaka in Bulgaria.' Mr. C. A. Doxiadis and his brothers had, in fact, to make a new start in life in Greece. Mr. C. A. Doxiadis has responded to this challenge by inventing a new profession and by using the experience and resources that this has given him for founding a new science—or rather, a new art. His profession is truly a new one; for 'town-planning', in the former rather perfunctory meaning of the term, would be an inadequate name for it. While Mr. Doxiadis has planned for Karachi and for Philadelphia, Pennsylvania, he is also planning for megalopolis; and, with the population explosion and the depopulation of the countryside always in mind, he is planning, not just for the next decade, but for the next century. He is working out a configuration for megalopolis that will allow for continuous expansion without producing an intolerable congestion round a static centre. Mr. Doxiadis has named this new art of his 'ekistics'. This imaginative approach and long-term view open up for future generations a prospect of mastering megalopolis instead of being victimized by it.

Yet, however vigorously and skilfully the new art of ekistics may be developed by Mr. Doxiadis and his disciples, congestion, to a hitherto unknown degree, is bound to be the consequence of the imminent tripling or quadrupling of the size of our planet's population. We are fast moving into a so far barely imaginable new world in which the largest surviving open spaces will be the airports for supersonic aircraft. There will be no room left for traffic on the surface. Goods that are too heavy to be carried by air will have to be transported underground. There will be no room left, either, for agriculture on land; streets and houses will occupy every acre of terra firma. Food production, if not fibre production, will be driven out to sea. We shall exterminate the sharks, cat-fish, and other predatory marine wild life, and shall stock the sea with flocks of herrings and with herds of whales, as we are already stocking our lakes and rivers with edible fresh-water fish. Our iron ration will be domesticated plankton.

While travel on business will be on a greater scale than ever before, travel for pleasure will probably tail off. The incentive for sight-seeing will disappear in a standardized world; for what will a man gain by visiting the Antipodes when there will be nothing to be found there but the ubiquitous megalopolis that will have been his starting-point and his accompaniment *en route*? If restlessness still drives him to undertake a journey that can no longer minister to his curiosity, the public authorities will intervene. For, though aeroplanes will abound, what will they be among so many? The authorities will be chary of issuing travel-permits. 'Is your journey really necessary?' they will ask, as they asked in Britain during the Second World War. 'Need you travel in person?' they will add. 'Cannot you travel vicariously, instead, by using the telephone, telegraph, radio, or TV?' Except for strictly necessary business purposes—and these will whirl people round the globe in a trice—the inhabitant of megalopolis will be more and more rigorously confined within the bounds of his own human-size quarters of the regional ward. What kind of a life will he and his neighbours be able to make for themselves within these oppressively narrow physical limits?

XII

Mechanization, Regimentation, Boredom

Some measure of regimentation is the inescapable price of any degree of sociality, and our ancestors could hardly have succeeded in becoming human beings if they had not been social beings already. The food-gatherer's life is the least severely regimented life that mankind has lived so far. Yet, when we meet any of our now rare fellow human beings who are still living this primeval life, we find that they are far from being free men and women. Their social organization is elaborate and rigid, and the initiation rites that are obligatory for them at each stage of life are exacting to the point of being penal. Each of the successive economic revolutions that have followed each other at an ever faster tempo in the course of the last 9,000 years, and that have, each time, bestowed greater affluence on mankind, have had to buy this boon at the cost of additional turns of the screw that has been clamping regimentation down upon us. The farmer and the nomadic herdsman are less free than the food-gatherer and the hunter. (The nomadic herdsman looks like a free man by comparison with the farmer, whose way of making his living roots him in his fields; but here appearances are deceptive; the nomadic herdsman's seasonal migrations between summer and winter pastures are practicable only if he submits to a discipline as strict as that of a professional army on the march.) The urban artisan and trader are less free than the farmer and the herdsman; and this gradual turning of the screw of regimentation has been speeded up since the advent of mechanization.

Mechanization means the replacement of the use of human and animal muscle-power by harnessing the inanimate forces of nature, which dwarf the physical power of any living creature in both potency and scale. Mechanization is now about 5,000 years old; for wind-power was harnessed at the dawn of civilization for the propulsion of ships, as an alternative to the muscle-power of oarsmen. Water-power was harnessed about 2,000 years ago. But it was not till 200 years ago that mechanization got up steam, and it is more recently still that the harnessing of steam-power has been followed by the harnessing of electricity-power, mineral-oil-power, and atomic power.

This progressive increase, through mechanization, in the potency of the material power commanded by Man has necessitated a proportionate increase in the regimentation of human life, and this for several reasons. The more high-powered our machinery is, the more dangerous it is to life and limb, the greater the care and the precision that are required for operating it, the greater its cost and therefore the greater the economic pressure to get the most lucrative possible performance out of it, and, finally, the greater the scale of its operations. Each of these aspects of high-powered machinery calls for greater human discipline on a larger social scale; and the scale and discipline tend to set the stamp of the machine on the life of the machine-tenders. In contrast to a human being or a domesticated animal, machinery is impersonal. It is true, as has been noted in Chapter VIII, that an element of impersonalness entered into human life already when, at the dawn of civilization, the size of human societies grew beyond the point at which a society could be held together by personal relations. The earliest use to which the art of writing was put was to serve as a medium for impersonal relations. It was used to compile lists of commodities and personnel, to record contracts, and to compose those official 'forms' that descend upon us in such quantities in our time. In our social life since then, personal relations have been supplemented, and overshadowed, by impersonal institutions that can hold together human beings who have never met each other, and never will meet each other, face to face. This impersonal element has always been present in civilization. The social effect of the recent progress of mechanization has, however, enormously strengthened and accelerated this previously existing tendency.

The scale of operations that our advancing mechanization now demands, and the cost of operations on this scale, are now too great to be within an individual human being's capacity. The Iowa farmer who still manages to own and operate a farm personally by means of mechanization is a lonely survivor from the vanished age of individual private enterprise, and even he cannot expect to survive much longer, in spite of his techno- logical and commercial prowess. He is doomed to be replaced by an impersonal corporation, and the corporation in its turn is doomed to become first the pensioner, then the creature, and finally one of the departments of a still more massive impersonal institution, the state. The structure of society that is presupposed in the Constitution of the United States and in the United Kingdom's Parliamentary Reform Bill of 1832 is one in which the typical citizen is a man who, on the economic level, is his own master. He is the farmer who owns his farm and stock, the storekeeper who owns his store and goods, and the professional man who charges a fee to his clients for his services. Between then and now, the typical citizen has come to be an employee of a corporation or else of some local or national or international public authority. 'State the name of your employer' is the first demand that is made nowadays on any form issued by any authority for any purpose. Occasionally the draftsman of the form has remembered to add in a footnote: 'If you are self- employed, enter your private address in the space here provided.' Self-employed persons are unpopular with all public authorities, including those whose official ideology is Individualism, while private employers are popular, even with Socialist régimes. A self-employed person is likely to be a nuisance to the officials through being unversed in the regulations, whereas a corpora- tion can afford to employ, and finds it worthwhile to employ, experts in the regulations to deal with the public authorities, and these private experts can be constrained by the officials to do a good deal of the officials' work for them at the private employers' expense.

The trend towards regimentation in all fields within my life-time is symbolized, for me, in what has happened within my life-time on the roads. In the year 1899, when I was ten years old, I was at school in a village that was within a mile-and-a- quarter of the road from Dover to London, about halfway between Dover and Canterbury. I used this section of the London-Dover road as a convenient place for teaching myself to ride a (pedal-driven) bicycle. I spent hours on that road mounting, falling off into the thick layer of soft white dust that covered the road's surface, mounting again, and repeating the performance till I had acquired the art. If one of my grand-children were to try to learn to ride a bicycle on the same road today, she would be run down and killed before any of the traffic police had had time to order her off. In my day, of course, there were no traffic police, because there were no vehicles on the road that were capable of being a danger either to each other or to anyone else. During the hours that I spent on that road alternately mounting my bicycle and falling off it into the dust, I was passed by nothing more dangerous than a rare charabanc. The rest of the wheeled traffic, such as it was, consisted of farm-waggons, dog-carts, donkey-carts, and wheel-barrows. If a donkey-cart had collided with a wheelbarrow, the damage would probably have been slight. The slow average pace of that traffic was inefficient, but it was safe; and therefore anybody could do anything on the London-Dover road that he pleased—he could, for instance, learn to ride a bicycle on it, as I did. Since then the invention of mechanized vehicles has enormously speeded up the pace of the traffic, but this at the cost of proportionately increasing the risk. The public authori-ties have therefore had to step in. For safety's sake, they have had to deprive road-users of their former liberty. The traffic regulations grow ever stricter, and the penalties for violating them grow ever more severe; yet the toll of casualties continues to mount. This story of what has happened on the roads be-tween 1899 and 1965 is the story of what has been happening in every department of life.

Regimentation has been imposed by mechanization not only on human beings themselves but on the products of their work. Mechanization has benefited mankind by overcoming the former scarcity and dearness of material goods. Things that were once luxuries are now produced in abundance at a price payable by ordinary purses. The means by which this socially valuable result is achieved is an elaborate and expensive initial outlay on setting up a manufacturing plant. Goods that were formerly produced in small quantities and at a high cost by a man whose only capital equipment was a hammer and chisel are now mass-produced by a whole battery of machines in a factory. Thanks to this, ordinary people now get much of what was formerly within the reach of a rich minority only. Ordinary people now get much of this, but not the whole; for goods cannot be mass-produced without being standardized. What is lacking to machine-made goods is the former hand-made goods' variety. The individual artisan could vary his product to meet the wishes of the individual customer. At the cost of being expensive, hand-made products could be adaptable. The machine, on the other hand, could not do its job of being prolific if it were capable, as a human worker is, of being 'a respecter of persons'; and, though this may be a vice in God or in a judge or in a civil servant, it is a virtue in an artist and would be a virtue in a machine, if a machine were capable of being the artist that its predecessor the artisan used to be.

Mechanization and regimentation and standardization have a psychological price, as well as a social and an aesthetic one. Their psychological price is boredom. It is boring to earn more and more money more and more easily by being employed to do more and more rigidly standardized work for a smaller and smaller number of hours in the week. In a completely mechanized economy, the work by which a human being makes his living is divorced from the zest without which our lives are not worth living and would, indeed, be unlivable. The machine-tender has to find his zest, outside his working hours, in 're-creation'; and this word itself is significant. It is an admission that something vital has been taken out of a human being by his work and therefore has to be put back into him in his leisure hours. 'Recreation' is like the artificial 'enrichment' of bread after the flour from which it has been made has been impoverished by being put through milling machinery that grinds too effectively to be efficient for its ultimate purpose, which is not just to grind but is to produce flour that will be nutritious.

This psychological sterilization of work is a new evil that mechanization has inflicted on mankind. Zest and work have never been entirely divorced from each other before. The food-gatherer's way of making his living is exciting because it is precarious. If he does not find a nest of grubs or a cluster of berries today, he may die of starvation tomorrow: so his day's research work is enlivened by hopes and fears and by corresponding thrills and pangs. The fascination of hunting and fishing is notorious; and even the farmer's relatively prosaic activities are, for him, entrancing. The capriciousness of Nature

keeps the farmer on tenterhooks. Will he be able to finish gar-
nering his harvest before the rain comes? Will his orange-crop
survive the frost unseared? Will his cow's coming calf be a bull
or a heifer? Will its colour be white or red? These uncertainties
are pleasurable for him just because they are also tormenting.
Such pleasures are denied to a factory-worker whose job is to
repeat the same streamlined motions, any number of times over,
as any number of specimens of the same standardized part of
some machine pass before him on a conveyor-belt that revolves
for twenty-four hours in the day in an atmosphere in which
the degree of the temperature and of the humidity is regulated
automatically. It is not surprising that the bored factory-
worker's 'recreation' in his leisure hours sometimes takes the
form of anti-social violence and destructiveness. This irrational
behaviour can be explained rationally, even if the victim of
mechanization is himself unaware of the reason why he is running amok. He is taking his revenge on society for an injury
that society has done to him; and this injury is a serious one.
In mechanizing his work, society has made the salt of his life
lose its savour for him. It has done to him, in fact, something like
what Tacitus, in a work cited in Chapter V, has pointed out that
the Augustan Peace did to the Roman art of public speaking.
When society is thoroughly well regulated, life becomes dull and
uninspiring.

XIII

Affluence and Leisure

The accelerating advance of technology is carrying us towards a novel state of society. Everyone is going to find himself in a position that has been enjoyed, hitherto, only by a privileged minority that has virtually monopolized the amenities of civilization since the dawn of civilization about 5,000 years ago. The abundance of money and leisure, which has been at the disposal of this minority in the past, is now going to be at the disposal of the masses. We are all going to be paid high wages for working for only a few hours in the week on rigidly standardized jobs. In the economically advanced countries this new economic régime is already within sight; but we can also anticipate an age in which affluence and leisure will have descended upon all the rest of mankind as well. Man is, among other and more important things, 'homo faber'. Human nature has an innate aptitude for technology; and, while it is true that creative technological inventions have been made at only a few times and places so far, it is also true that, when once they have been made somewhere by someone, they are not difficult for other people to master and to adopt. All technological inventions that have been made hitherto have spread widely over the face of the globe in the course of time, and the new mechanized form of technology is spreading faster today than any earlier form of it, thanks to the revolutionary improvement in means of communication which this mechanized technology has already achieved.

Thus we can look forward to seeing everyone in the World endowed with money and leisure sooner or later. But, when all mankind has them, all mankind will not be able to benefit by them as the privileged minority has benefited hitherto, so long as the majority has still been having to earn its living by hard daily work. To extend a privilege to everyone is tantamount to withdrawing it from everyone. When everyone has plenty of money, everyman's money will not be able to buy the amenities that money has bought for the privileged minority in the past. Everyman's money will not even be able to buy necessities; for everyone else will have plenty of money too; so why should anyone any longer be willing to work overtime during the five days of leisure in the week, when the two working days will bring him in more money than he will now be able to use? And what will people do with their five vacation days, when everyone else will be on vacation simultaneously, so that there will be no one left on duty to provide holiday-makers with amusements?

The sabbath day's rest has been an opportune institution for an industrial society. The hardest-working farmer or shepherd is saved from being worked to death by the dependence of his work on the rhythm of Nature, with its alternating spurts and pauses. Homo mechanicus has made himself independent of Nature by enslaving himself, instead, to machines that are capable of keeping him at work unceasingly. Only a man-made pause can give the factory-worker and the office-worker the respite that they need. For them, therefore, an arbitrary black-out of one day in the week is a boon. Even the two days' black-out which is customary in advanced countries now is a timely offset to the increasingly hectic tempo of mechanized life, though this two days' black-out has perceptibly slowed down the World's work—particularly any kind of work that involves correspondence. However, the reduction of the number of weekly working days through mechanization is not going to stop at the present point. We can foresee a time, not far ahead, when not only factories, offices, and post-offices, but restaurants, theatres, cinemas, hotels, banks, stores, hospitals, chemists' shops, and clinics will be closed, not just for two days in the week, but for five.

Already one can get a preview of this impending world-wide dearth of amenities by visiting present-day Australia or New Zealand. On the door of a restaurant or a hotel dining-room in these two ultra-advanced countries you will find a notice warning you that 'dinner service stops at 6.30 p.m. *sharp*'; and sharp is the word; for, if you present yourself at 6.33, you will have to wait to be fed till next morning. You may have arrived, exhausted, after having flown halfway round the globe. Your late arrival will have been the pilot's fault, or the weather's, not yours; but no plea will win you pity or indulgence. The 6.30 rule is one of the trades-union regulations, and these are as immutable as the laws of the Medes and Persians. In Australia and New Zealand it is not only inadvisable to arrive even three minutes after closing hours at a restaurant; it is also imprudent to fall sick or to die between 6.00 p.m. on a Friday evening and 9.00 a.m. on a Monday morning. If you fall sick between those hours, you may get no medical attention; and, if, in consequence, you die, you will certainly not be able to get yourself buried till Monday comes. Translate this meticulous two days' black-out into a five days' one, and you have the world of the future—a world in which, thanks to the progress of mechanization, everyone is going to have time and money on his hands. Even if the workers' two-day stints are staggered to cover all seven days of the week, they will cover them so thinly that the affluent world will still be a most inconvenient and uncomfortable world to live in.

Technology is proving as malicious as the gods were when they granted foolish Midas' prayer that whatever he touched might turn to gold. This magic 'golden touch' threatened Midas with immediate starvation. His food duly turned to gold in his fingers before he could carry the inedible metal to his mouth, and food that has turned to gold is as useless for food's purpose as gold is for gold's purpose if gold cannot be exchanged for food or for any other goods or services. In Australia and New Zealand you become conscious of the number and the importance of the things that money can no longer buy. It cannot buy domestic service, of course, and this is no grievance; even in rather less advanced countries, money can no longer buy that. It is more serious when money cannot buy the help without which a man cannot operate a productive economic enterprise. In one of the eastern states of Australia in 1956, I spent a weekend with the owner and operator of a large and profitable cattle-station. The stock and the pasture were fine; and the owner was rich. He had been a generous benefactor of the local university. But his money could not buy him the help of a second herdsman besides himself, however high the wages that he might offer. No one needed the job and no one wanted it. The station-owner himself was resolute and hard-working. Every morning at 6 a.m. he rode the rounds, rain or fine. But he was now in his sixties, and so was his wife. How much longer would they be able to carry on their strenuous productive life unaided? And, if and when old age at last constrained them to retire, what would become of the cattle and the pasture? The couple had more than enough money to retire on any day; but, when they did retire, Australia might lose a valuable piece of the productive side of her economy.

In retirement, this couple would find it as difficult to spend their money on meeting their needs as they were finding it while they were still at work. How would they spend their leisure if they were to live on into the imminent age in which the number of black-out days in the week would be, not two, but five?

Of course, there are some people for whom a black-out of even seven days in the week would present no problem. These are those happy few for whom leisure is an opportunity for work— the few who are spurred into working by a passion to create or by a passion to satisfy their curiosity or by an ambition to achieve power or even merely fame. For such people, the lengthening of the average expectation of life, thanks to modern medical skill, is derisorily meagre, considering the amount of the things that they are eager to accomplish. Their agenda is practically infinite; eternity itself would hardly suffice for carrying their agenda out. The most fortunate among them are the artists and the writers who do all their work with their own minds, and most of it with their own hands as well. These are almost independent of their neighbours' time-tables. They can still go on doing their own work for seven days in the week when their neighbours' working week has dropped to a two-day stint. Less fortunate, because less autarkic, are the eager scientific researchers who need laboratory assistance and the ambitious politicians who need auditors and, if possible, constituents. Yet even they are less dependent on the economic régime of their time than the office-workers and the factory-workers are; for these must stop working when the office or the factory closes, whereas the candidate for the Presidency of the United States can and will work night and day for years on end in pursuit of his objective. Let us reckon the politicians and the scientists among the independents, and let us add them to the writers and the artists. Even so, when we have bracketed all these rare birds together, we have accounted for no more than an infinitesimal fraction of mankind. In the majority the psychological stimuli that move this minority to exert itself are feeble or dormant. We must therefore leave this happy minority out of account. Their exceptional freedom to contract out of the coming two days' working week does not contribute appreciably to the solution of the problem that five days of leisure in the week are going to present to ordinary mortals.

How to spend five non-working days on which none of your fellow human beings will be working to provide you with amusement? Well, in the age of mechanization, one's dose of amusement need not be taken 'live'; it can be taken 'potted'. The record can be reproduced on one's gramophone, without any other human beings having to be mobilized for the purpose at the moment. Moreover, this 'potted' amusement need not all be frivolous. No doubt, unaccustomed leisure and newfangled gadgets will be used frivolously, for the most part, at first; but already we are being offered, through mechanical media, a modicum of more satisfying cultural fare in the shape of classical music, informative lectures, and discussions of current issues in which the conflicting views are fairly and instructively presented. Still, viewing and listening are passive ways of passing one's time. Human beings will hardly be satisfied with being perpetual spectators of the game of life without ever becoming players again. What openings, if any, for action will the affluent society offer?

One opening will be offered to everyone by everyone's unwillingness to do the World's work, now that economic pressure will not constrain anyone to do more than his weekly two days' stint of work of the kinds that can be standardized and mass-produced. To mend shoes or to clean watches by this method seems likely to be beyond the power of even the most refined and most ingenious automation. Accordingly, cobblers and watch-repairers will become extinct; and then, when one's shoe wears down at the heel or one's watch gets a piece of grit into its works, one's only economic recourse will be to throw this pair of shoes or this watch away and buy a new one. This lavish alternative to the ancient expedient of getting things repaired will be economically sound in the Age of Affluence. We shall all have enough money in our pockets to pay for it. Indeed, to begin with, we may even be glad to get rid of some of our money in this way, since we shall 'have money to burn'. However, the sport of 'burning money' will probably soon grow stale, and it will also do little towards helping us to burn our leisure, which will weigh as heavily as our money will on our idle hands. Sooner or later, therefore, it may occur to us that, though it has now become impossible for us to get our shoes mended and our watches cleaned by paying someone else to do it, it is still possible for us to perform these services for ourselves. After all, we shall have five days in the week for teaching ourselves, and then practising, the cobbler's and the watch-cleaner's arts. So, instead of letting these ancient arts fall out of use, we shall transfer them from the economic realm, in which work will still be done for pay during two days in the week, to the recreational realm, in which, for the other five days in the week, we shall be free to practise these useful arts as amateurs 'for love'.

While the useful arts are likely to be the first field in which we shall find some active way of occupying our leisure, it seems probable that we shall not be content to limit our amateur activities to these; for there are also the fine arts, which have been cultivated since the Upper Palaeolithic Age and have been pursued intensively since the dawn of civilization. The beauty of the works of art that have been created within these last 5,000 years takes our breath away each time that some new cache of them is disinterred by our present-day archaeologists. We are having to rely more and more on the archaeologists to remind us of this creative form of human activity, since, in our time, it is fast becoming extinct. One of the ironies of the affluent society is that it is too rich to be able any longer to afford to pay for the creation of beautiful things. Human labour has become so expensive that it is now not economic to hire it for any work except standardized mass-production; and standardization irons the beauty out of the mass-product. If you want to find works of art that are still being created for sale, you have now to go to some relatively secluded country—a mountain-fastness, say, such as Ethiopia or Afghanistan—where a mellow civilization is combined with a backward economy and where wages are therefore still low because the cost of living there is still cheap. But these relics of unmechanized life are evaporating, as one 'developing' country after another achieves its ambition of becoming a 'developed' one.

Is man-made beauty doomed, then, to disappear from the face of the Earth during the last 2,000,000,000 years of Man's presence here? Fortunately not. What is doomed is only the creation of works of art for pay instead of for love, and this is not a bad thing; it is a good thing. It is a good thing because the beauty of the paid-for works of art has been marred by the brand on it of social injustice. These ancient works of art were not created for the benefit of everyone, and, above all, not for the benefit of their creators. They were produced for the benefit of a privileged minority which misused its privilege by exploiting the majority, artists included, economically. We cannot be sorry that works of art should now cease to be created on these inequitable conditions. We can, and surely shall, do with the fine arts what we are going to do with the useful arts. We shall do with them what President Roosevelt did, during the Second World War, with the products of the United States that were shipped to Britain under the 'lease-lend' dispensation. We shall expunge the dollar sign from the transaction. One cannot commission works of art for purchase without 'sweating' other people's labour. 'Sweated' labour is the only labour that is cheap enough for creating, on an economic basis, works of art that ought to be 'labours of love', but that can be created only by men and women who 'live laborious days'. One will live laboriously by compulsion if one is constrained by economic pressure; but one can also live laboriously by choice, out of love for the act of creation. 'Do it yourself' for your own delectation during your five days a week of leisure, instead of doing if for someone else at a 'sweated' wage, which is the inequitable way in which works of art have mostly been produced in the past. In the Age of Mechanization, 'do it yourself' will be the talismanic formula for inspiration. We shall paint pictures, chase silver, and carve wood and marble for love, besides mending our own shoes for love and cleaning our own watches for it.

The creation of works of art for love will be the affluent society's first step towards saving human souls from the occupational psychoses of wealth and leisure. This will redeem our days of leisure from the curse of boredom and will re-animate them with the zest that will have ebbed out of our paid work when we are being paid for working at the conveyor-belt for two days in the week. But is art enough to give significance and purpose to life? Can we, and should we, practise 'art for art's sake'? When we ask ourselves this question, we remember how recent the coining of the slogan is. Traditionally, art has not been practised for its own sake. Even the privileged patrons of the 'sweated' artists of the past did not commission the artists' works merely for the patrons' personal and private pleasure.

Traditionally, works of art have usually been commissioned for the service of religion. The Pyramids, the Parthenon, and Giotto's paintings on the walls of the church at Assisi were all commissioned, not for art's sake, but for the glory of God. We may justifiably find fault with the patrons of the creators of these wonderful works. We may convict those patrons of having been either hypocrites or self-deceivers. The god Pharaoh who immortalized himself in a pyramid was in truth only a man, and that an egotist. Pericles was misappropriating trust funds contributed by Athens' allies when he used these for glorifying the Athenian people's collective power by building-operations that put pay into the Athenian workman's pocket. Brother Elias was prostituting beauty to the service of publicity. He was 'selling' the Franciscan Order to a materialist-minded world by repudiating his master Francis's espousal of holy poverty. In these notorious cases, and in many others besides, the patrons' motives have been impure. At the same time they have not been wholly worldly. In being moved by mixed motives, Pharaoh and Pericles and Elias were behaving as the morally imperfect creatures that all we human beings are. In them, too, the concern for the glory of God was partly sincere; and a sincere concern for Man's quest for the ultimate spiritual presence behind the phenomena of the Universe has been the principal inspiration of the greatest works of art throughout the ages.

This traditional dedication of art to religion suggests that the true end of art is not 'art for art's sake' and that the true end of Man is not art but is religion. This has always been Man's true end since our ancestors became human. The quest for ultimate spiritual reality is inborn in human nature. In the past, some human beings have eagerly embraced this common birthright of ours, while others have sought to be quit of it. We are now moving into an age in which it will be more difficult to ignore the truth. In this coming age of mechanization, atomic power, affluence, and leisure, religion will surely come into its own as the one boundless field for freedom and for creativity that is open for the unlimited aspirations of human nature.

This is a hard saying for modern Western Man. It is perhaps an even harder one for the non-Western intelligentsia that has been remoulding itself in Western Man's image. During the last three centuries, Western Man has been putting more and more of his treasure into another quest which is also as old as humanity. He has been concentrating on the perennial human enterprise of mastering non-human nature. He has now deliberately turned his attention outward towards the material facet of the Universe. He has allowed his human gift for spiritual contemplation to grow rusty through disuse. It will be painful and terrifying for him to reverse the modern tide of Western life and to look inward again. It will be painful to resume the use of a faculty that has been out of action for so long. This will also be terrifying; for, when Western Man does look inward again, he will be facing himself and, beyond himself, will be facing 'the dweller in the innermost'. This is a vision from which modern Western Man has shied away. When he has found himself being led back towards it by some of the shattering experiences that he has brought upon himself, he has been seized with panic and has sought escape, like Jonah, by fleeing from God to the ends of the Earth. He has redoubled the impetus of his external activities—grinning like a dog and running about through the city,[1] in the futile hope that even aimless outward action may make him immune against a spiritual experience that might carry him whither he would not.[2]

Fortunately, this distraught mood of modern Western Man's is both recent and abnormal. It would have surprised his medieval ancestors, as it surprises his Hindu contemporaries in so far as the modern Hindus have not become infected with the modern Westerner's psychosis. St. Thomas or Shankara would have asked why it was necessary to write a book—even a rather short book—to lead up to the statement of a truism. It would indeed be a truism to say that religion is the true end of Man if one were saying this to any representative of the human species except the modern Western one. However, modern Western Man

[1] Psalm 59, 6, in the Anglican Book of Common Prayer.   [2] John 21, 18.

is temporarily dominant; and therefore to remind him of his blind spot may not be a waste of ink and paper.

What are the prospects for the West and for our Westernizing World? Is Western and Westernizing Man likely to succeed in recovering the use of the human faculty for spiritual contemplation? If this faculty were to atrophy in use, we should forfeit our birthright of being human, and, in the Atomic Age, the course of our relapse into sub-human animality would certainly be 'nasty, brutish, and short'.[1] It is possible, however, that the human impulse to seek God may be ineradicable, however hard we may try to pluck it out and cast it from us. 'What is the chief and highest end of Man? Man's chief end is to glorify God and to enjoy Him for ever.' This question and answer do not come from any of the Hindu scriptures or from any medieval Western Christian theological work. They are the opening words of the shorter Westminster Catechism which was composed in 1648 and was adopted by the Calvinist Church of Scotland. In these words, modern Western Man is, in spite of himself, declaring the truth that he has been seeking to elude. He is giving evidence against himself; and this confession is a plea in his favour and is a hope for his redemption. To glorify God and to enjoy Him for ever is to partake of eternal life here and now, without waiting for Man's still unspent 2,000,000,000 years of life on Earth.

[1] Thomas Hobbes, *Leviathan*, Part I, Chapter 13.

INDEX

'Abbas, the Prophet Muhammad's uncle, 135–6
'Abbasid Caliphate, 93, 124, 126–7, 135–6
Abyssinia, 80, 147, 181, 223
Administration, 60, 63, 79
Advertisement, 170, 190, 191
Aegean basin, the, 72
Affluence, 201, 215–16, 218–27
Afghanistan, 223
Africa: East, 56, 80; North, 76, 80; North-West, 83; physical barriers to penetration of civilization in, 95; Tropical, 56, 83, 95; Union of South, 84, 143; West, 59
Agadé, 71, 117, 126
Agriculture, 4, 31, 37, 60, 61, 62–3, 94, 104–7, 162–3, 172, 202–3, 207, 210, 212, 213–14, 216–17, 219
Ahmadabad, 200
Akkad, 64–7, 82, 117
Akkadian language, the, 65
Alexander the Great, 83, 126
Alexandria, 76, 152
'Ali, Caliph, 135–6
Alphabets, 62, 65
Amaterasu, the Japanese sun-goddess, 134
Amazon, River, 95
Amenities, dearth of, in affluent world, 201, 219–20
America: Central, 142; Latin, 81, 143, 145; North, 151; see also UNITED STATES OF AMERICA
Americas, the: diasporás in, 83, 86; occupation of, by peoples from Old World, 57, 80, 144; opening up of, 95; pre-Columbian civilizations in, 62, 69, 83, 99, 156, 181; religion in, 77, 181
'Ammān, 178
Amorites, the, 117
Amun, the Theban (Egyptian) god, 185
Amun-Re, 133, 185
Anatolia, 64, 65, 72, 129
'Ancients' and 'moderns', dispute over relative merits of, 23
Andean Civilization, the, 83, 99, 184–5
Angevins, the, 131, 132
Animals, domesticated, 60, 61, 77–9, 94, 105, 106, 107, 172, 213

Anthropology, 13, 59, 89
Antioch, in Syria, 127
Antonine Age, the, 97
Arab Empire, the, 120–1, 123–4, 127, 186; see also 'ABBASID CALIPHATE; UMAYYAD CALIPHATE
Arabia, 80
Arabs, the, 73, 86, 119, 121
Aragon, 187
Aramaeans, the, 118
Aramaic language, the, 86, 152
Archaeology, 10–11, 22, 57, 59, 68, 93, 98, 144, 223
Architecture, 68
Arequipa, 205, 206, 208
Aristeides, Aelius, 120
Aristotle, 179, 195
Armaments, socialization of, 175
Armenians, the, 82, 86
Arsacid (Parthian) Empire, the, 126–7
Arts, the: beauty of works of art, 223–4; cave paintings, 22, 26; commissioning of artistic works for religious purposes, 225; creativity in, decline of, in affluent societies, 223; incommensurability of schools of art, 22, 23; flourishing of, in fractured structure of society, 91, 93; Mexican painting, 156; motifs of works of art, 68; production of works of art for payment or for love, 223–5; useful, 223, 224
Aryans, the, 145
Ashoka, the Maurya Emperor, 75, 103
Asia: Central, 77, 121; Eastern, 74, 75, 77, 143, 158; Pacific coast of, 83; South-East, 41, 74, 83; South-West, 65, 76, 77, 80, 82, 83, 94, 118, 152, 169, 189
Assisi, 225
Assyria, 49, 64, 65, 82, 117, 125, 126
Astronomy, 4, 8, 9, 20, 179
Atatürk, Mustafā Kemāl, 154, 155
Athena, the Greek olive-goddess, 106, 173
Athens (Greece), 38, 106, 111, 173, 206, 208, 209, 225
Atlantic Ocean, the, 41, 57, 78, 80, 95, 151
Atomic energy: discovery of technique for harnessing, 32, 35; peaceful use of, 34, 35; power generated by, 213, 226; waste, problem of, 35, 39, 46,

reactions against, in Roman Empire, 185, 190; recession of, in modern West, 169–70; repudiation of, by Nazis, 18–19; revelation, belief in, 165, 167, 180; schisms in, 84, 109, 161; social justice, neglect of, in Marx's time, 174; subversiveness of, from Roman Government's point of view, 122–3; totalitarian period in history of, 51–2, 92; uniqueness, claim to, 166, 167; valuation of human souls in, 174; *see also* names of Christian churches

Cicero, 93

Cimmerians, the, 118

City-states, 82, 83, 91, 93, 96, 98, 106–7, 141, 142, 149, 155, 172, 173

Civilization: distinctive features of, 62; divisive feeling increased at dawn of, 105; extension of benefits of, to majority of mankind, 35, 218–19; impersonal relations through institutions a feature of, 141–2; radiation of, beyond homeland, 65, 67, 69, 71–2, 78, 79, 80, 82, 151–3; religious and economic changes at dawn of, 62–3, 106–8; surplus of food-production in relation to, 63, 66, 172

Civilizations: Age of the, 24–5, 60, 63; failure of first generation of in Old World to reunify mankind, 65–72; geneses of, 60, 62–72, 94–5, 172; geographical expansion of, 64–5, 67, 71–2, 79, 82; number of, 69; successive, breach of cultural continuity between, 130, 156; *see also* names of individual civilizations

Clement IV, Pope, 131

Colonialism, 40, 41

Commerce, 60, 65, 69, 76, 82, 91, 147, 170, 207, 210–11

Communication, means of, 58, 59, 61, 77–8, 79–80, 82, 101, 146, 191, 192, 210–11, 218

Communism, 27, 51, 52, 110, 115–16, 129, 130, 170, 171, 173–5, 190

Communist International, the, 190

Comnenian avatar of the Roman Empire, the, 128, 130

Computers, 139

Conciliar movement, the, 182

Confucianism, 74, 94, 150, 169, 186

Confucius, 12, 151, 186

Consciousness, 13, 28, 30, 31, 33, 57, 89, 102, 168

Constantine, the Roman Emperor, 52, 124, 129, 185, 186

Constantinople, 128, 129, 133

Cook, Captain, 80

Corichanca, 185

Corinth, 106

Corporations, 39, 214

Cortés, Hernando, 154

Cosmic time-scale, the, 20

Creativity, 94, 124, 223, 224, 226

Creeds, the Christian, 152

Cross, the Christian, 170

Crusades, the Western Christian, 121

Ctesiphon, 127

Cultural aggression, alternative responses to, 151–4

Cultural interpreters, role of, 152–5

Curiosity, 15–16, 20

Cybele, worship of, 155

Cyrenaica, 75

Cyrus the Great, the Persian Emperor, 117, 126, 186

Czardom, the, 129

Damascus, 127

Danube, River, 83

Darius I, the Persian Emperor, 13, 117, 186

De Gaulle, President Charles, 40

Dea Roma, 185

Dead, the, disposal of, 13, 22

Death, 14, 16, 44–5, 139, 176

Death-rate, the, reduction of, 34, 35, 36, 39, 45, 46, 48

Delhi, 136; Sultanate of, 127, 135

Denver, Colorado, 207

Deportation, 83–4

Deutero-Isaiah, 164

Diasporás, 81–7, 192

Diocletian, the Roman Emperor, 128

'Disciplines', 88–9

'Displaced persons', 84, 208–9

Distance, 'annihilation' of, 38, 61, 77, 81, 95, 101, 146, 158, 192

Disunity, advantages of, 90–9

Dostoyevski, F.: *The Brothers Karamazov*, 123, 124

Douglas-Home, Sir Alec, 40

Doxiadis, C. A., 209–10

Dutch, the, 147, 181

Dutch language, the, 143

Eannatum, King of Lagash, 107, 108

Earth, the: age of, 20; expectation of life on, 48, 52, 181, 207, 224, 227

East Roman Empire, the, 128, 129, 131, 133

Eastern Orthodox Christian Church, the, 128–9, 133, 177

Eastern Orthodox Christian Civilization, the, 128–9, 188

Economic regress, improbability of, 200–1

Edom, 107, 151
Education: religious conversion by
means of, 188–9; transmission of
social and cultural tradition by, 17,
45, 59; universal primary,
importance of in Westernizing
world, 156
Egypt, 65, 67, 71, 76, 80, 83, 125–6,
135, 142, 205
Egyptian Civilization, the, 25, 65,
67–8, 71, 76, 79, 93–4, 98, 107,
116–17, 125–6, 152, 172–3
Egyptian Empires, successive, 71, 74,
79, 93–4, 98, 104, 108, 116–17,
125–6, 133, 172–3, 184, 185
Ekistics, 210
Elam, 64, 67, 68
Electricity, 21, 213
Elephantinê, 83
Elias, Brother, 225
Endurance, as a reaction to evil, 52–3
Engels, Friedrich, 190
English language, the, 81, 143
Enlil, the Sumerian wind-god, 106, 173
Epicurus, 165
Epirus, 75
Erivan, 86
Ertoghrul, 136
Ethical codes, different, 13–15
Ethiopia, *see* ABYSSINIA
Eugenius, would-be Roman Emperor,
50, 51
Euphrates, River, 63, 64, 66, 72, 78,
80, 106, 107, 117, 127, 172
Europe: Central, 85; Eastern, 85;
nations of, in eighteenth century,
92; South-Eastern, 77, 129; Western,
77, 80, 81, 83, 86
Experience: collective, 3, 5; future
findings of, 181–2; individual, 3, 5;
limited use of, for dealing with
human affairs, 5–6, 8; value of,
3, 4, 5

Family-planning, 36–7, 45–6, 201–2
Famine, 37, 39, 54
Fanaticism, 27, 109–10, 170, 174
Fertile Crescent, the, 80, 94
'Fifth columns', 191
Fire-making, art of, 57, 59
Flags, national, 111, 170
Florence, Union of, 129
Food-gatherers, nomadic, 22, 55–61,
64, 66, 69, 81, 102, 104–5, 107, 116,
141, 142, 207, 212, 216
Food-production: application of science
to, 37–8, 47, 202, 205; changes in,
to meet the needs of megalopolis,
210; control of, by a world-
authority, question of, 37–9, 47, 54,

138–9, 157, 199, 202; financial
aspect of distributing surplus, 202–3;
increase in, at dawn of civilization,
62–3; raising general standard of
nutrition by increase in, 47, 195,
199, 202; release of part of a
community's labour force from, 63,
66, 172; surplus of, in advanced
countries, 202–3
France, 40, 41, 43, 132, 133, 158, 173
Francis of Assisi, Saint, 225
Franconian Western Roman
Emperors, the, 130
Frankish avatar of Roman Empire,
the, 130
Frederick II, Emperor, 130–2
Free enterprise, 174, 175
Free will, 5, 6, 7, 10, 13, 14, 17, 29,
44, 46, 139
French language, the, 153
French Revolution, the, 97, 99
Future, the: guesses about, 5, 10;
planning for, 3, 4–5

Gandhi, Mahatma, 12, 45, 155, 156,
200–1
Garrisons, 83, 84
Gautama, Siddartha, 165; *see also*
BUDDHA
Genesis, Book of, 55
Genetics, 4, 8, 9, 17, 88
Genocide, 44, 49, 50, 51
Germany, 18–19, 26, 51, 84, 93, 111,
132
Ghost-dance religion, the, 151
Gibbon, Edward, 91, 93, 96, 97, 99,
125; *General Observations on the Fall
of the Roman Empire in the West*,
quoted, 92
Giotto, 225
Glass, unbreakable, 124
God, 165, 167–8, 174, 227; *see also
under* UNIVERSE
Goethe, Johann Wolfgang, 19
Good Hope, Cape of, 80
Graeco-Roman Civilization, *see*
HELLENIC CIVILIZATION
Greece: ancient, 42, 91, 93, 94, 96,
106, 149, 173, 225; *see also*
HELLENIC WORLD
Greece, modern, 86, 206
Greek language, the, 80, 81, 86, 120,
152
Greeks, the, 83, 86, 119, 120, 128–9,
152
Gregory VII, Pope, 132
Guatemala, 156
Gujeratis, the, 83, 86
Gupta Empire, the, 127
Gutaeans, the, 118

Habits: changes in, possibility of, 18, 138, 145–6, 202; diversity of, 145–6
Habsburg Monarchy, the, 85, 131
Hadhramawtis, the, 83
Hammurabi of Babylon, 117, 126, 185
Han dynasty, the, 118, 120, 129
Harsha, Emperor, 127
Hawaii, 143
Health, public, administration of, 34, 36, 39, 54
Hellenic Civilization, the, 23, 32, 106, 109, 120, 128, 130, 149, 151, 152, 155
Hellenic World, the, 75, 94, 99, 108, 111, 130, 149, 150, 152, 155–6, 181
Hellenic world-state, the, *see* ROMAN EMPIRE
Herod the Great, 151
Herodians, 151, 154
Herodotus, 13
Hindu Civilization, the, 74
Hinduism, 73, 76, 77, 84, 147–8, 156, 161, 164, 165, 169, 177–8, 186, 187, 227
Hindus, the, 143, 156, 177–8, 226; *see also* CASTES
History: man's social and cultural heritage as field of, 19; objective and subjective meanings of word, 19; as collective experience, 3, 5
Hitler, Adolf, 18, 49, 51, 111
Hittite Civilization, the, 72
Hittites, the, 64, 65, 67
Hobbes, Thomas, 132, 227
Hokkaido, 162, 163
Holy Roman Empire, the, 130–1
Homer, 23
Hominids, different species of, 10–11, 21, 144
Homo faber, 11, 29, 30, 56, 218
Homo neandertalensis, 22, 144
Homo pedester, 56, 57
Homo sapiens, 10, 11, 21, 57, 144, 145
Homsis, the, 83
Huguenots, the, 84
Human sacrifice, 49, 146–7, 184
Hume, David, 93, 96, 109, 124, 125, 132, 194; *Of the Rise and Progress of the Arts and Sciences*, quoted, 91–2
Hungary, Kingdom of, 131
Hurrian language, the, 65
Hyksos, the, 125

Iamblichus, 185
Ideologies: approximation towards each other, 174, 175; as a reversion to the worship of human power, 27, 171, 173; contest between, 171, 174–5; failure of, to help individuals, 27, 176, 193; imposition of, by force, 51; prospects of, 171–6; servitude to community re-imposed by, 176–7; spreading of, throughout world, 170; variety in, desirability of, 191; *see also* COMMUNISM; INDIVIDUALISM; NATIONALISM
Inca Empire, the, 83, 119, 184–5
India, 45, 74–7, 80, 83–6, 103, 119, 127–8, 135–7, 143, 145, 147–8, 151, 154, 156, 169, 177–8, 187, 190, 200–1, 208
Indian Mutiny, the, 136–7
Indian Ocean, the, 78, 95
Indian Union, the, 128
Indians, the American, 31, 96, 154, 162, 163
Individualism, 27, 110, 170, 171, 173–5, 182, 190, 214
Indo-European languages, the, 65, 80
Indonesia, 83
Indus Culture, the, 68–9, 72, 78, 98
Indus, River and Valley, 63, 68–9, 72, 78, 80
Industrial Revolution, the, 99, 174
Industrialism, 60, 62, 63, 104, 204, 207, 208, 213, 215–17
Insects, social, 12–13, 16, 17, 26, 44, 176
Intelligentsia, the, 153–5, 181, 226
Iowa, 162–3, 203, 204, 207, 213–14
Iran, 93
'Irāq, 25, 63, 64, 69, 83, 95, 127, 135, 205–6
Iron Curtain, the, 171, 174, 175
Irrigation, 63, 66, 106, 107, 127, 172, 200, 205
Isis, worship of, 155
Islam, 27, 51, 73, 74, 79, 84, 109–10, 121, 123–4, 128, 135, 143, 145, 155–6, 161, 164–7, 169, 175, 179, 186, 188–9
Islamic World, the, 151, 181, 182, 188
Isolationism, American, 41–2, 44–5
Israel, 107, 183; modern state of, 86
Italian Renaissance, the, 23, 93, 109
Italy, 22, 93, 94, 128, 132
Iuppiter Dolichenus, 155
Ivan IV, Grand Duke ('the Terrible'), 129

Japan, 18, 37, 43, 46, 75, 147, 154, 158, 162, 163, 169, 181, 206
Japanese Empire, the, 134–5, 137
Jericho, 142, 206
Jesus, 12, 32, 74, 86, 122–3, 166, 182–3
Jews, the, 32, 51, 73, 88, 122, 143, 151, 152, 179, 186; *see also* ISRAEL; JUDAISM
John XXIII, Pope, 177, 182